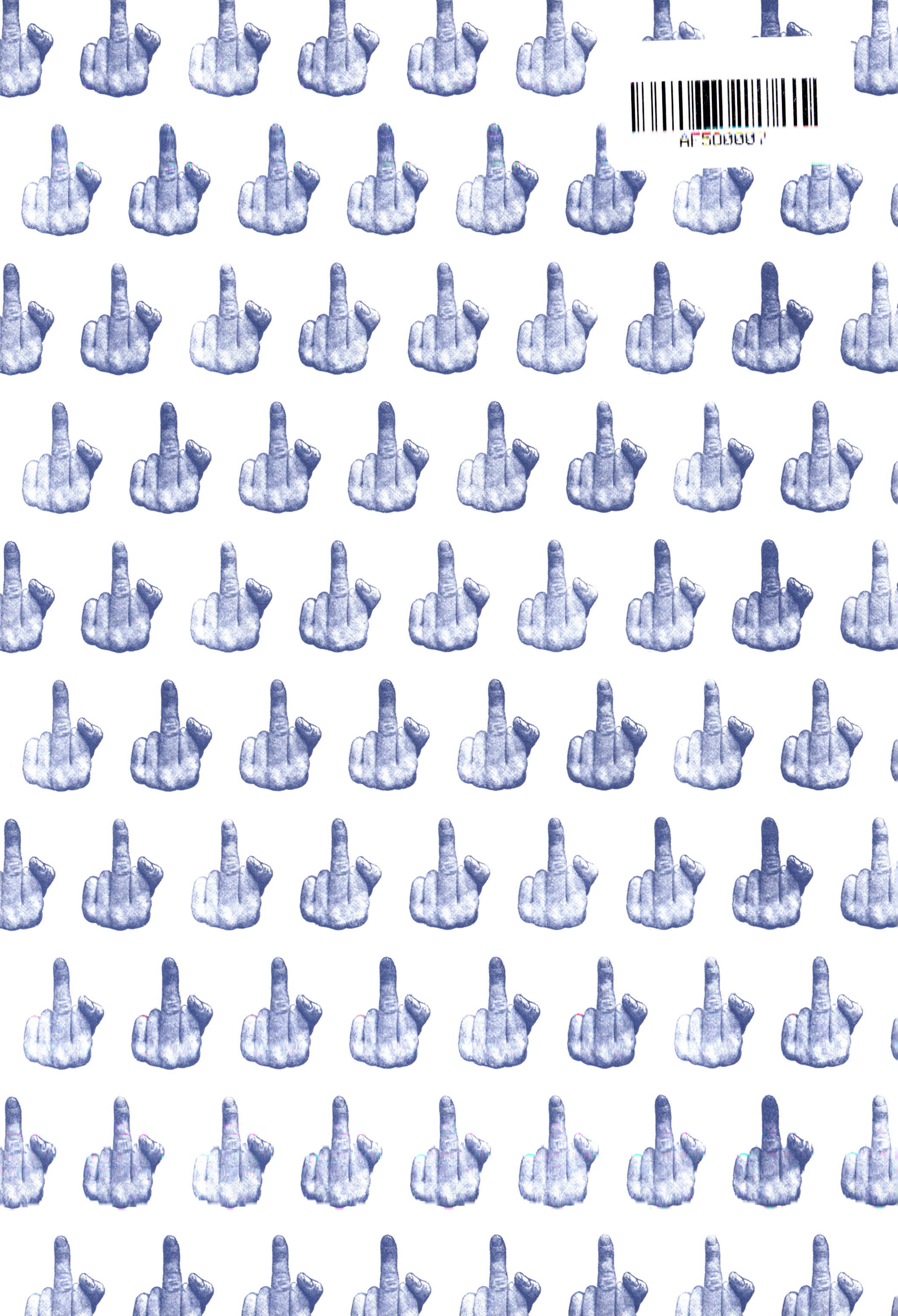

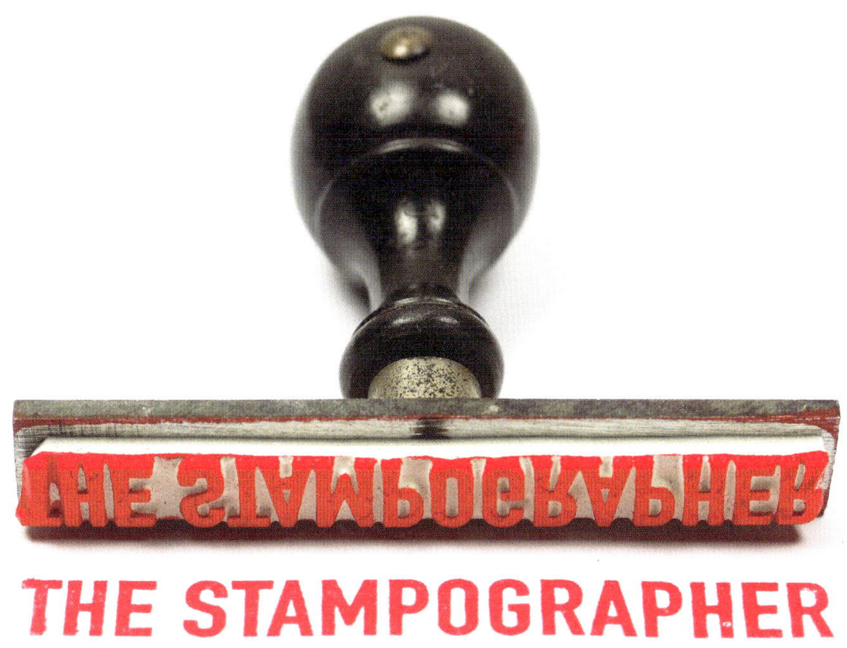

VINCENT SARDON

siglio NEW YORK 2017

Editors: Richard Kraft and Lisa Pearson
Translator: Philippe Aronson

Thanks to those who assisted with the insults: Laura Park, Maureen Forys (English, pages 8-9), Mia Trifa (Romanian, page 39), Ryoko Sekiguchi (Japanese, page 40), and Dr. Laurent Zarnitsky and J-L Mélenchon (Trotskyist, page 38).

Special thanks to Eva Aebischer.

FIRST EDITION
ISBN: 978-1-938221-16-3
Printed and bound in South Korea

siglio uncommon books at the intersection of art & literature
PO BOX 111, Catksill, New York 12414 p 310-857-6935
www.sigliopress.com publisher@sigliopress.com

Available to the trade through D.A.P./Artbook.com
75 Broad Street, Suite 630, New York, NY 10004
Tel: 212-627-1999 Fax: 212-627-9484

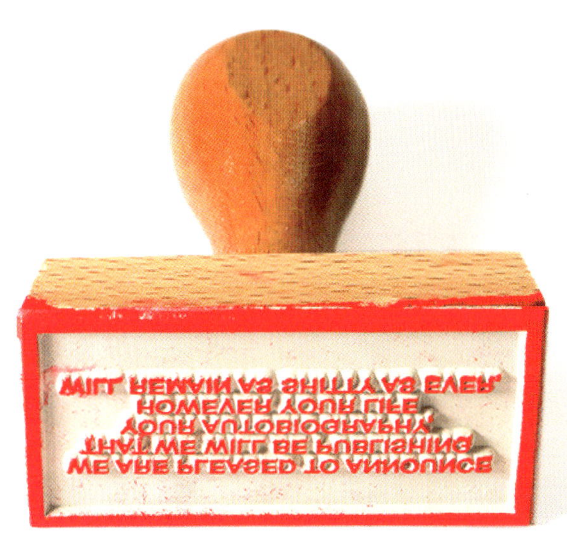

WE ARE PLEASED TO ANNOUNCE
THAT WE WILL BE PUBLISHING
YOUR AUTOBIOGRAPHY,
HOWEVER YOUR LIFE
WILL REMAIN AS SHITTY AS EVER.

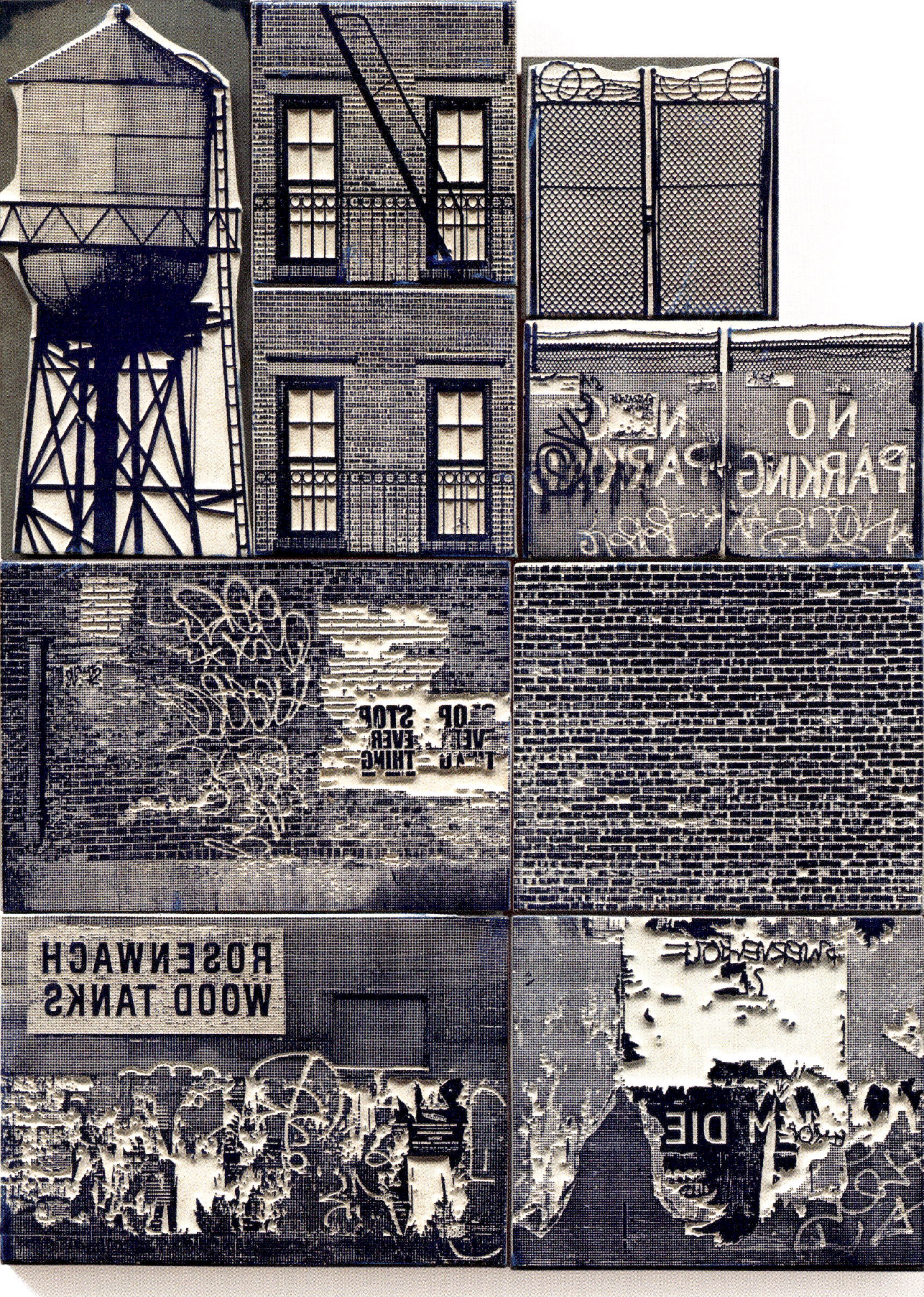

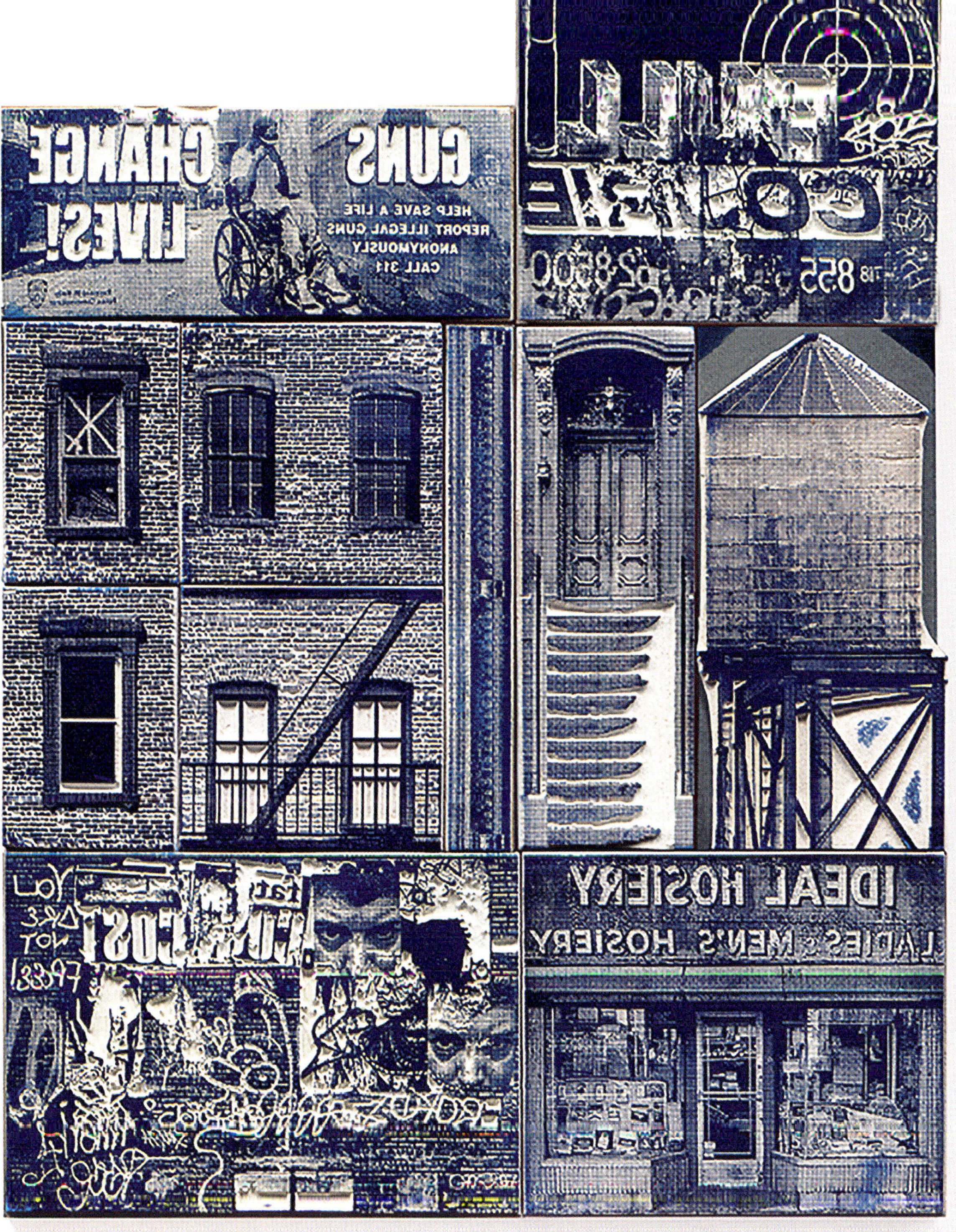
GUNS
CHANGE LIVES!
HELP SAVE A LIFE
REPORT ILLEGAL GUNS
ANONYMOUSLY
CALL 311
GO VIA
IDEAL HOSIERY
LADIES MEN'S HOSIERY

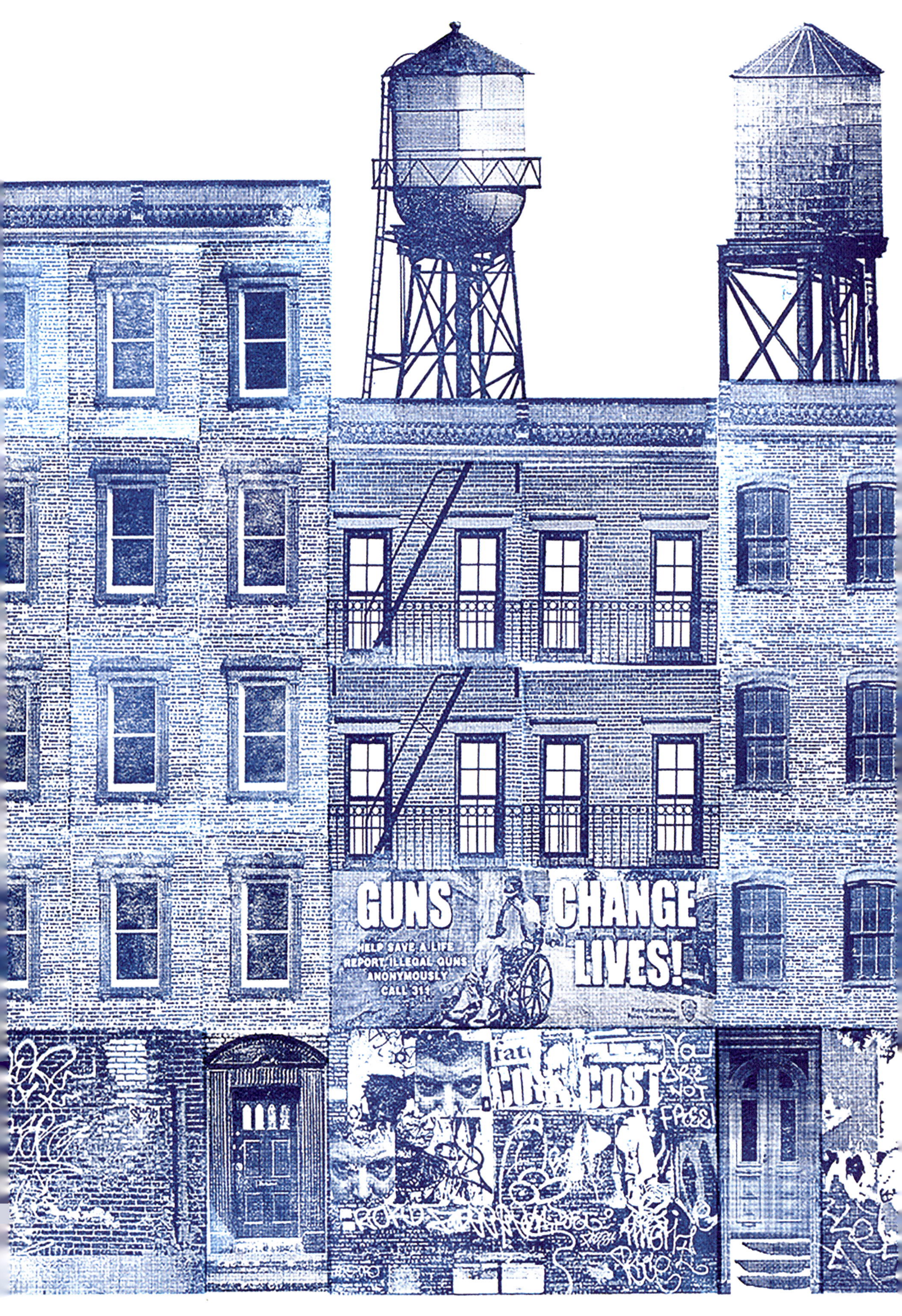
GUNS
HELP SAVE A LIFE
REPORT ILLEGAL GUNS
ANONYMOUSLY
CALL 311
CHANGE
LIVES!
COST
YOU ARE NOT FREE

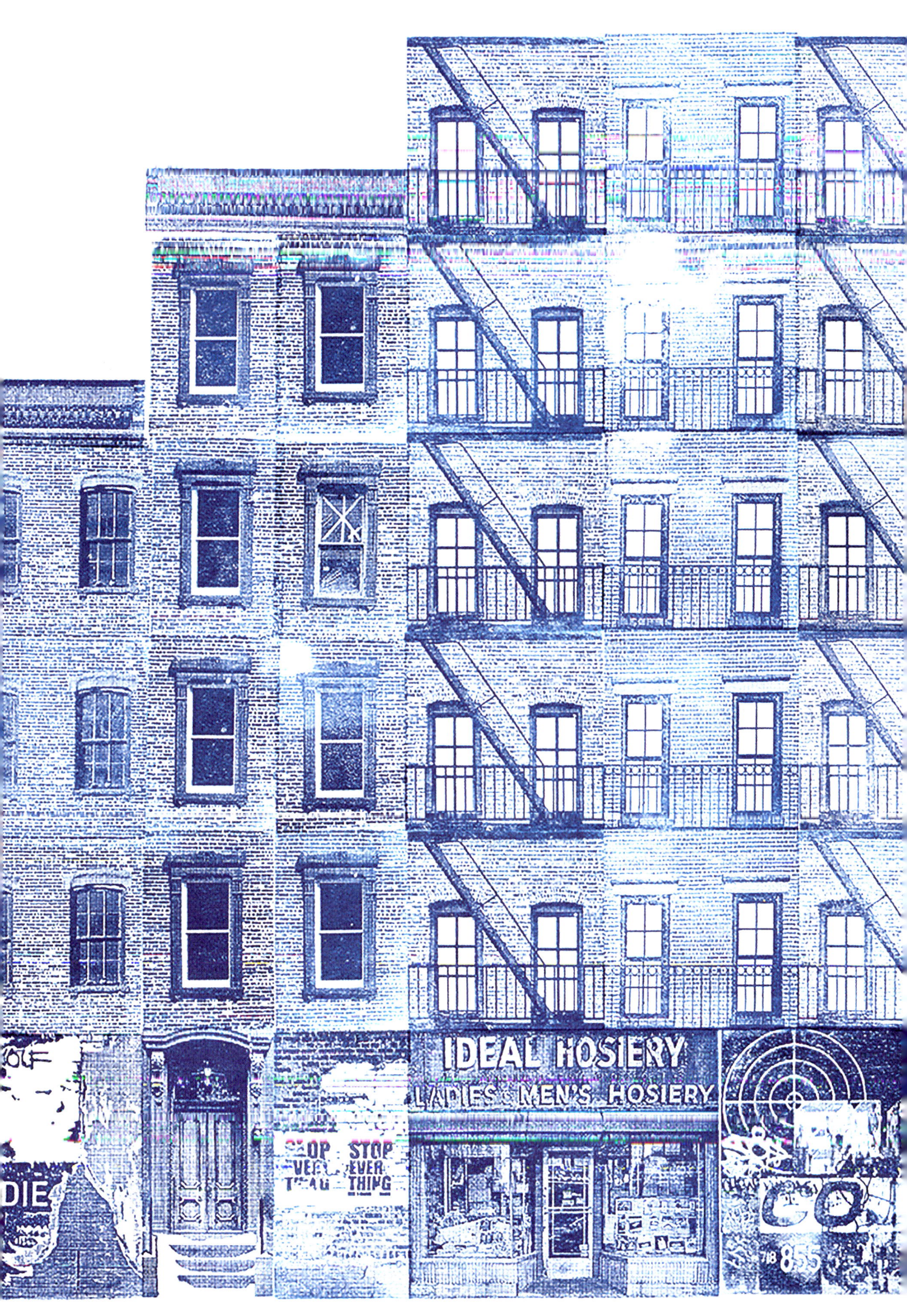
IDEAL HOSIERY
LADIES & MEN'S HOSIERY
STOP
EVER
THING

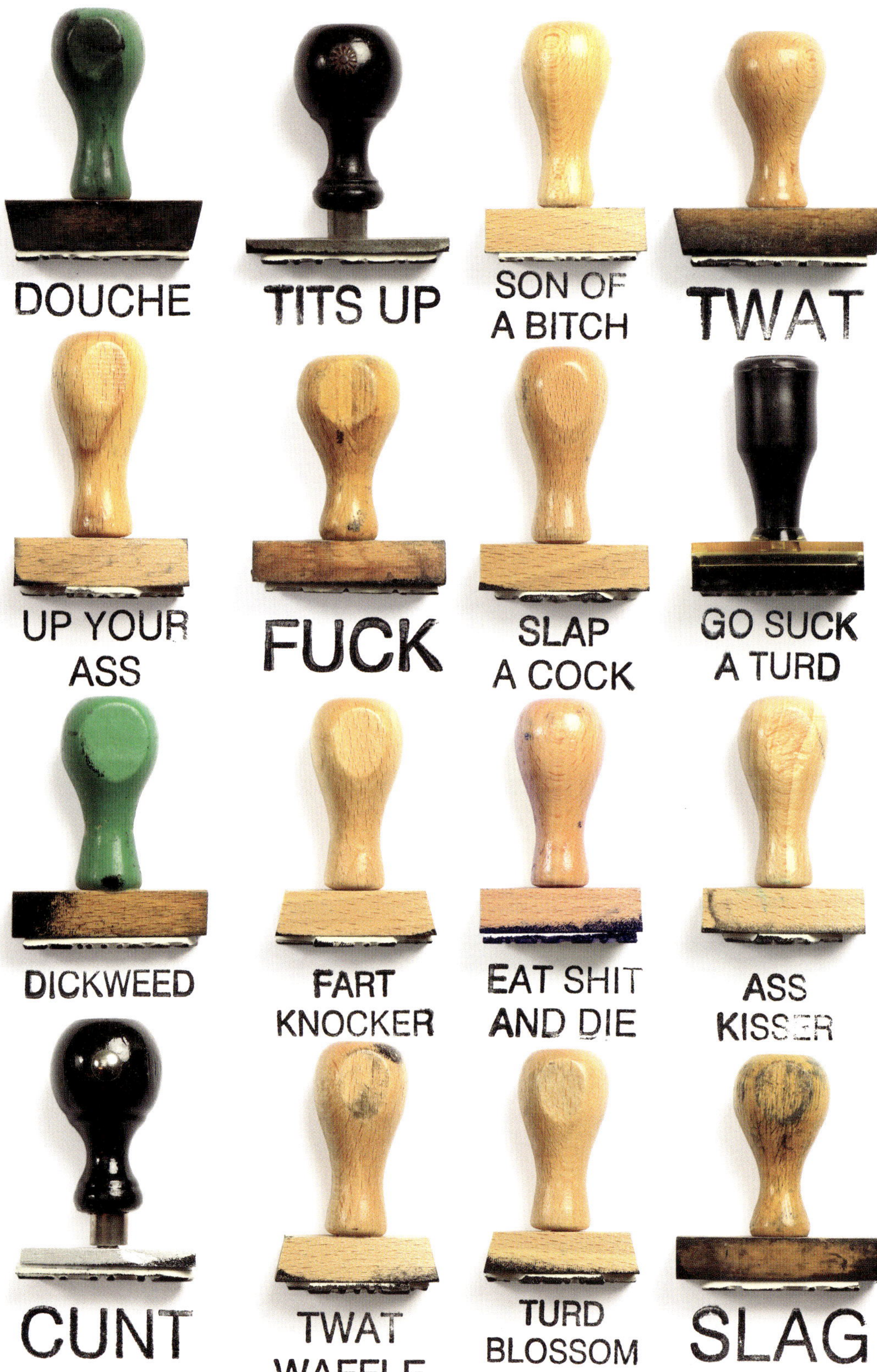
DOUCHE
TITS UP
SON OF
A BITCH
TWAT
UP YOUR
ASS
FUCK
SLAP
A COCK
GO SUCK
A TURD
DICKWEED
FART
KNOCKER
EAT SHIT
AND DIE
ASS
KISSER
CUNT
TWAT
WAFFLE
TURD
BLOSSOM
SLAG

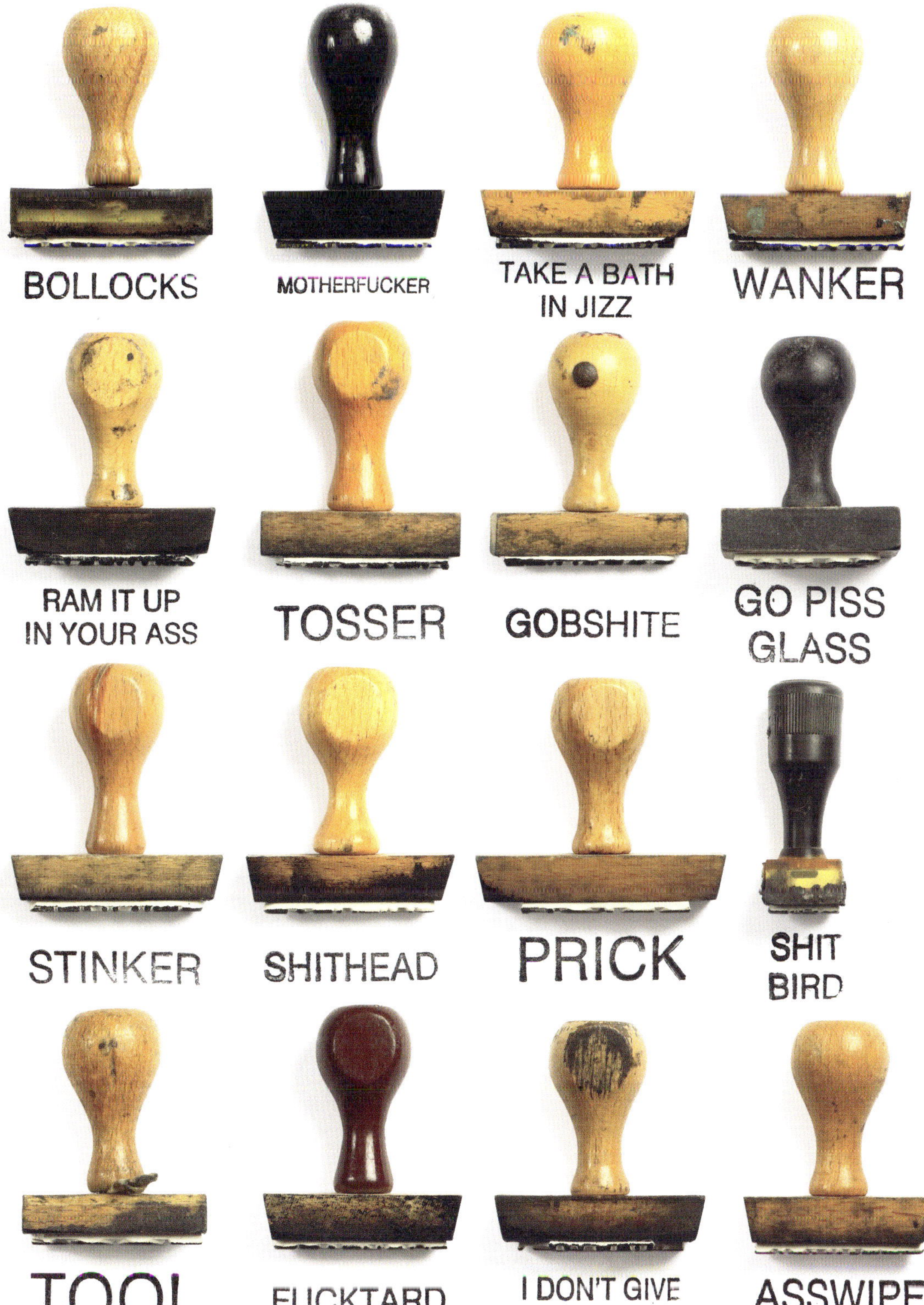
BOLLOCKS
MOTHERFUCKER
TAKE A BATH IN JIZZ
WANKER
RAM IT UP IN YOUR ASS
TOSSER
GOBSHITE
GO PISS GLASS
STINKER
SHITHEAD
PRICK
SHIT BIRD
TOOL
FUCKTARD
I DON'T GIVE A FUCK
ASSWIPE

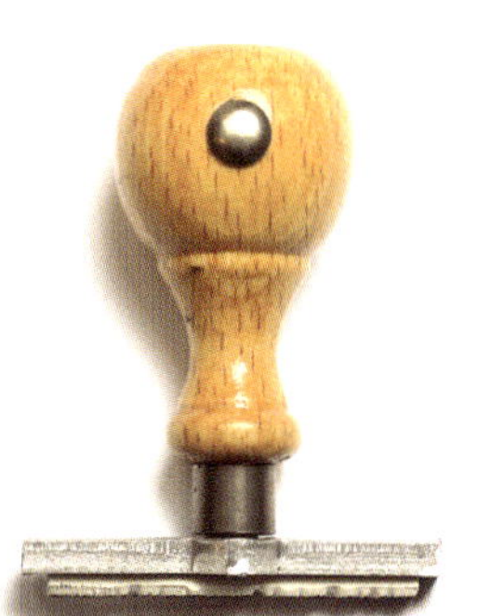

PETIT RENTIER DE L'AVANT-GARDE

little independently wealthy avant-gardist

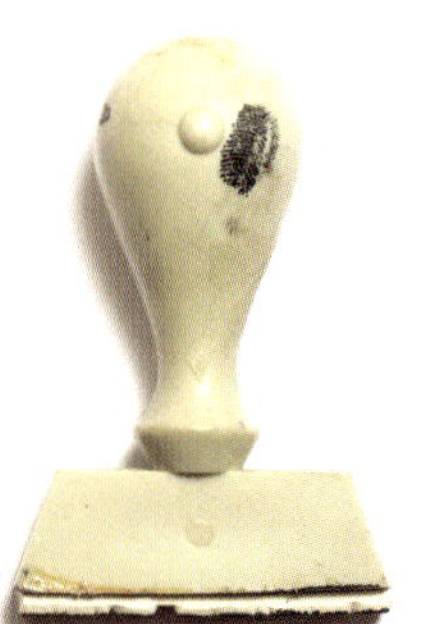

ADAPTÉ SOCIAL

Socially adapted

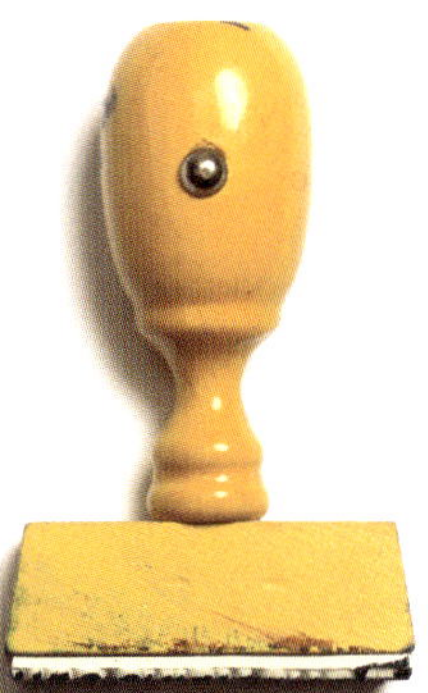

CAFARD DE VERNISSAGE

art opening cockroach

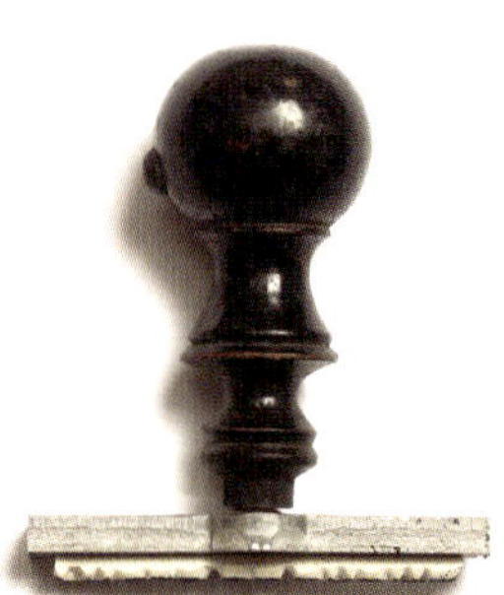

FAIS-TOI VASECTOMISER

go get a vasectomy

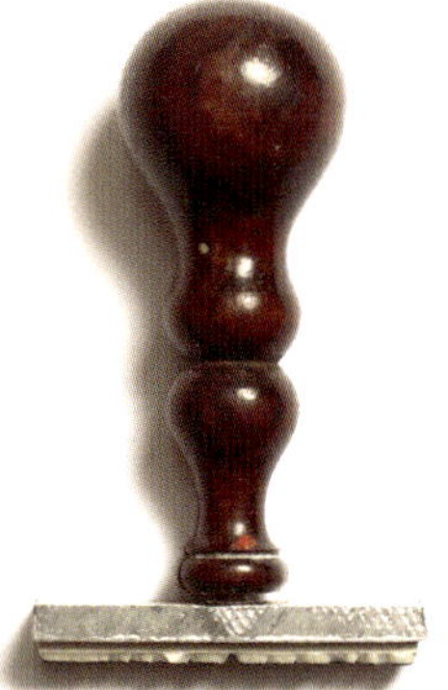

RENTRE CHEZ MAMAN

go home to momma

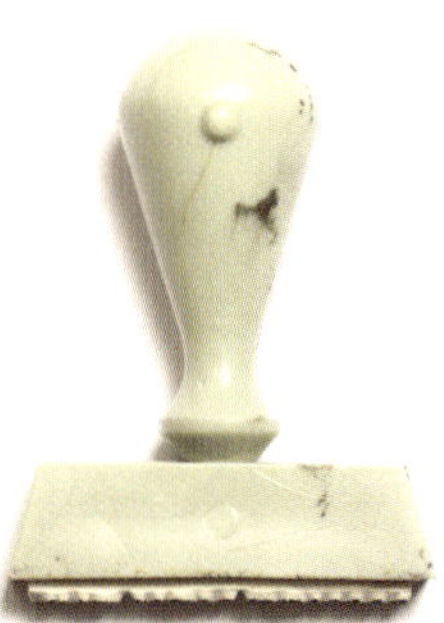

IDIOT UTILE

Useful idiot

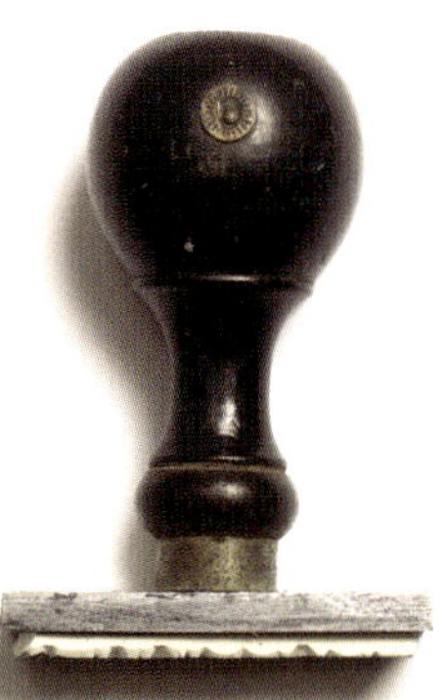

VERMINE OPPORTUNISTE

Opportunist vermin

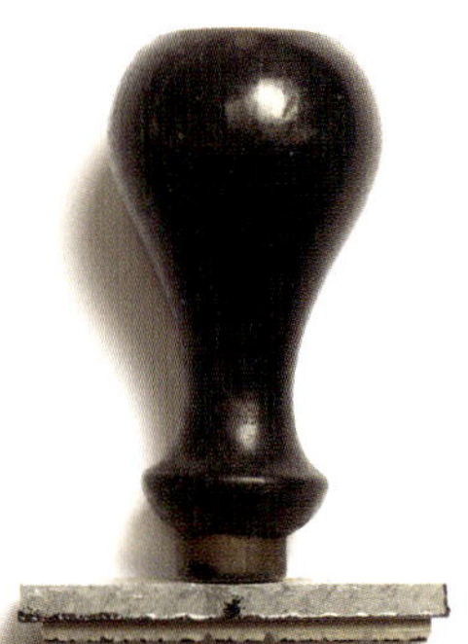

PELOTEUR DE STAGIAIRES

Intern fondler

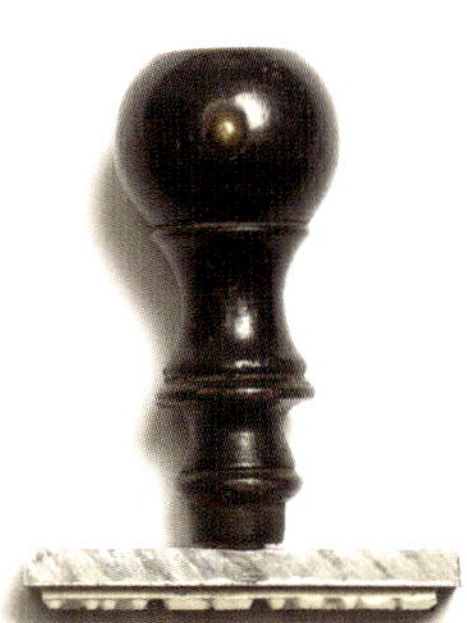

FLIC CULTUREL

Cultural cop

VA CHIER DANS TA CAISSE

go shit in your car

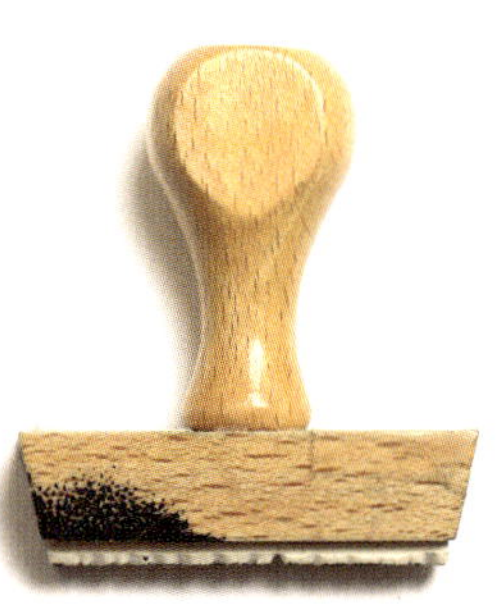

STREET-ARTISTE SOURNOIS

Shady street-artist

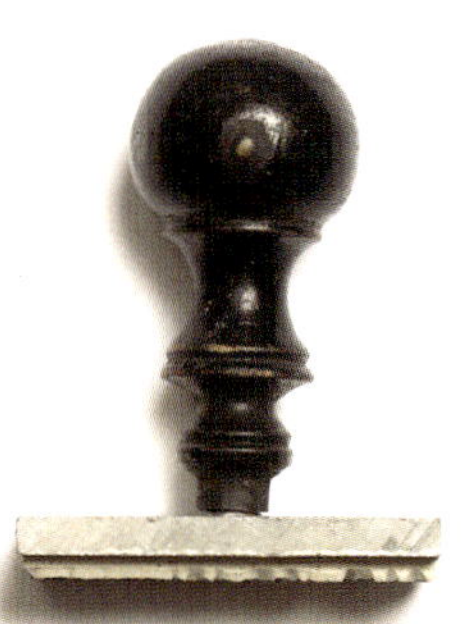

PERSONNE NE REMARQUERA TA MORT

Nobody will notice when you're dead

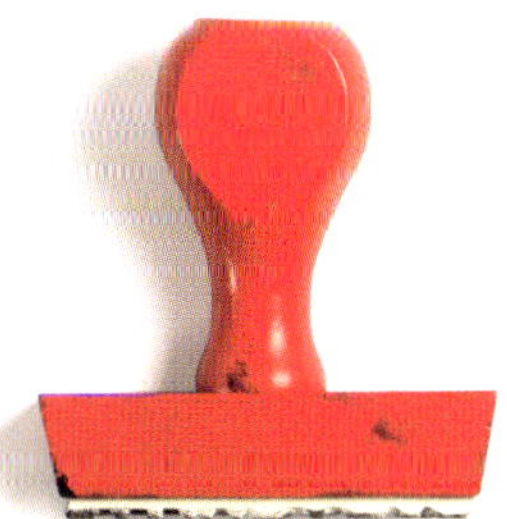

VA POURRIR À LA
VILLA MÉDICIS

*Go die in
Villa Medici*

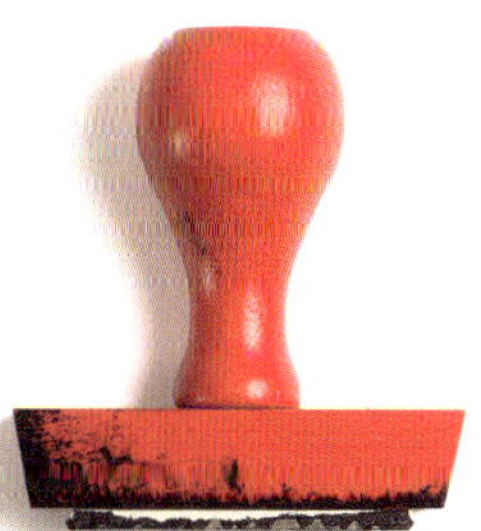

CURATEUR
DE MON CUL

Curate my ass

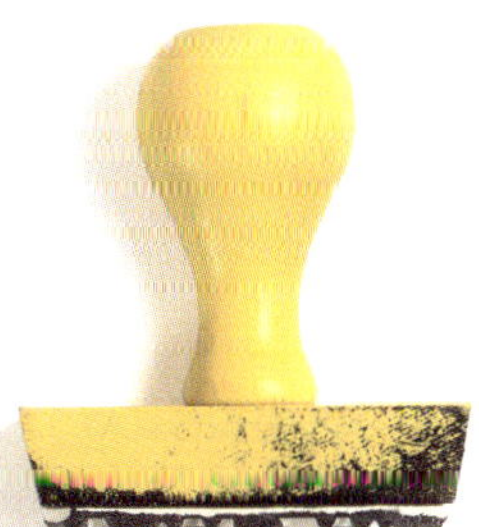

VAMPIRE
À SUBVENTIONS

*Endowment
vampire*

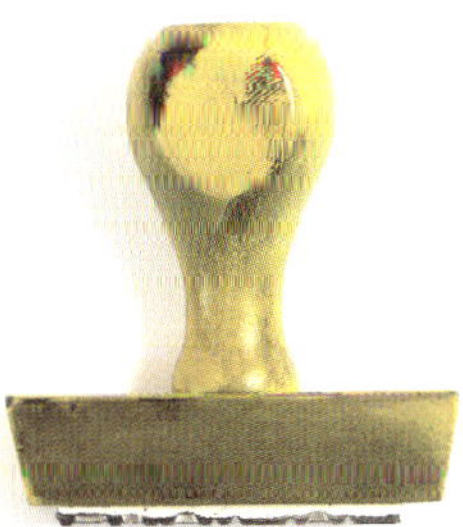

ARTISTE
MODERNE D'ÉTAT

*Modern artist
of State*

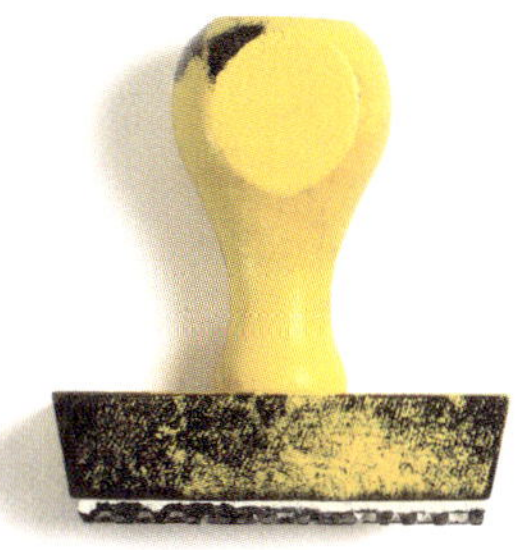

JETTE-TOI
DANS UN LAC

*Go jump
in a lake*

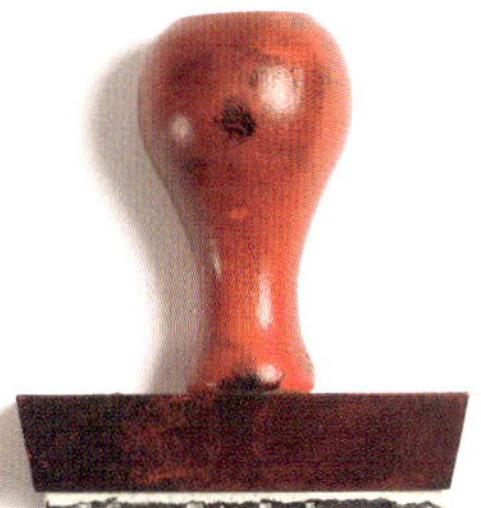

HYÈNE
DACTYLOGRAPHE

typist hyena

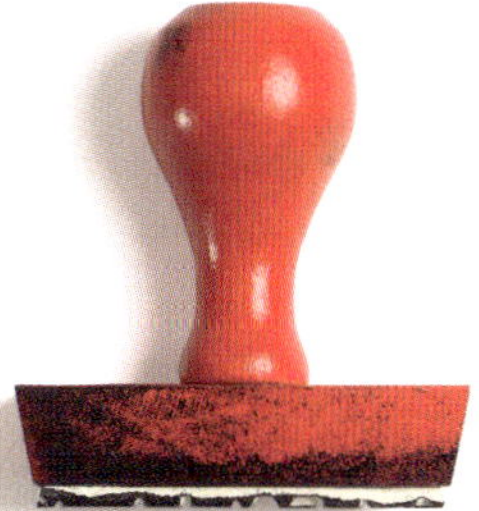

VA FAIRE TON
ART-THÉRAPIE

*Go art-therapy
yourself*

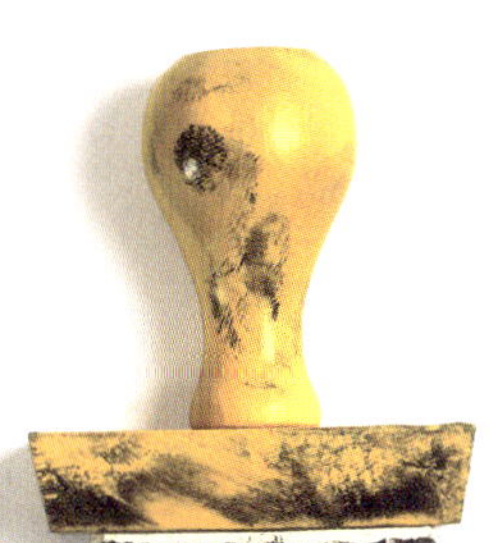

MORT-VIVANT

Zombie

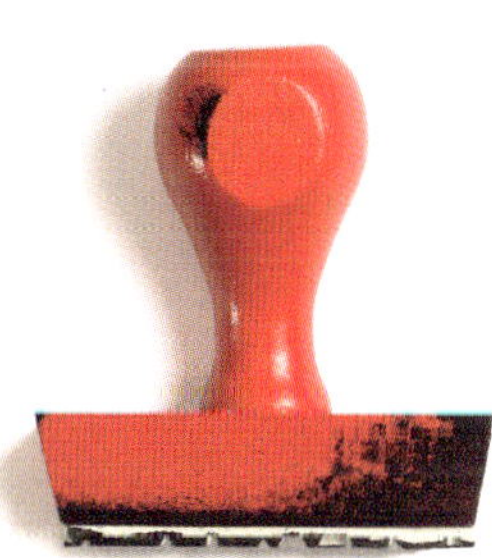

ARTISTE
MUNICIPAL

*municipal
trash-can*

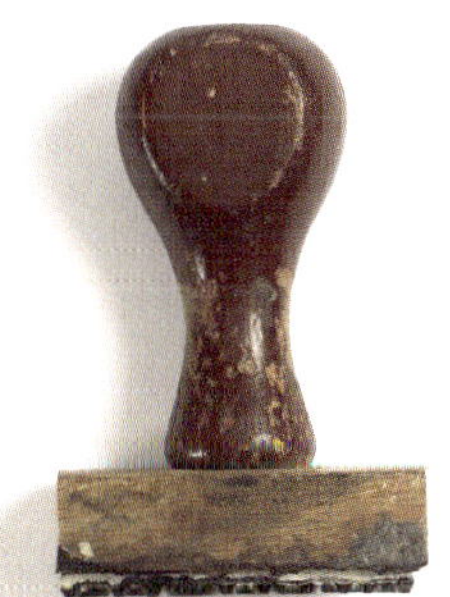

PUNK DE
DROITE

*Right-wing
punk rocker*

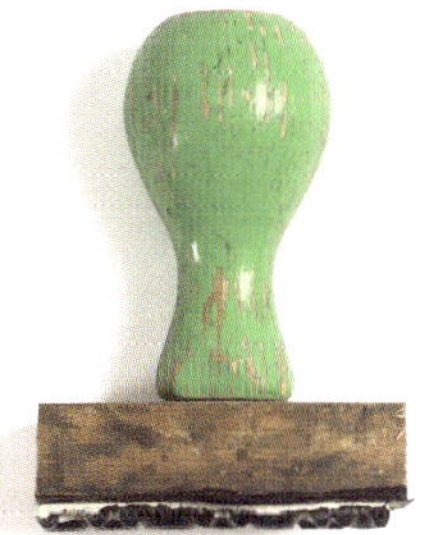

T'ÉTAIS MOINS CON
QUAND TU BUVAIS

*You were less
insufferable
when you were
still drinking*

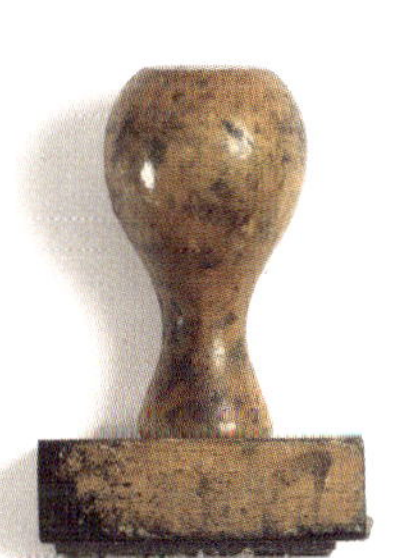

TON EXISTENCE
N'A AUCUN SENS

*Your life is
meaningless*

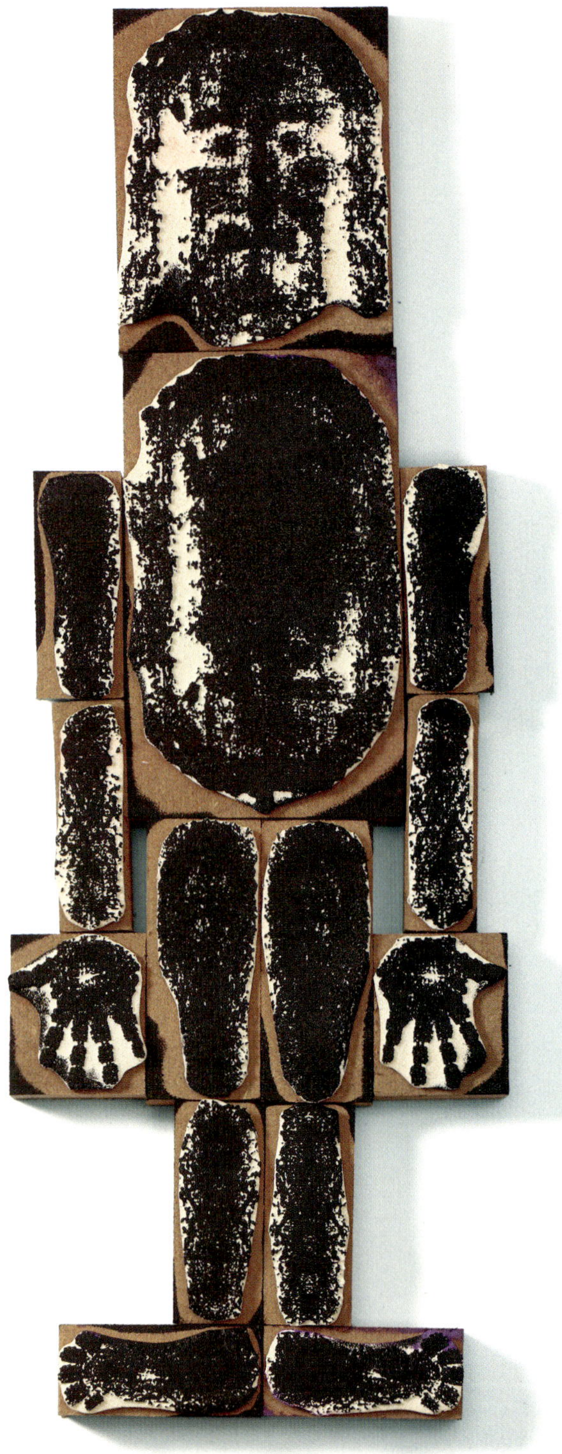

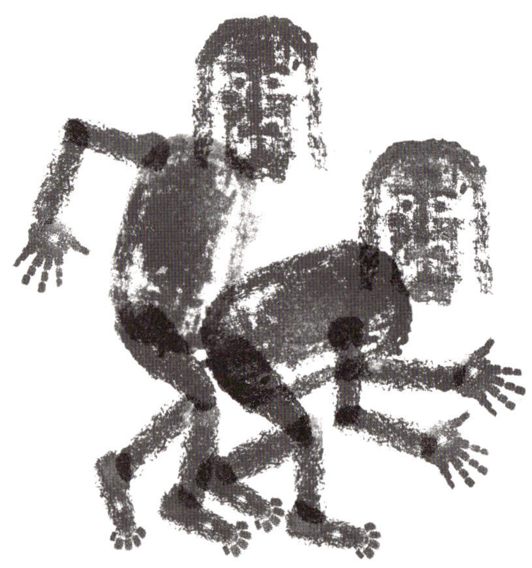

little galilean choo-choo train

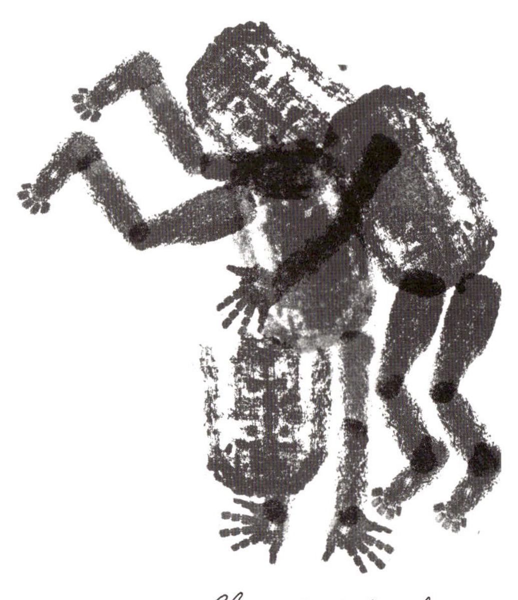

Clarinet of Jericho

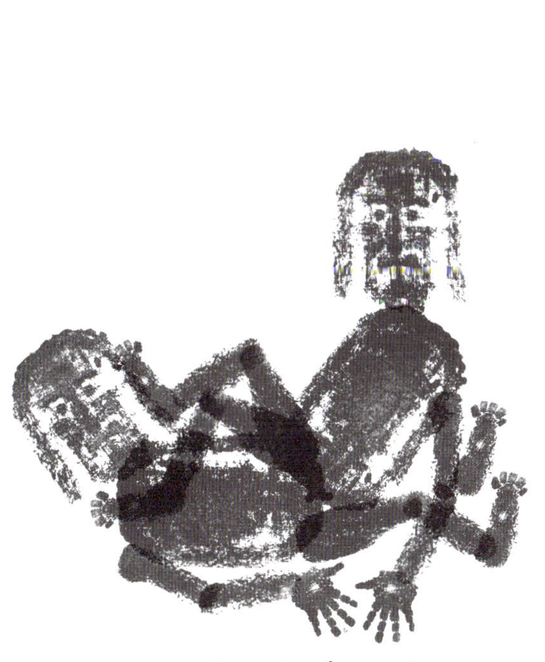

the Golgothan slide

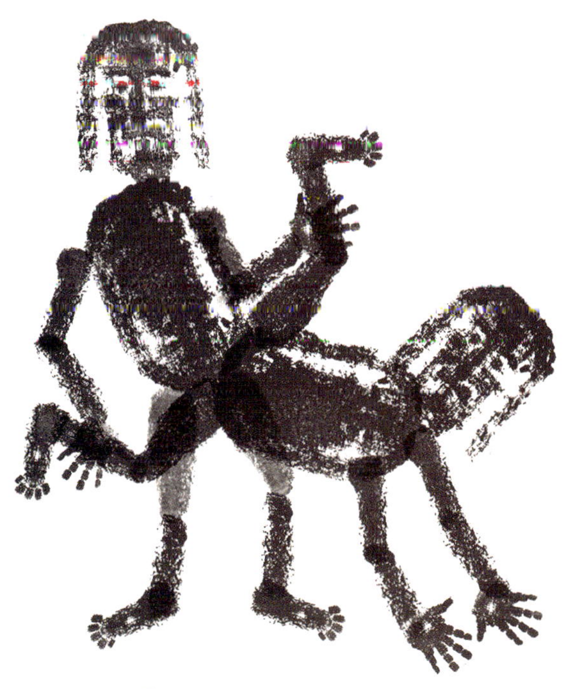

Bethlehem wheelbarrow

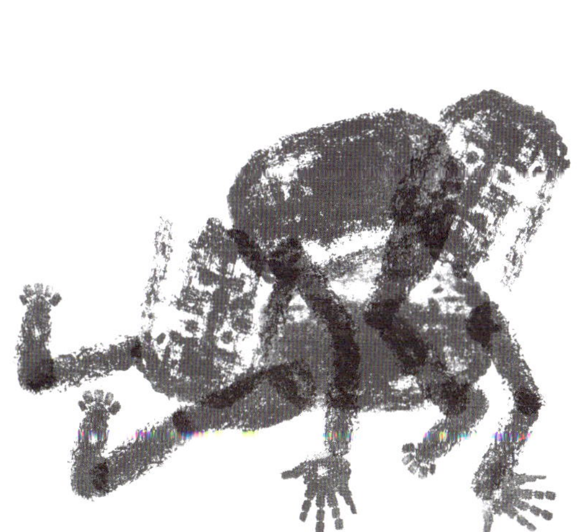

the palestinian tourniquet

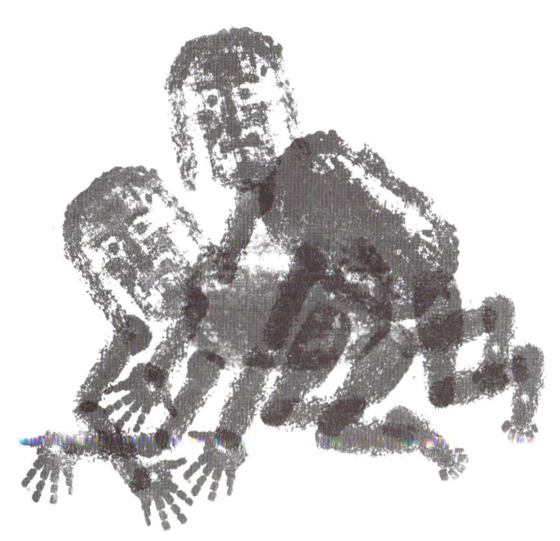

Jerusalem's little backdoor

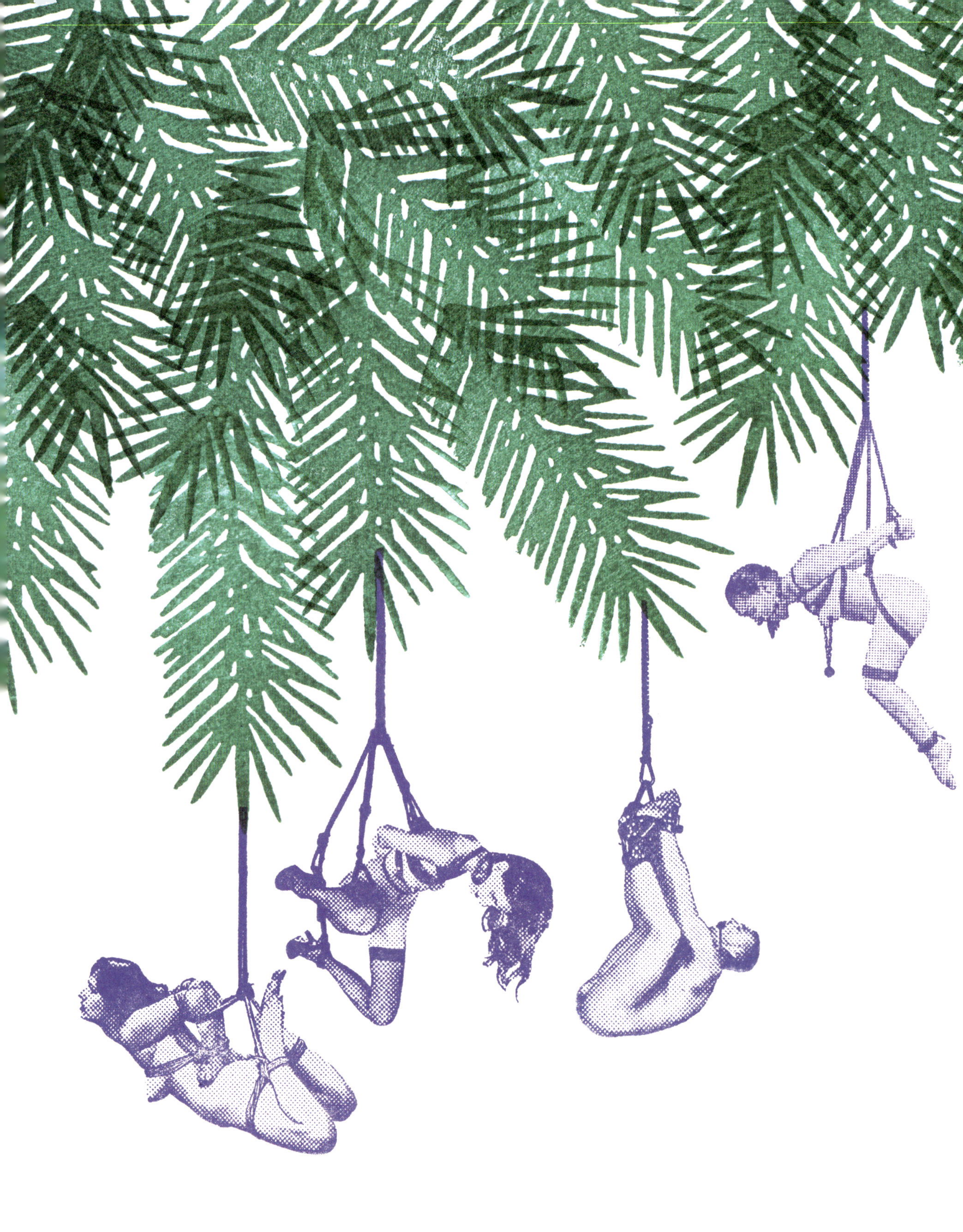

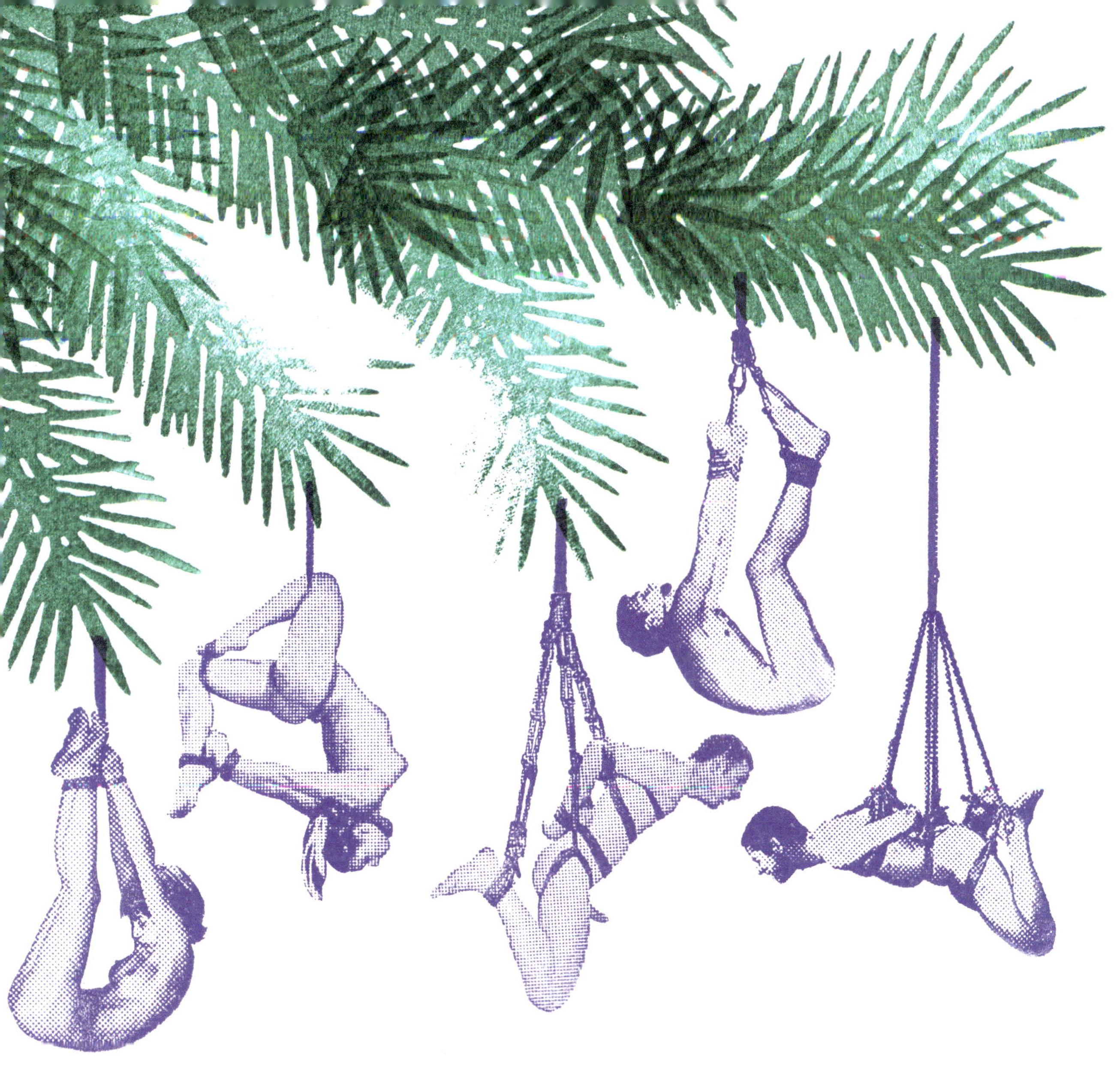

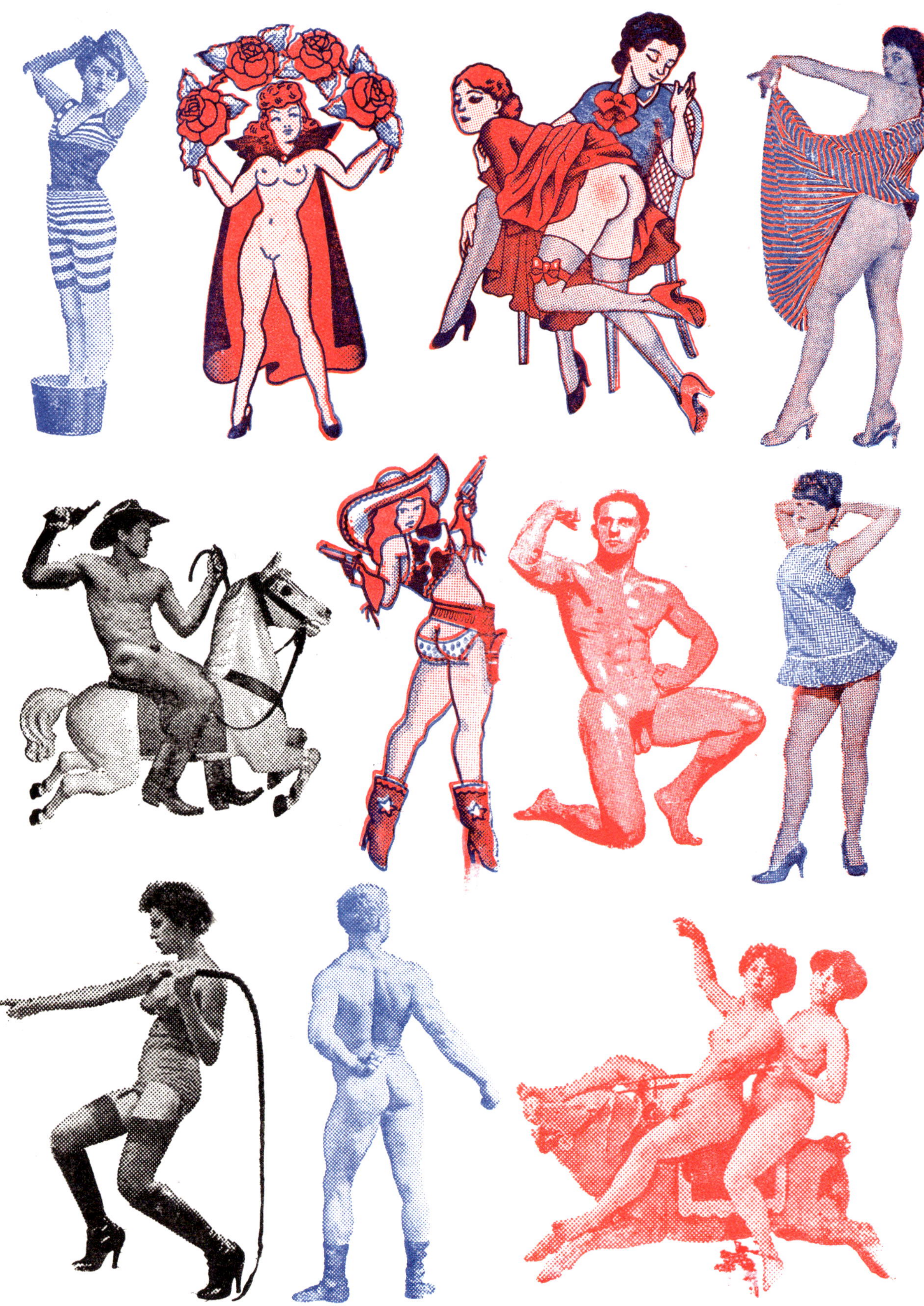

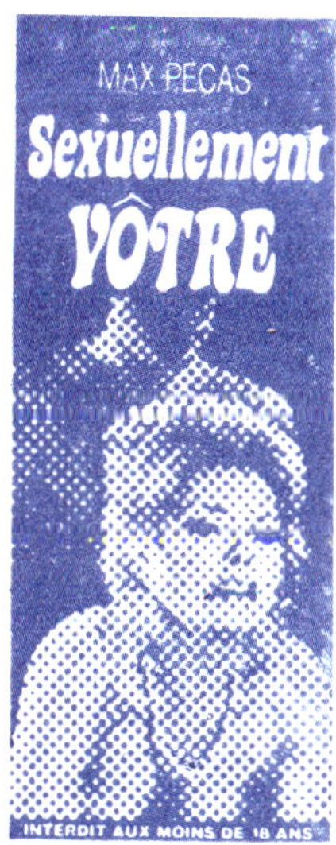
MAX PECAS
Sexuellement
VÔTRE
INTERDIT AUX MOINS DE 18 ANS

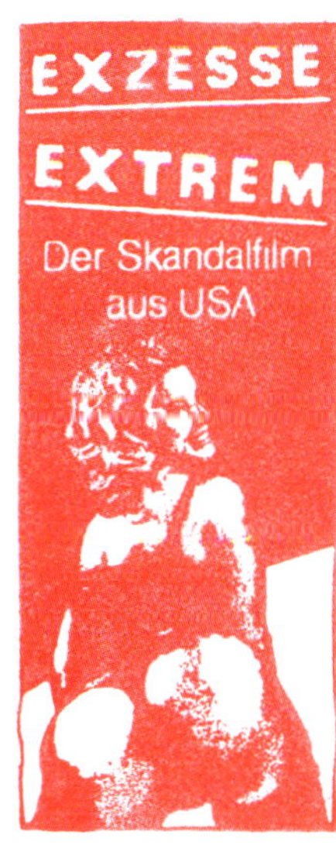
EXZESSE
EXTREM
Der Skandalfilm
aus USA

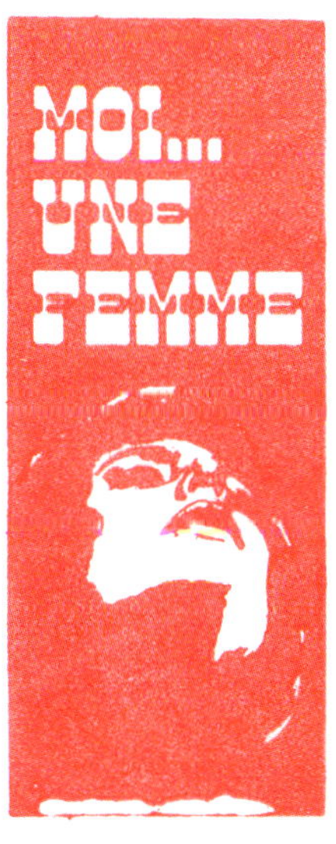
MOI...
UNE
FEMME

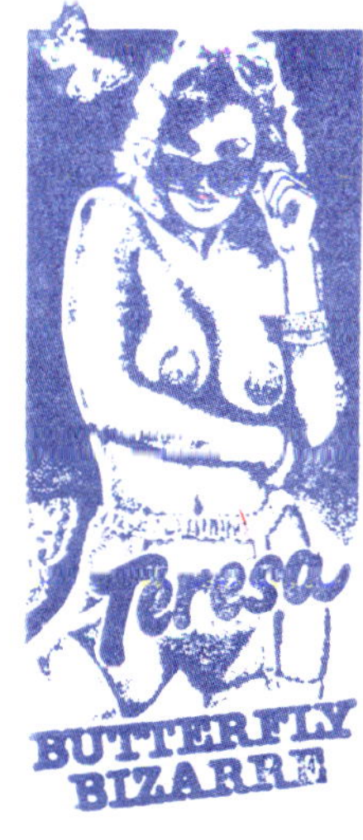
Teresa
BUTTERFLY
BIZARRE

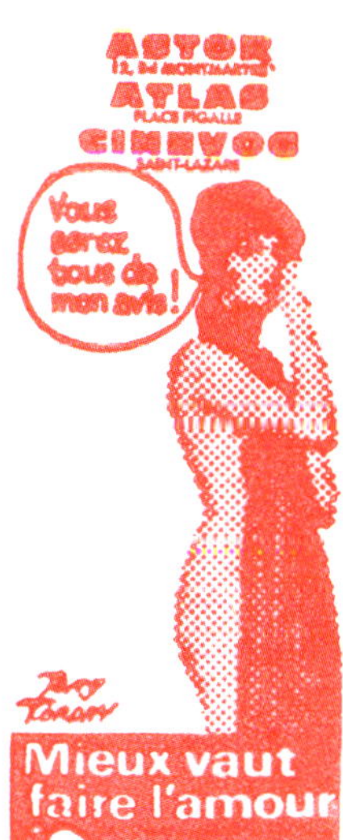
ASTOR
ATLAS
PLACE PIGALLE
CINEVOG
Vous
serez
tous de
mon avis!
Mieux vaut
faire l'amour

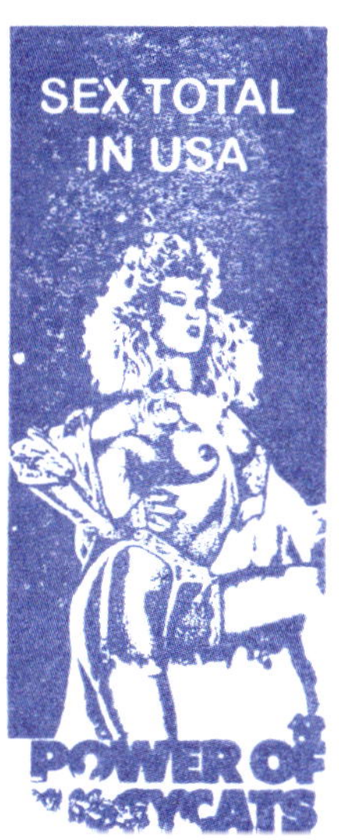
SEX TOTAL
IN USA
POWER OF
CATS

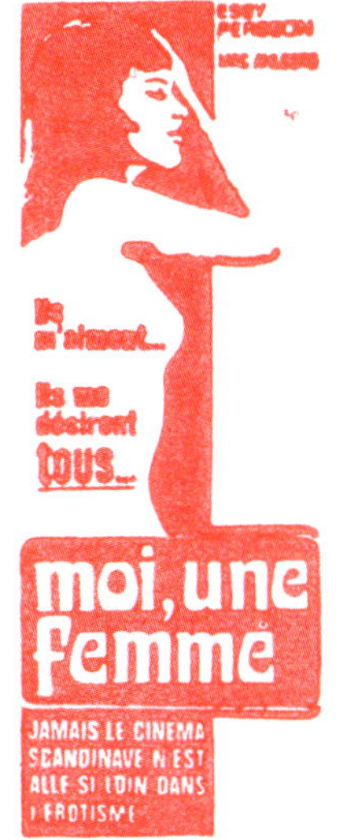
TOUS...
moi, une
femme
JAMAIS LE CINEMA
SCANDINAVE N'EST
ALLE SI LOIN DANS
L'EROTISME

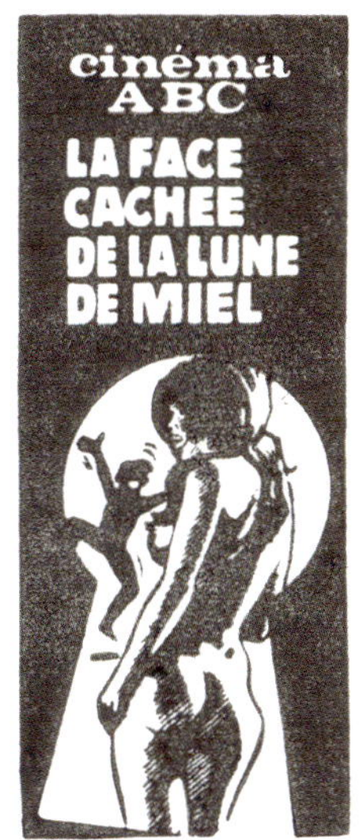
cinéma
ABC
LA FACE
CACHEE
DE LA LUNE
DE MIEL

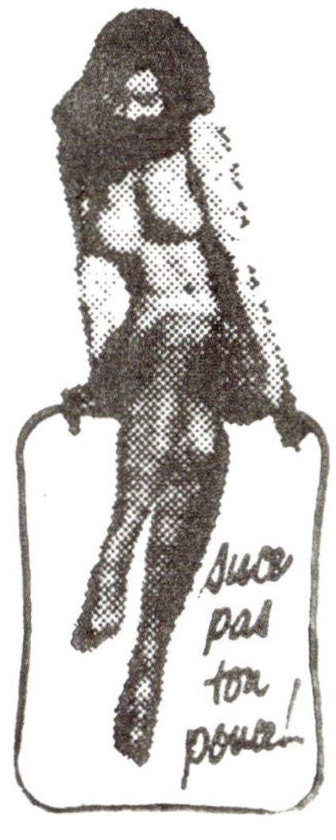
Suce
pas
ton
pouce!

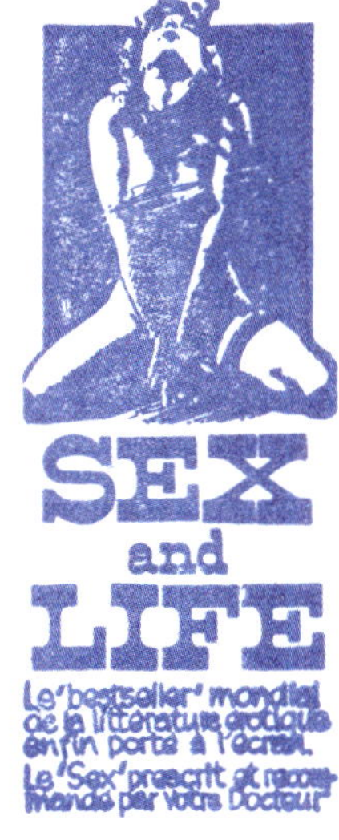
SEX
and
LIFE

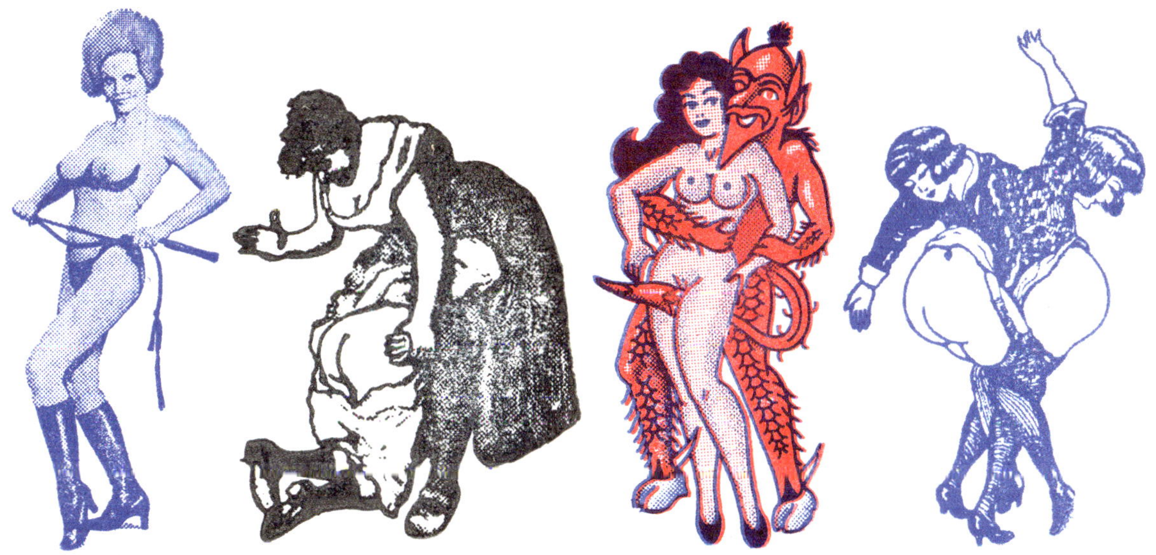

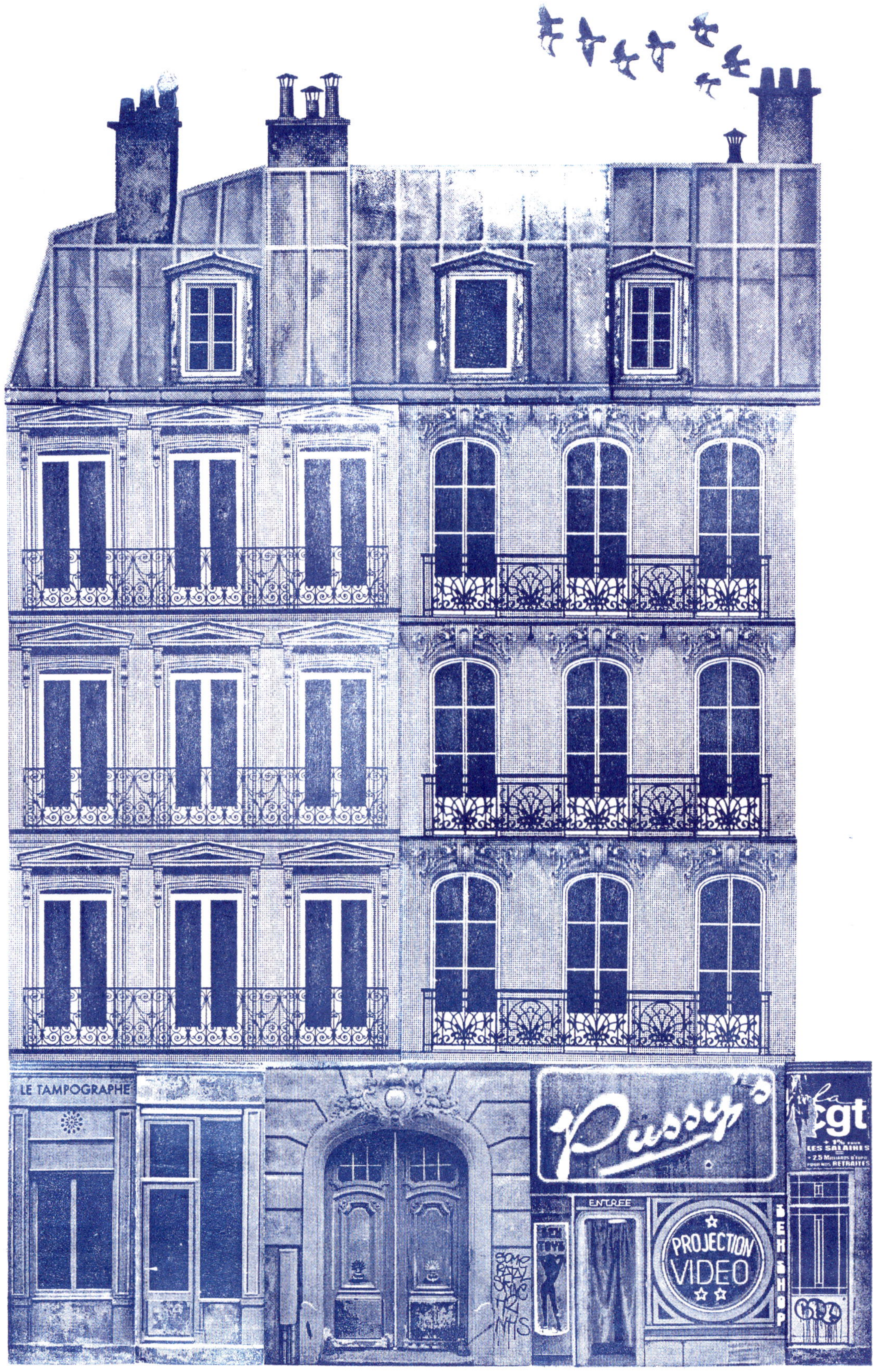
LE TAMPOGRAPHE
Pussy's
ENTREE
PROJECTION VIDEO
SEX SHOP
la cgt
+ 1% pour LES SALAIRES
+ 25 Milliards d'euros pour nos RETRAITES

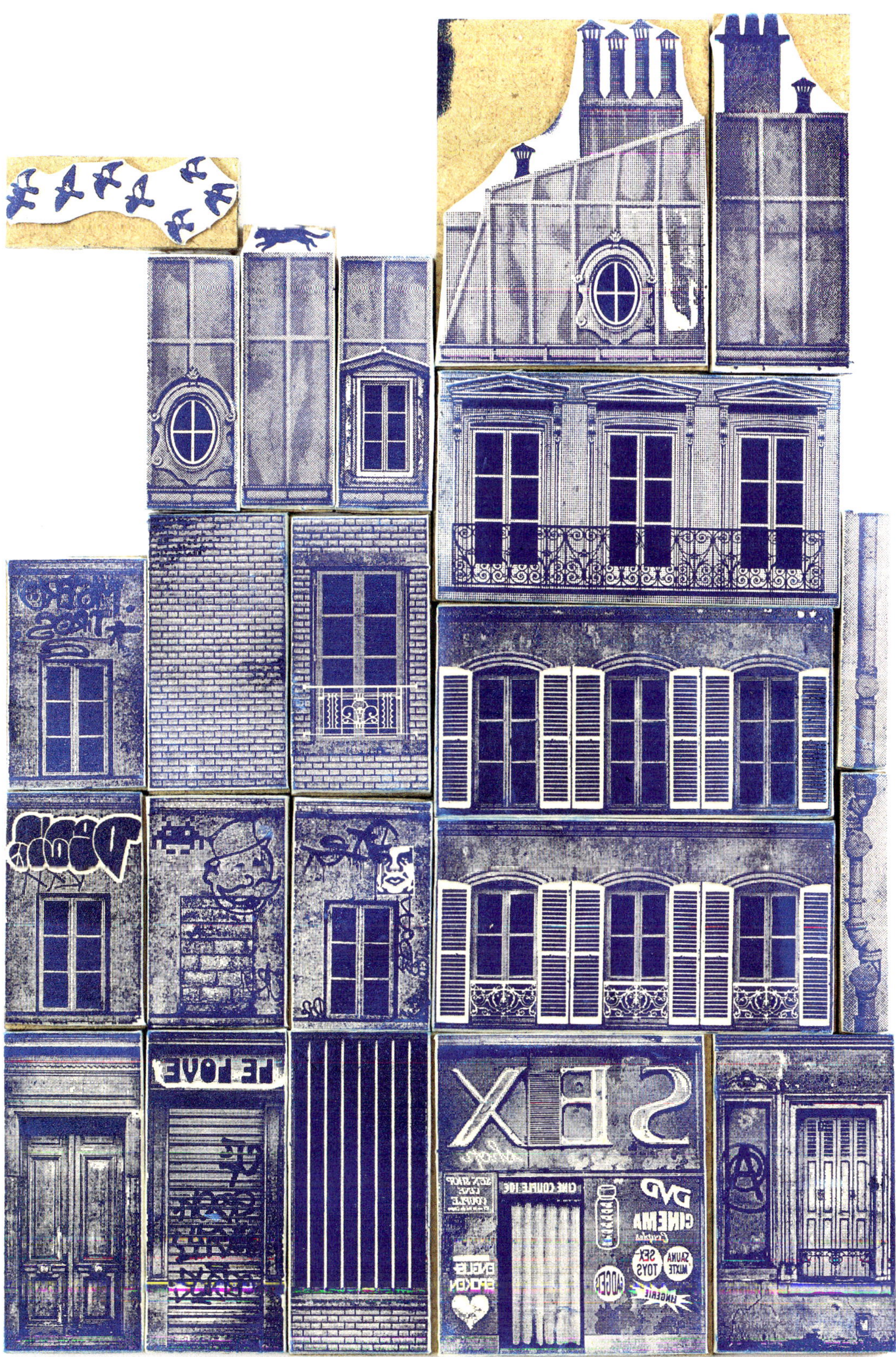
LE LOVE
SEX
DVD
CINEMA
SAUNA MIXTE
SEX TOYS
LINGERIE

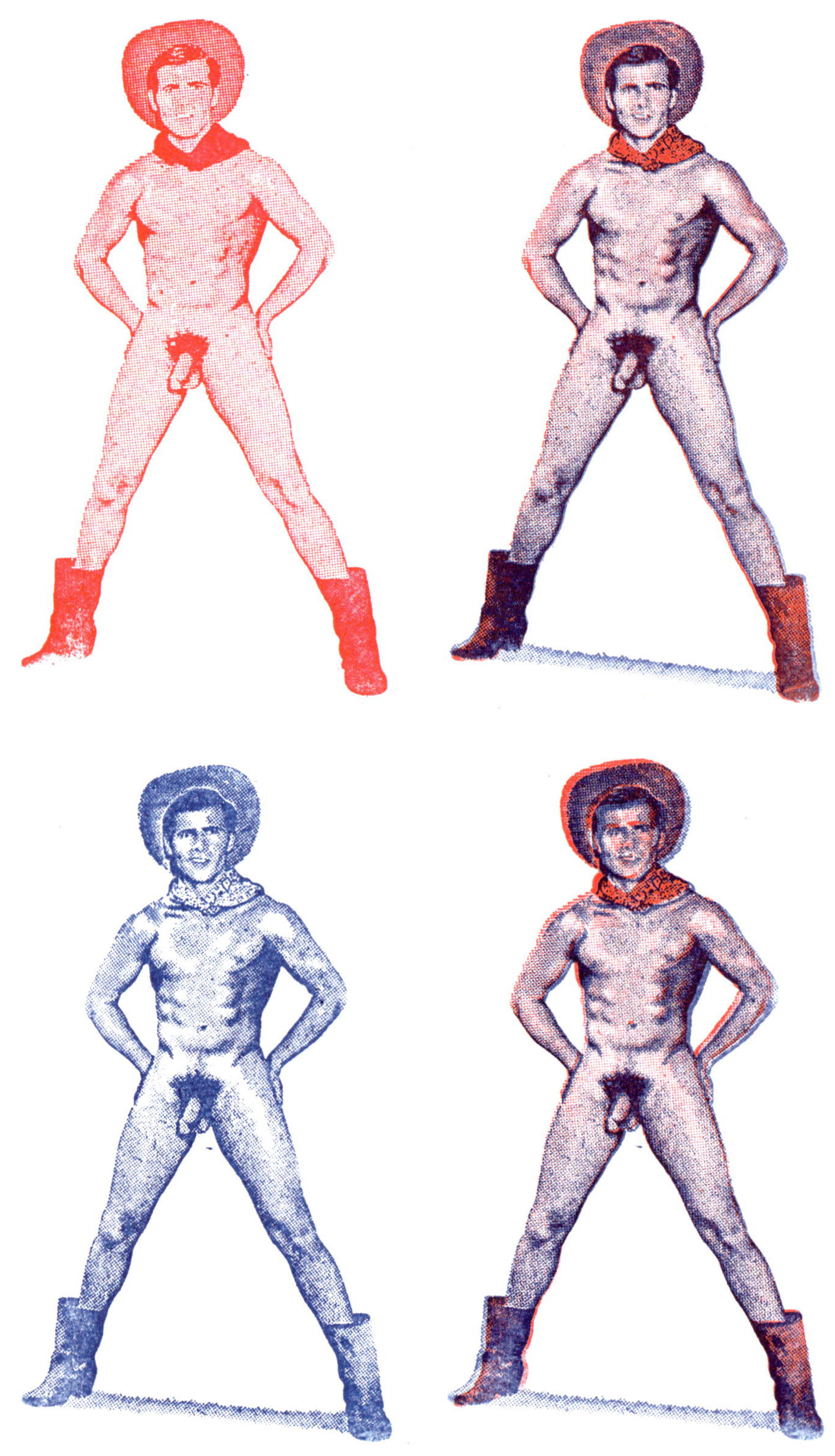

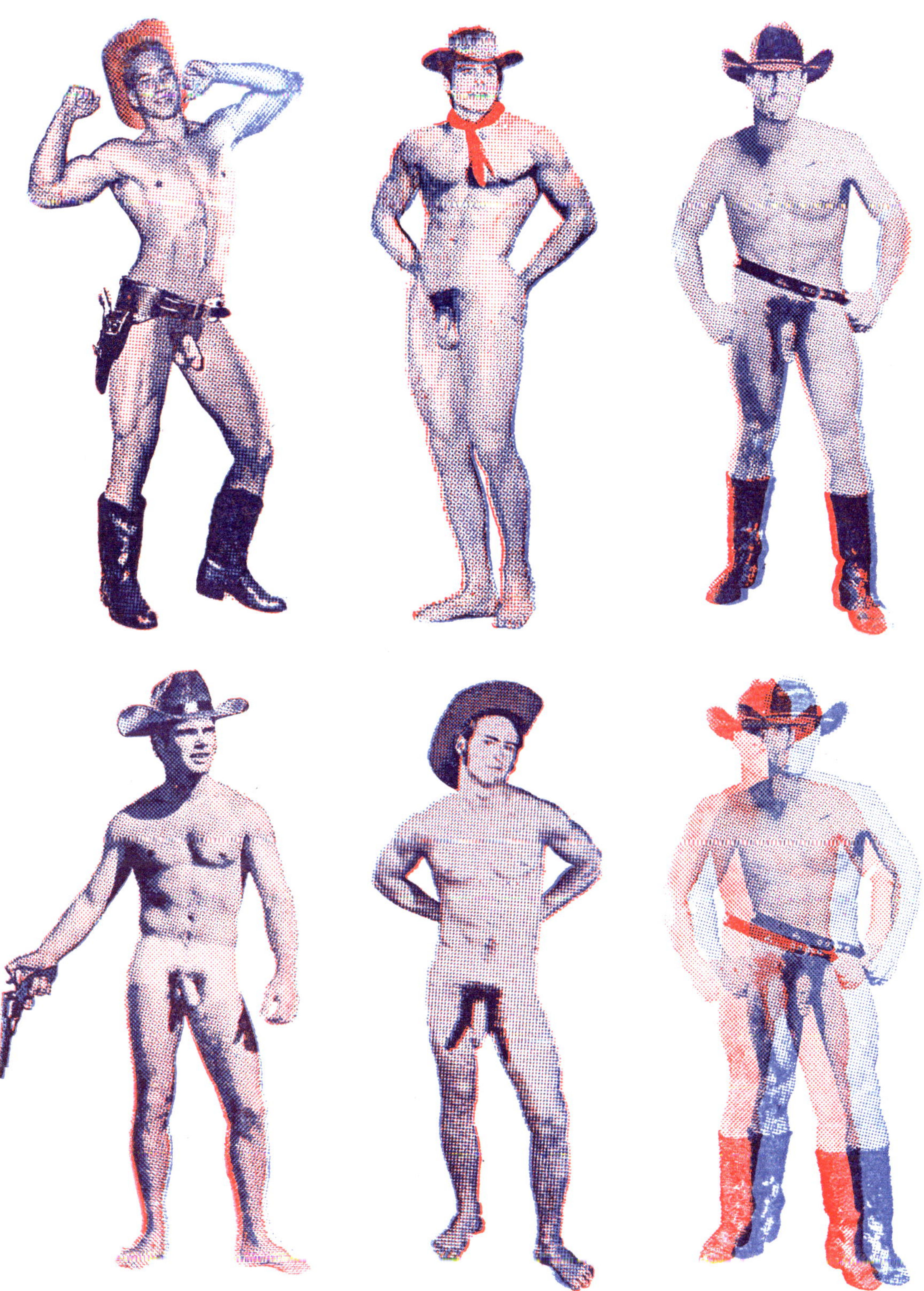

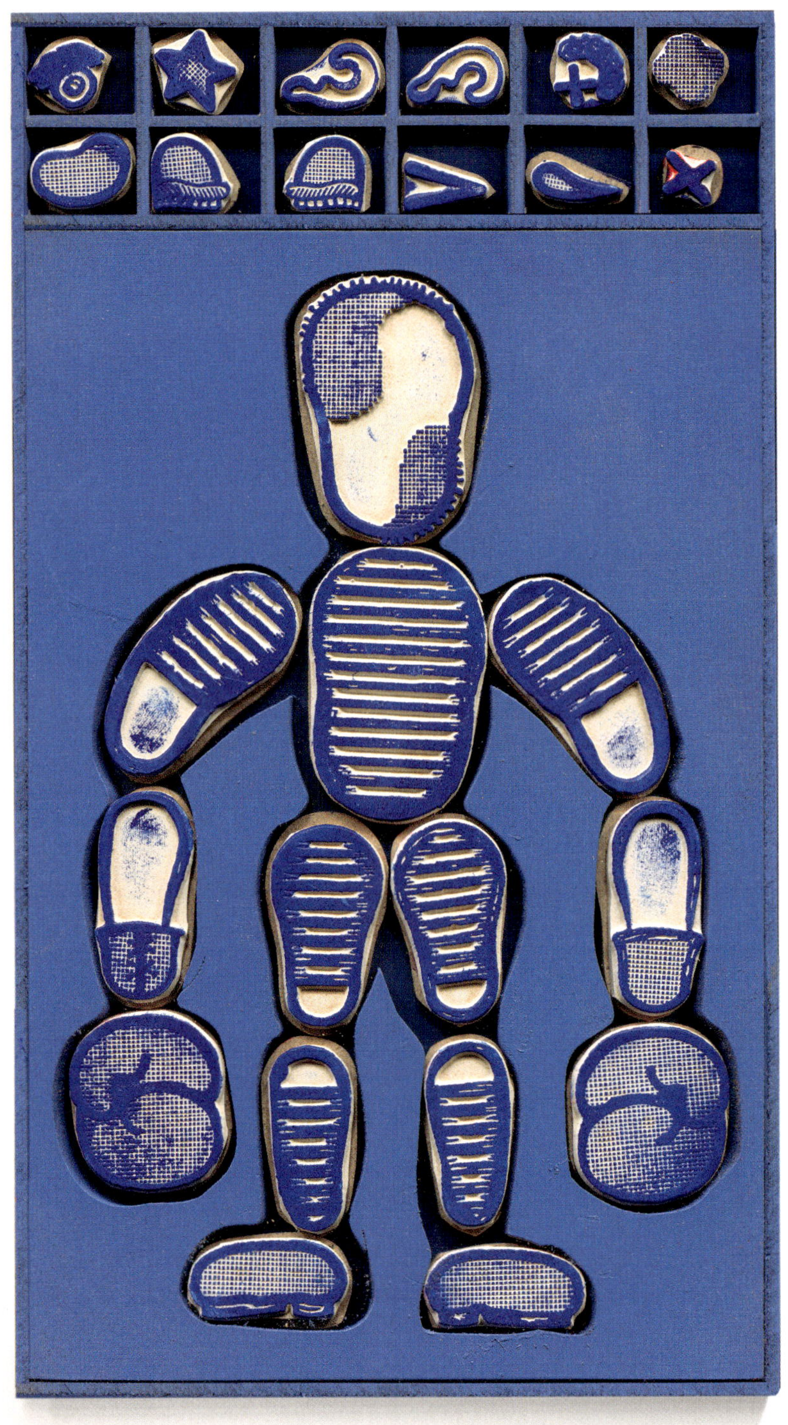

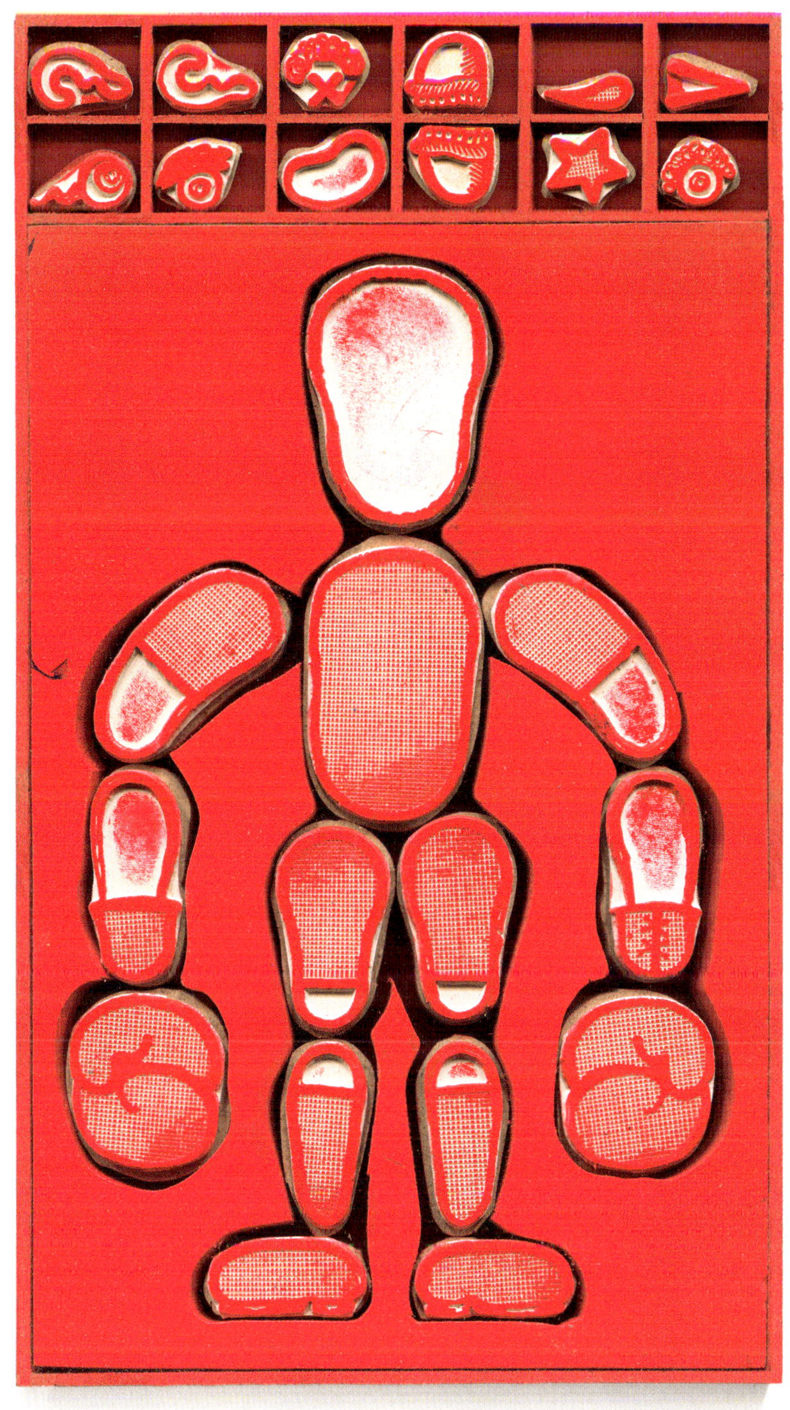

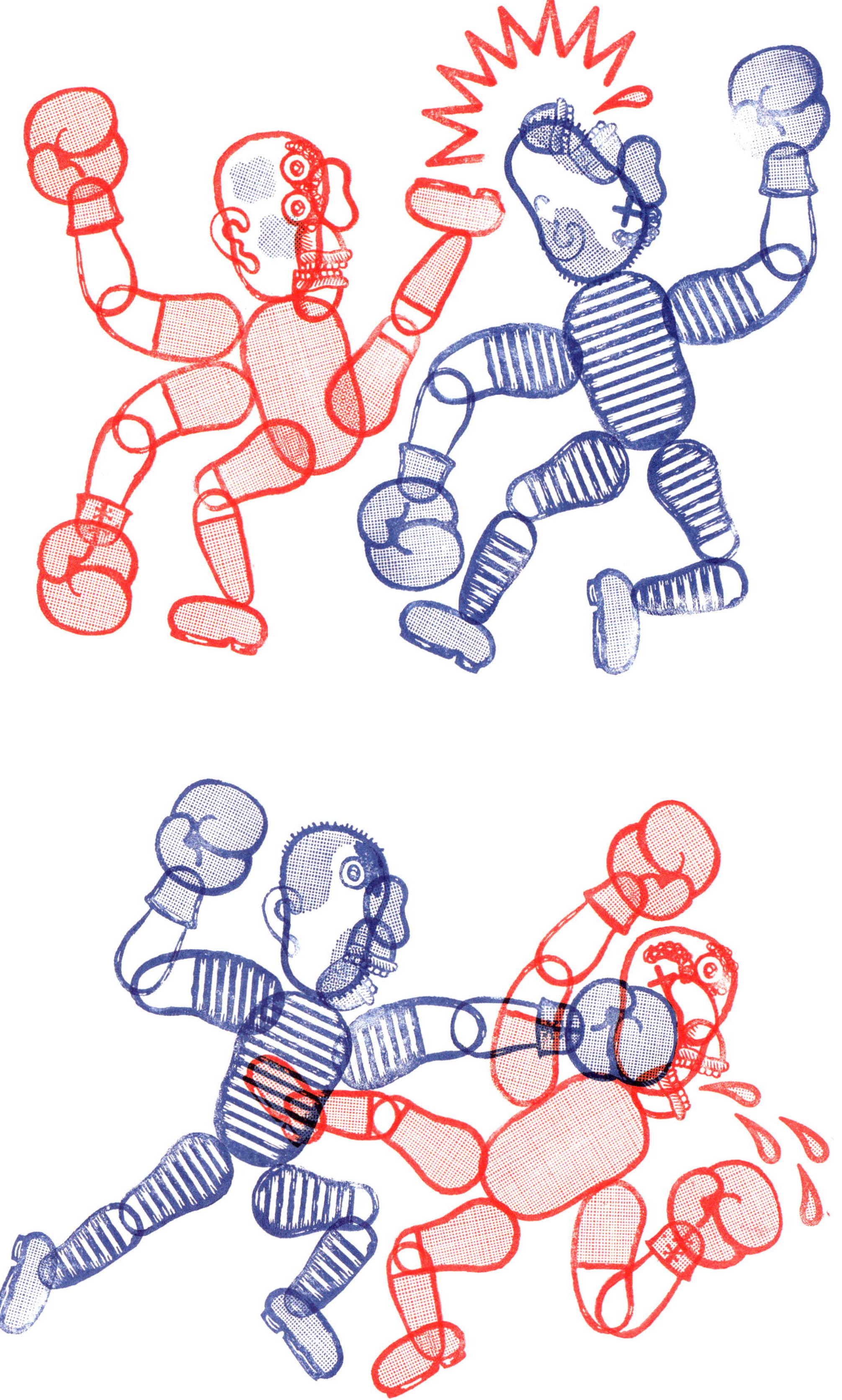

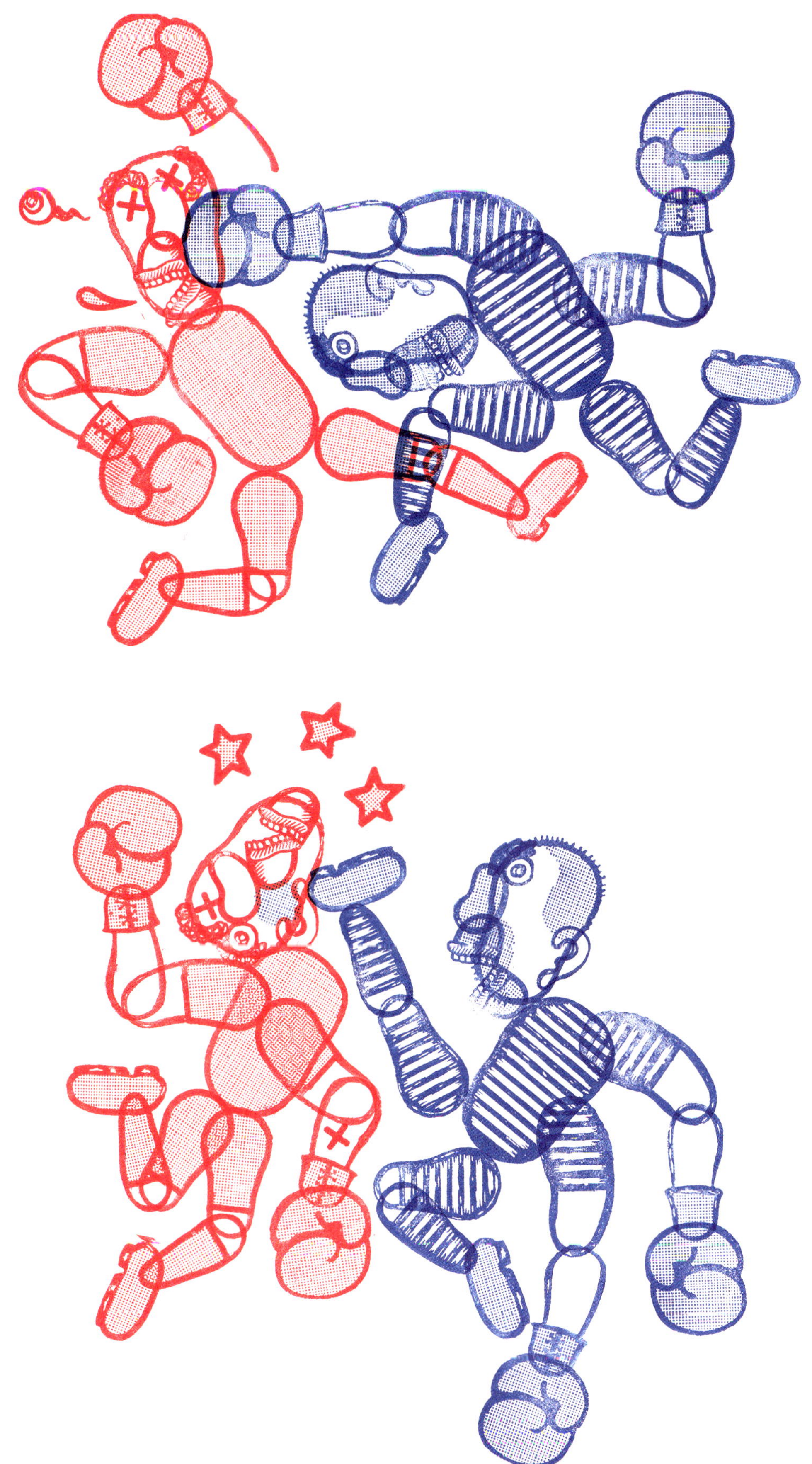

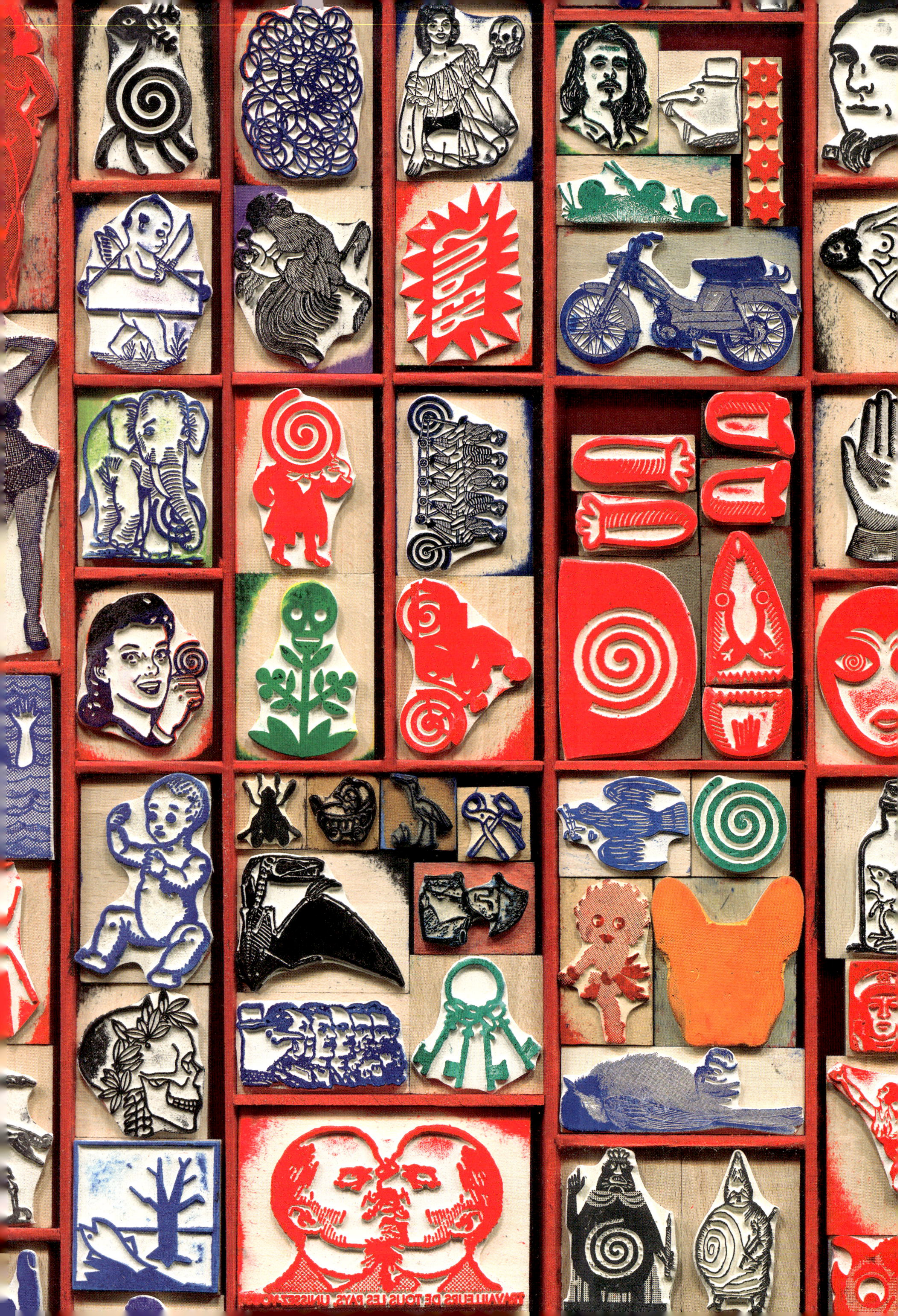

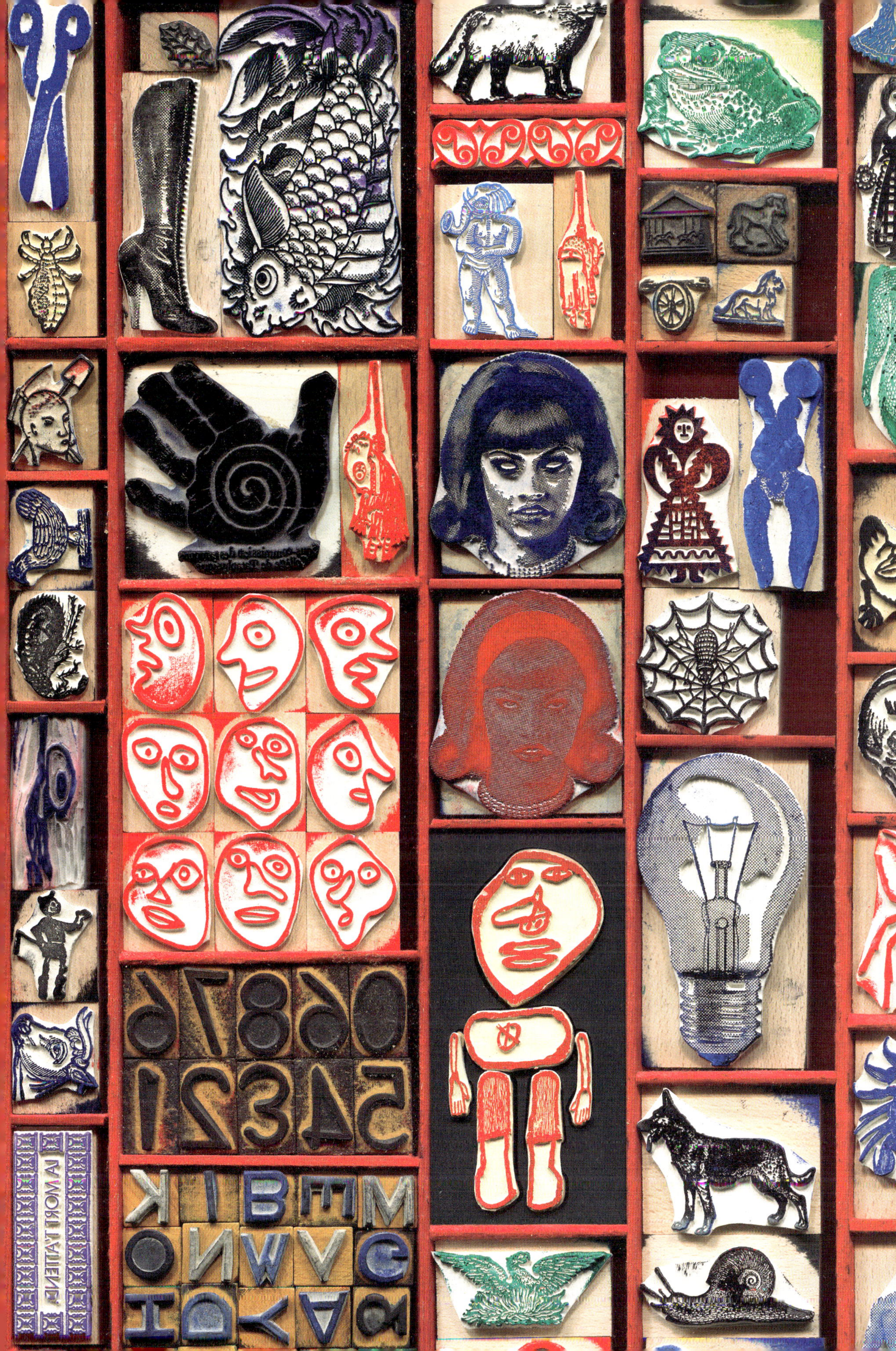

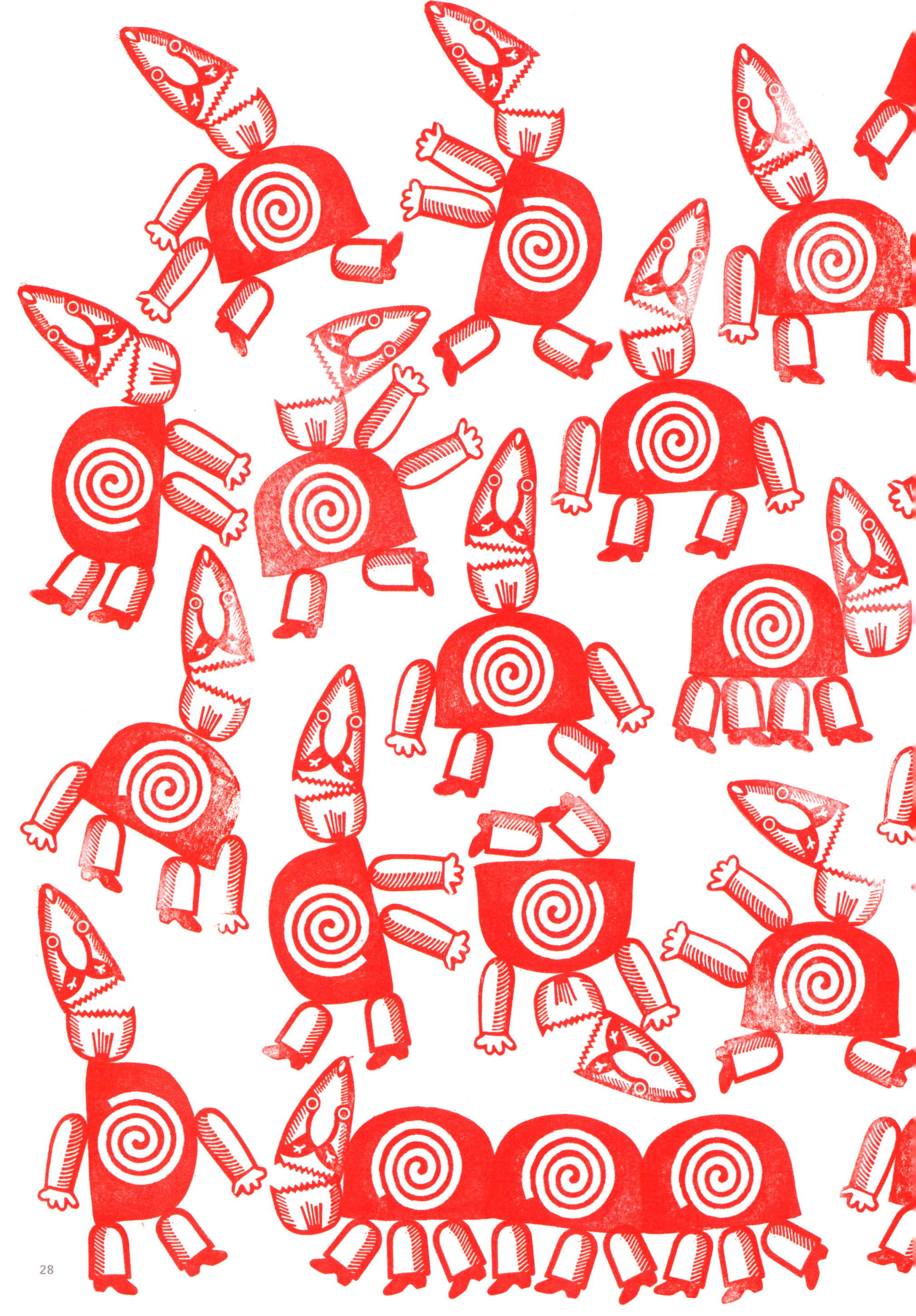

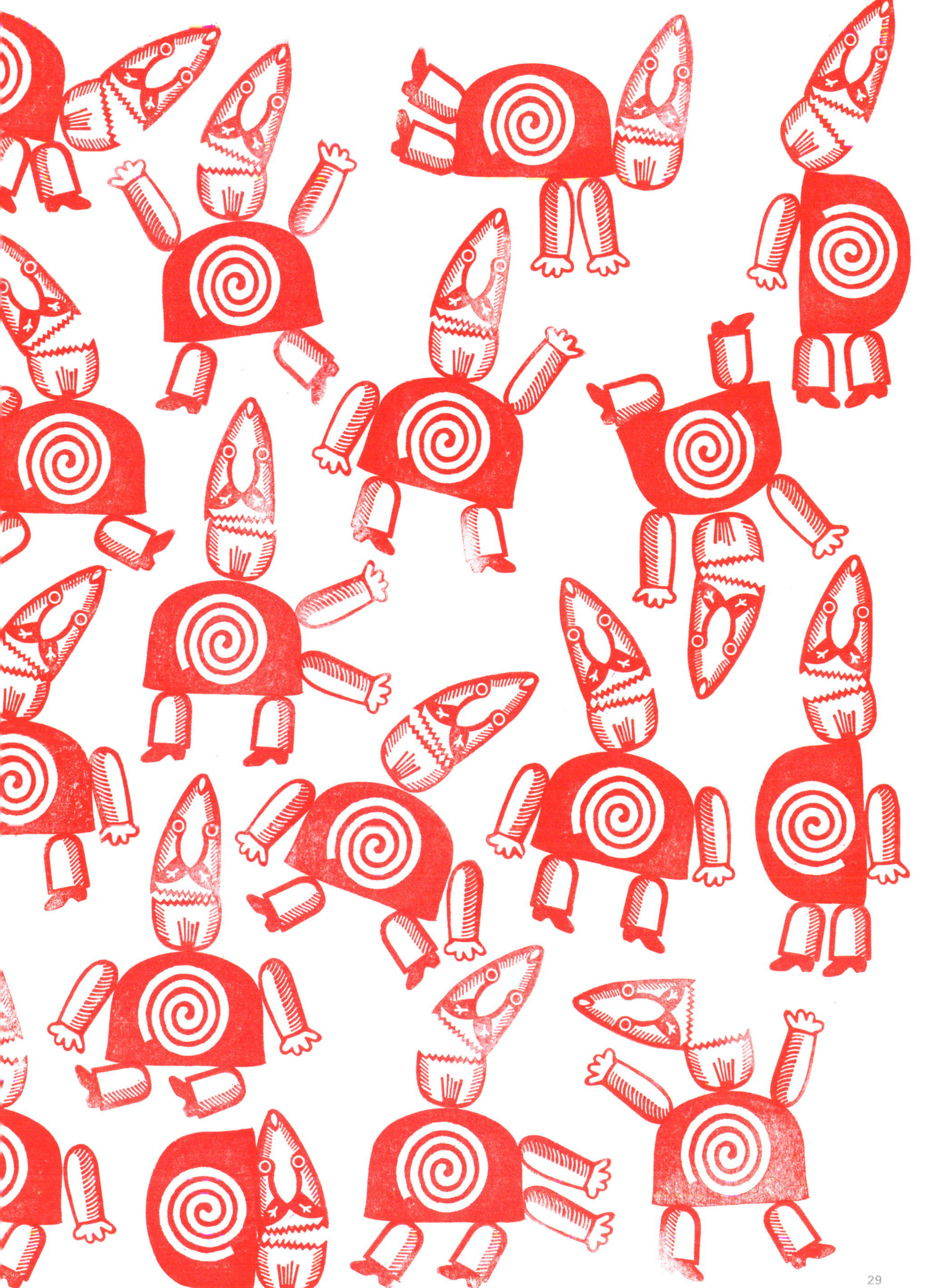

YOUR MANUSCRIPT
IS NOT ENTIRELY WITHOUT MERIT:
GROUND TO A FINE POWDER
AND MIXED IN YOGURT,
IT APPARENTLY PROTECTS
AGAINST THE STOMACH FLU.

DO NOT TOSS THIS BOOK ON THE GROUND.
PLACE IT DIRECTLY IN A TRASH CAN.
BY BURNING THIS BOOK, YOU WILL PRODUCE
SUFFICIENT ENERGY TO KEEP
A 60-WATT LIGHT BULB LIT FOR 10 MINUTES.

IF YOU KEEP SENDING US
YOUR SHITTY MANUSCRIPTS
WE ARE GOING TO HIRE
A TEAM OF GYPSIES
TO COME TO YOUR HOUSE
AND FUCK YOU UP.

I AM HAPPY TO ANNOUNCE
THAT YOU HAVE BEEN SELECTED
FOR INCLUSION ON THE SHORTLIST
OF PUBLISHERS WORTHY OF PUBLISHING MY WORK.

I HEREBY AUTHORIZE YOU
TO SEND BY RETURN MAIL
A HANDWRITTEN LETTER OF MOTIVATION
INCLUDING A FINANCIAL PROPOSITION
ACCOMPANIED BY SUPPORTING DOCUMENTS
FROM YOUR BANK.

YOUR MANUSCRIPT IS SO BAD
THAT WHILE CONSIDERING IT,
OUR ENTIRE READING COMMITTEE
GOT CANCER AND DIED.

ADVANCE READING COPY.
CANNOT BE SOLD.
IF YOU SELL THIS
AND WE GET A HOLD OF YOU,
WE WILL MAKE YOU
EAT YOUR PRESS CARD
THROUGH YOUR ASS.

ATTACHED YOU WILL FIND MY MANUSCRIPT.

I ENCOURAGE YOU TO READ IT SLOWLY,
OTHERWISE THE AESTHETIC WALLOP IT PACKS
MIGHT BLIND YOU, GIVE YOU BRAIN DAMAGE,
OR KILL YOU INSTANTLY.

WE ARE PLEASED TO ANNOUNCE
THAT WE WILL BE PUBLISHING
YOUR AUTOBIOGRAPHY,
HOWEVER YOUR LIFE
WILL REMAIN AS SHITTY AS EVER.

SORRY, NOT INTERESTED

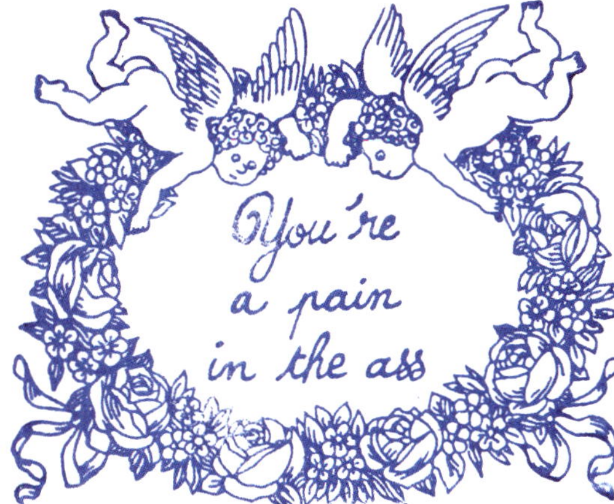

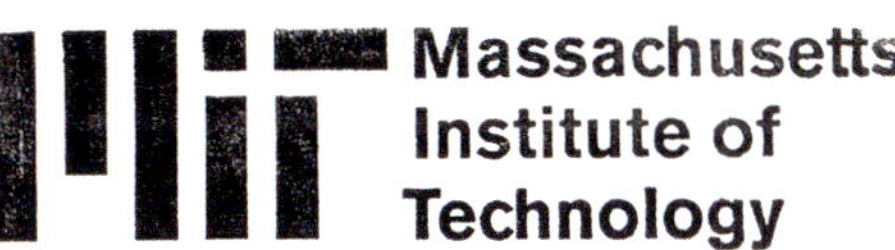

Interdisciplinary institution for research on killer robots and the cloning of porn actresses.

THIS BOOK WAS STOLEN FROM THE LIBRARY OF:

....

FOR MY DEAR......................

WITH ALL MY FRIENDSHIP,

SINCERELY.

SIGNATURE:.......................

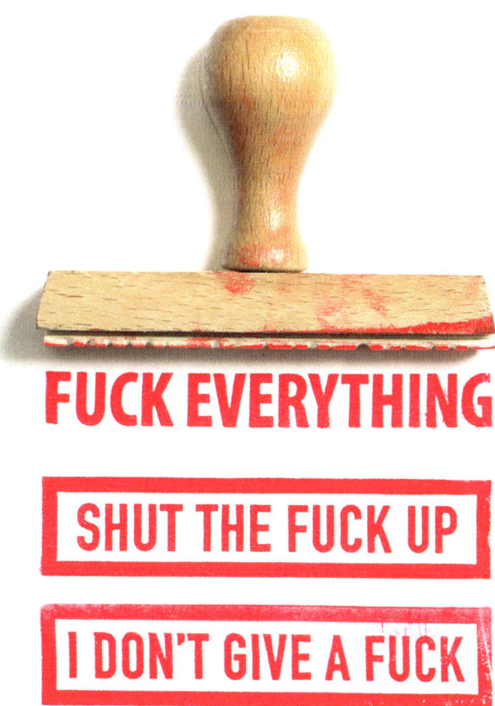

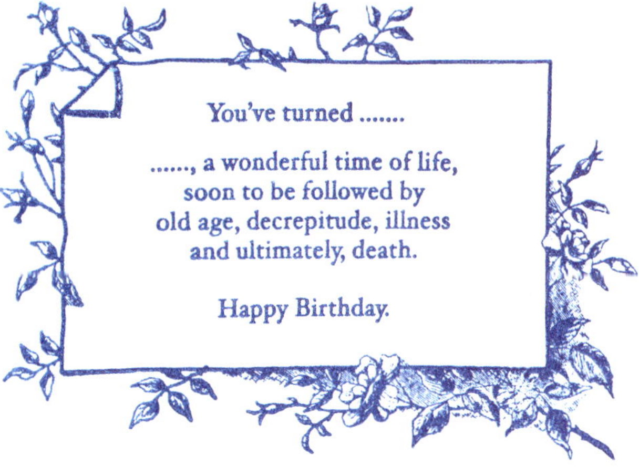

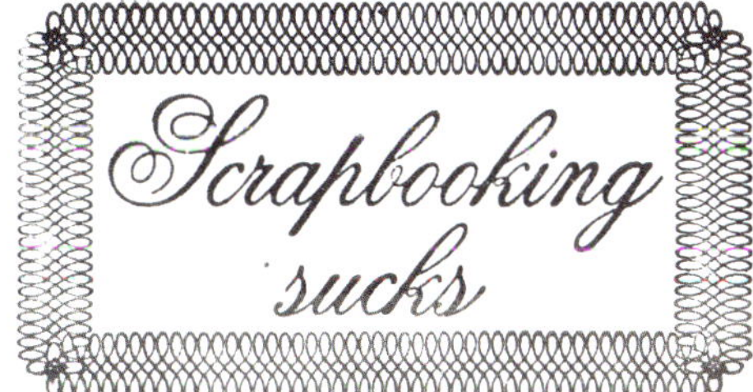

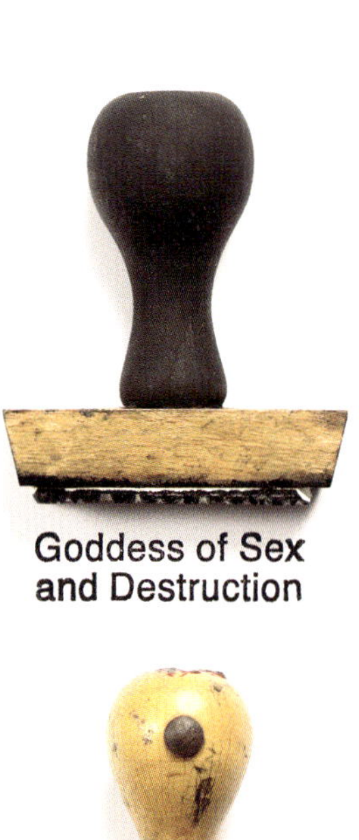

Goddess of Sex and Destruction

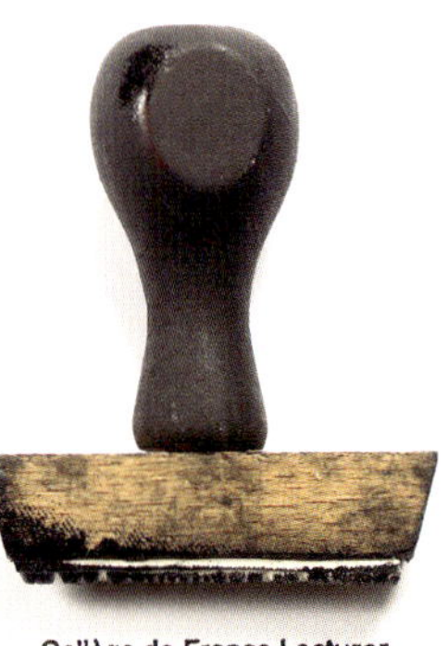

Collège de France Lecturer in Comparative Pornography

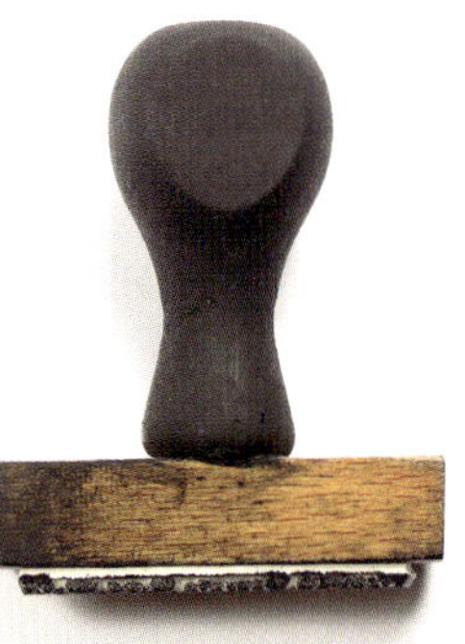

Alsatian Female Free-Fight Champion

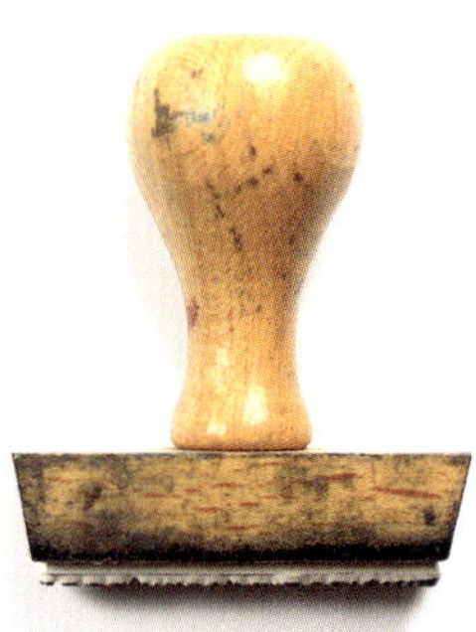

1988 Miss Angoulême

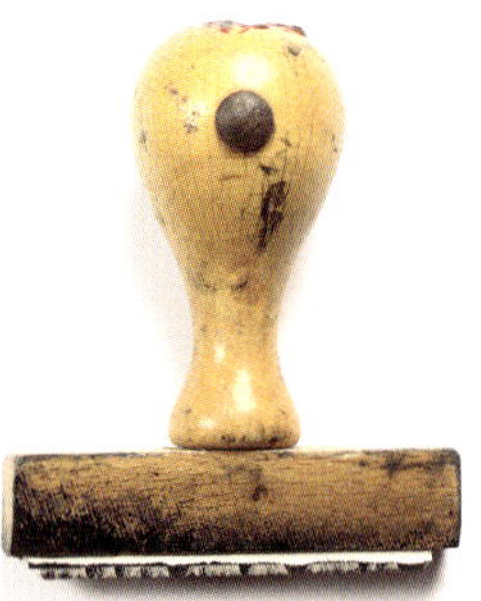

Eighteen Previous Convictions for Assault

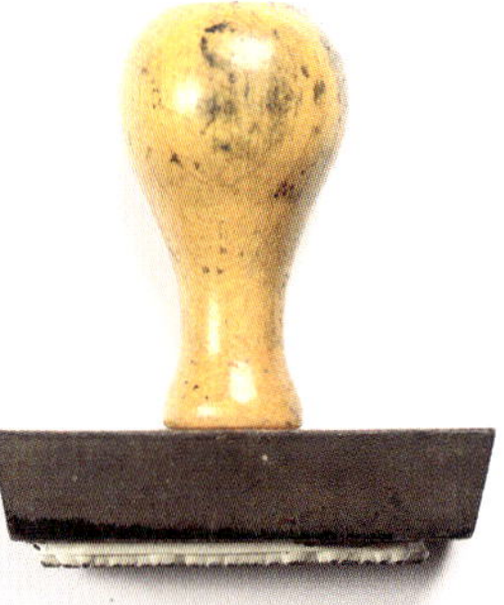

North German Female Beer-Guzzling Champion

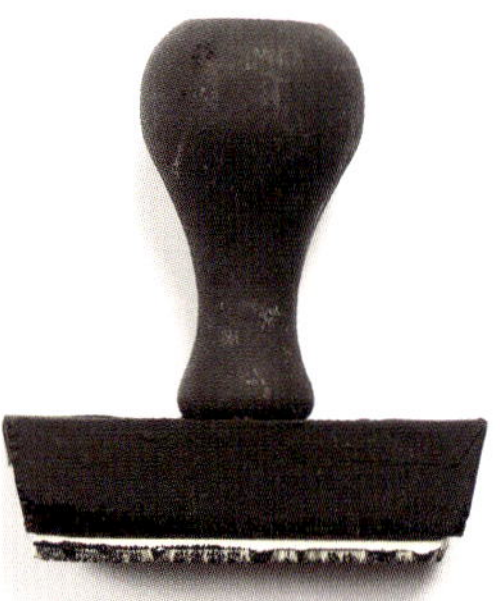

Fifth-Degree Dan Black Belt in Judo, sans Kimono

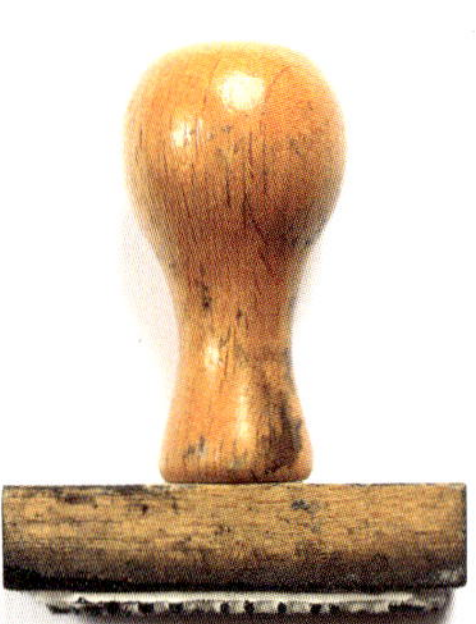

The Height of Arts, Letters and Sciences

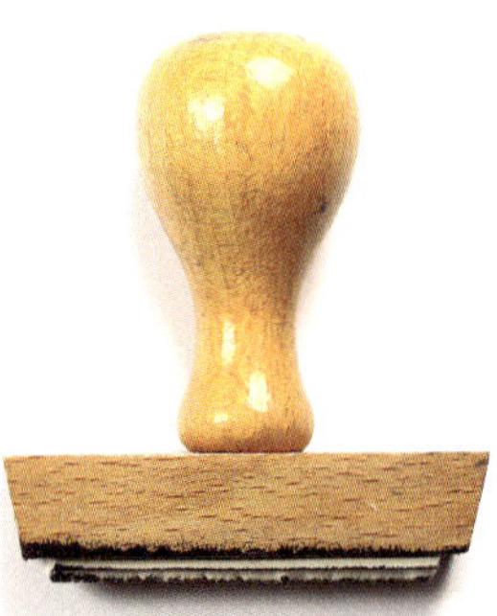

Black Belt in Lap-Dancing

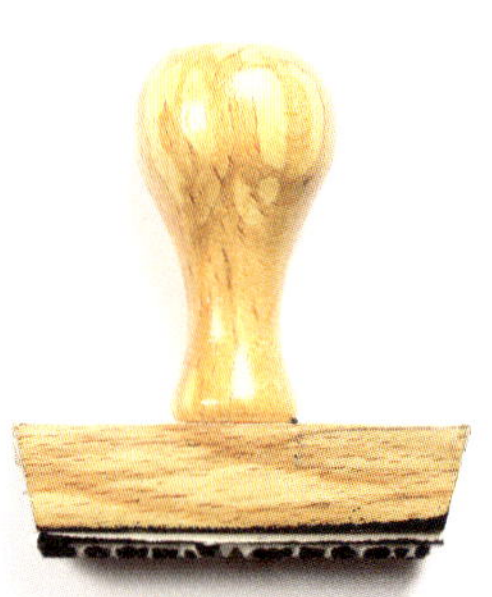

Beauty Queen

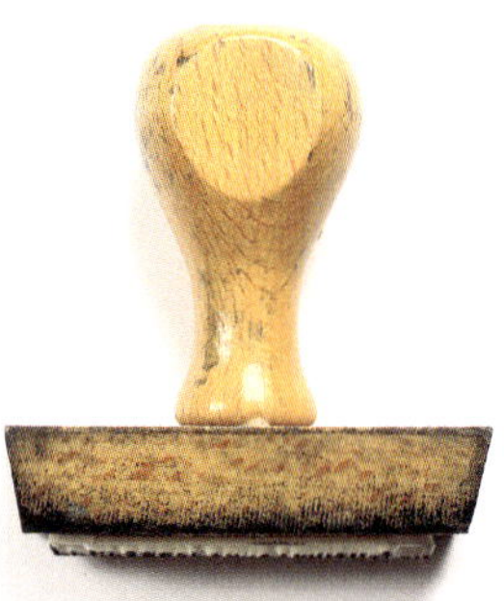

Descendant of the Prophet

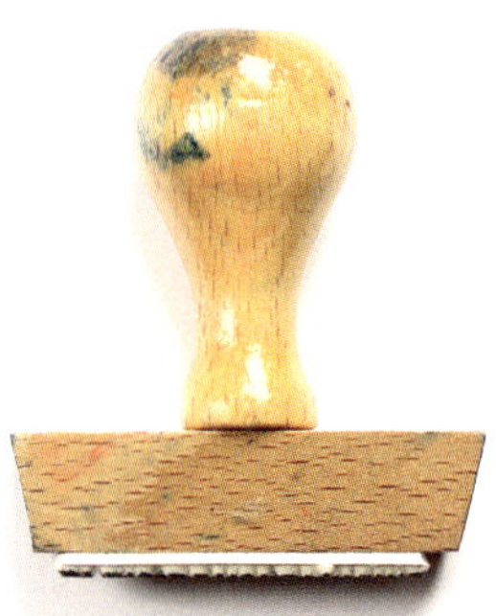

Madam President of the Soviet Supreme

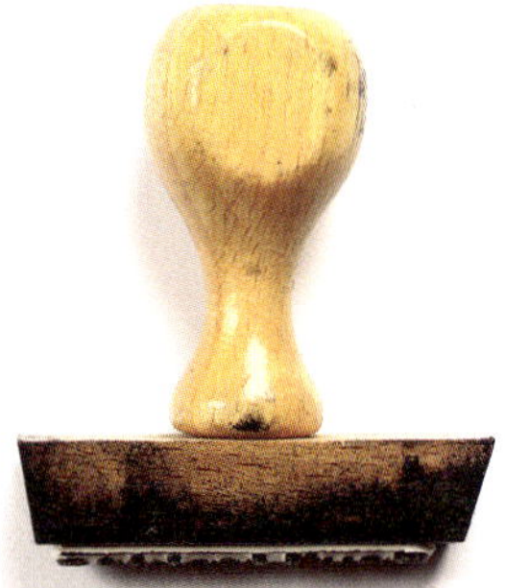

Sex Machine

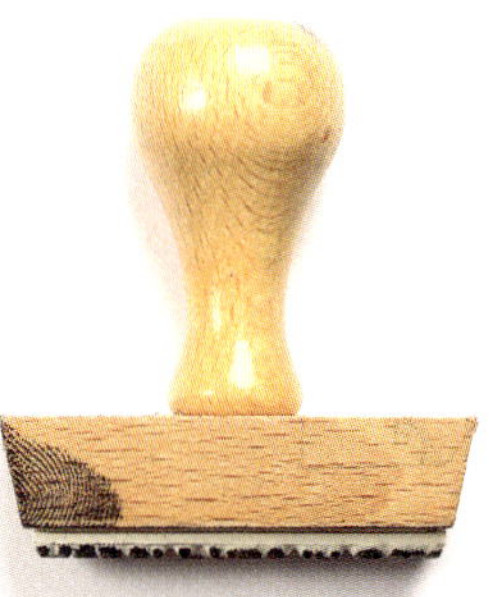

Nobel Prize in Sex

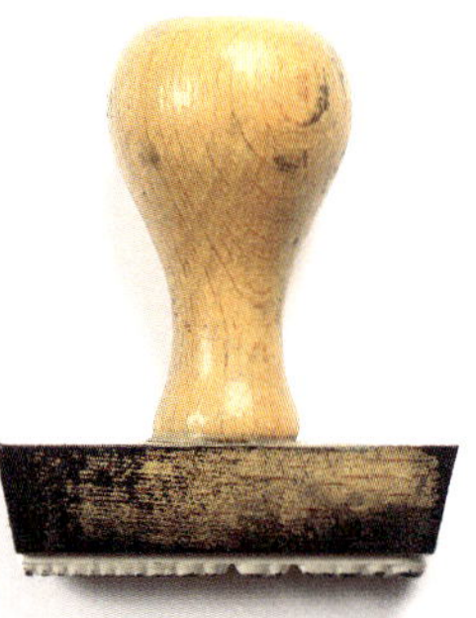

Matador of Love

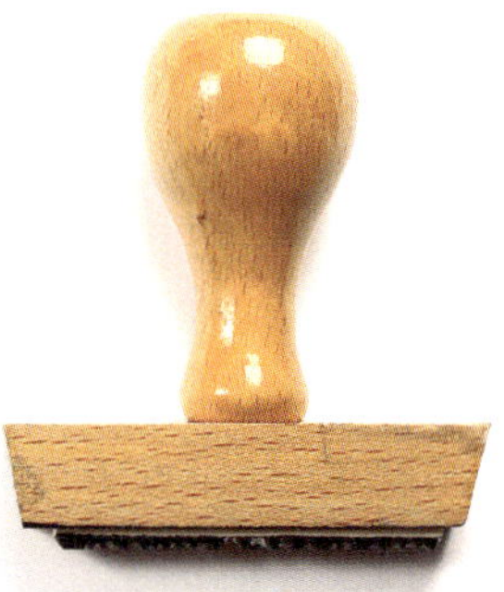

Living Human Treasure

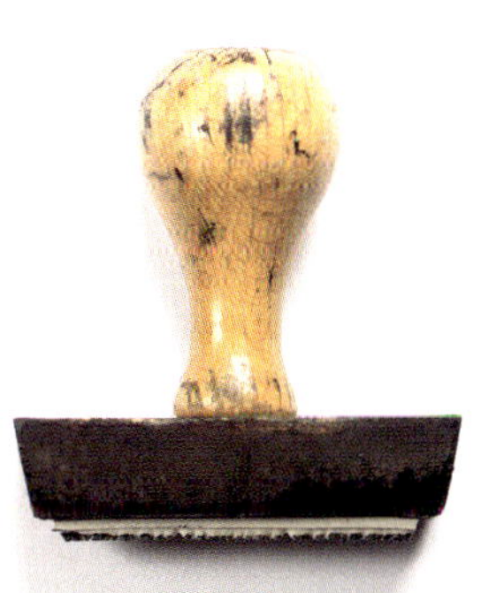

Maiden Name: Dracula

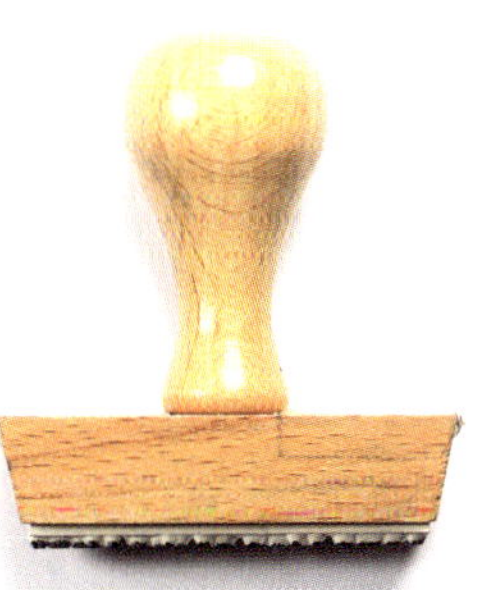

1978 Man of the Year

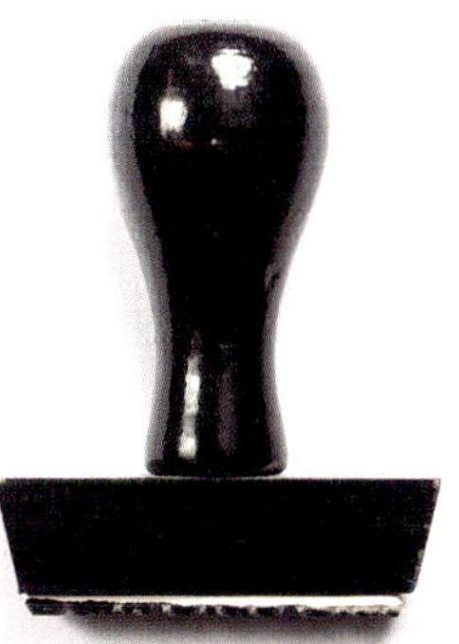

Dark Side Slut

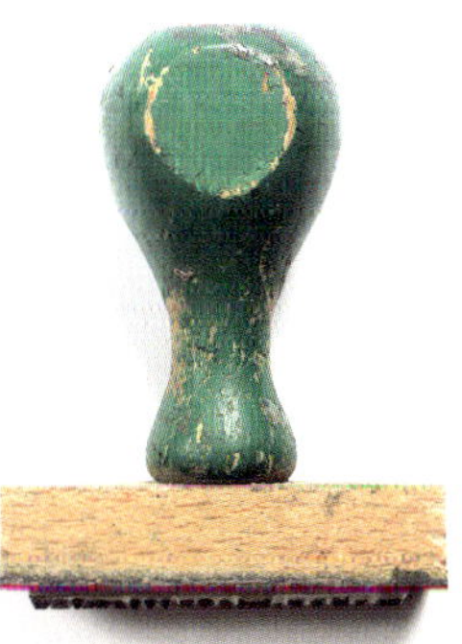

Dance-Floor Warrior

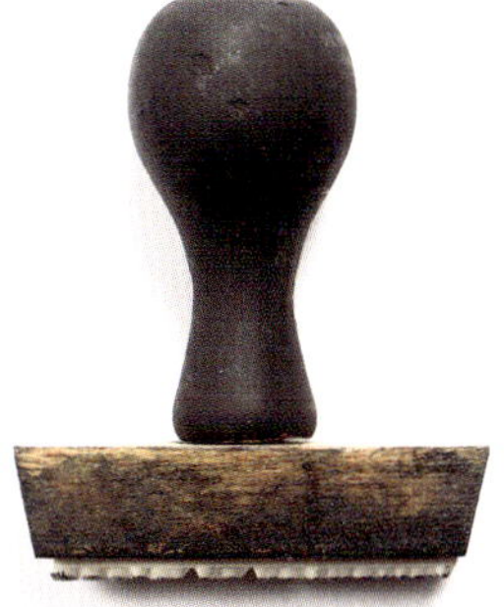

Inventor of Disco

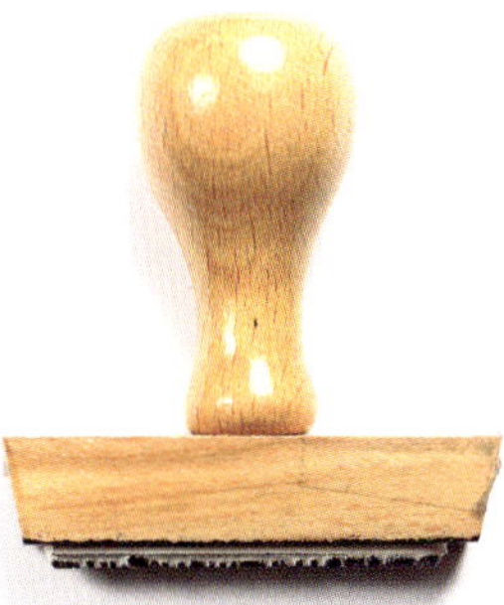

Best-dressed man in Paris

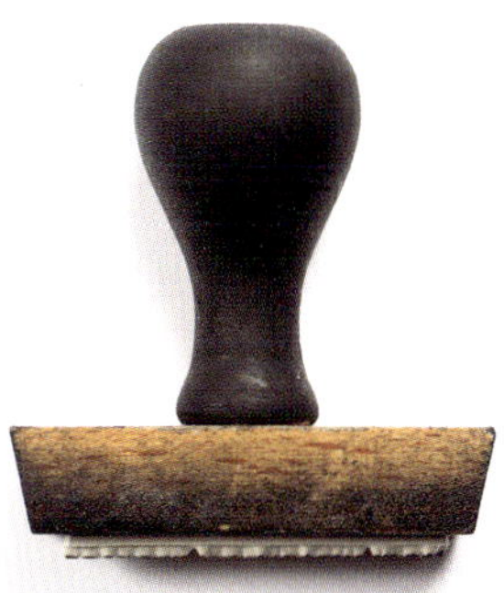

Jedi waterbed master

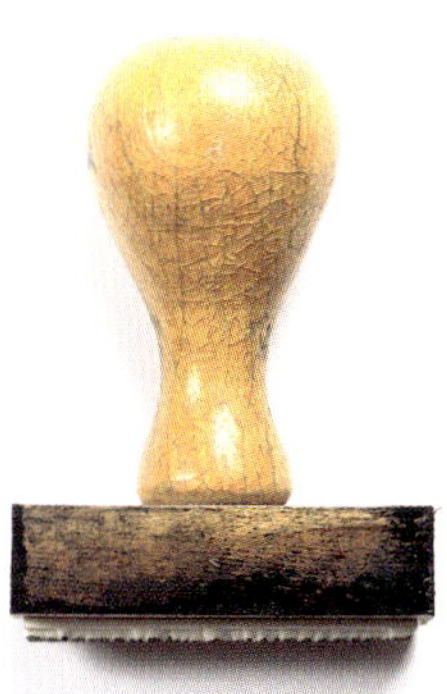

European Air-Sex Champion

Darling,

Here is some money for your birthday.

Love, Grandma

Last Frenchwoman
to be Sentenced to Death

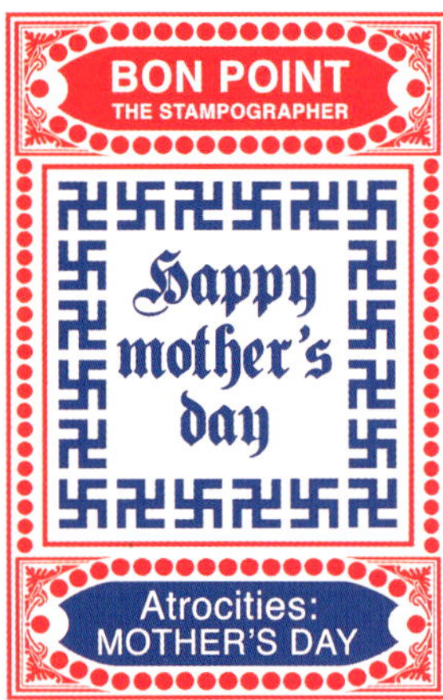
BON POINT
THE STAMPOGRAPHER
Happy mother's day
Atrocities:
MOTHER'S DAY

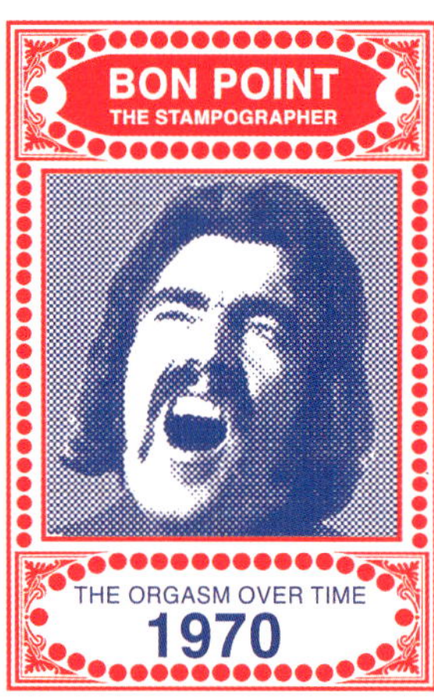
BON POINT
THE STAMPOGRAPHER
THE ORGASM OVER TIME
1970

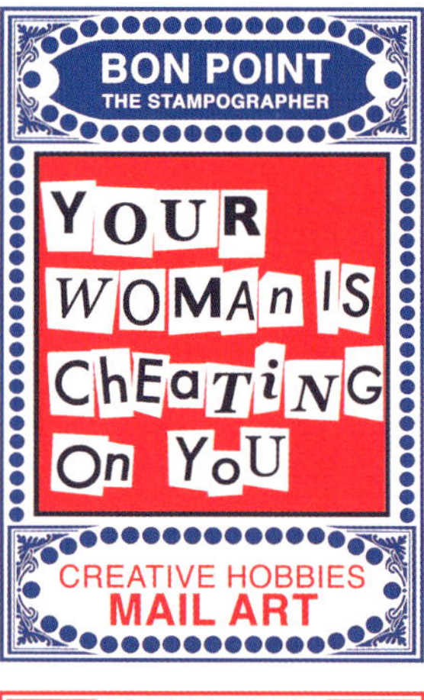
BON POINT
THE STAMPOGRAPHER
YOUR WOMAN IS CHEATING ON YOU
CREATIVE HOBBIES
MAIL ART

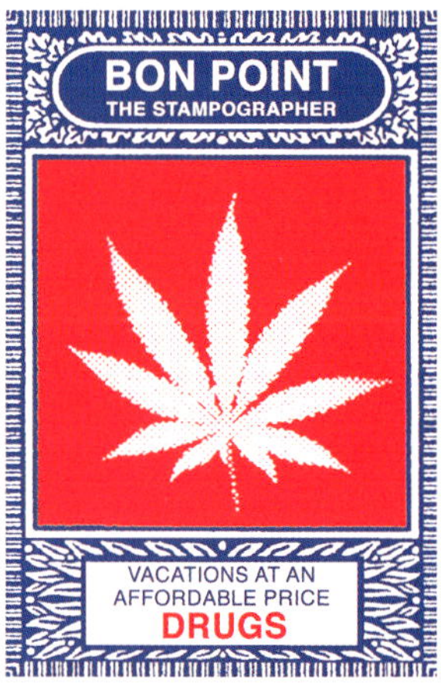
BON POINT
THE STAMPOGRAPHER
VACATIONS AT AN
AFFORDABLE PRICE
DRUGS

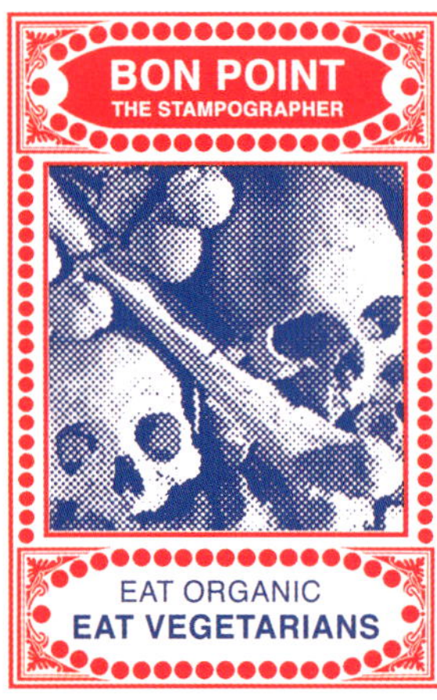
BON POINT
THE STAMPOGRAPHER
EAT ORGANIC
EAT VEGETARIANS

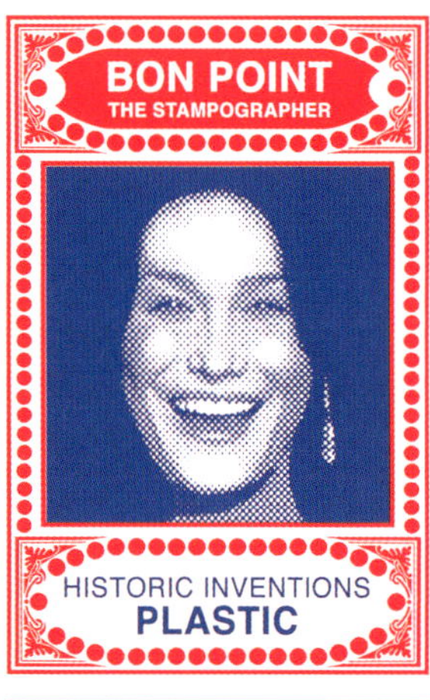
BON POINT
THE STAMPOGRAPHER
HISTORIC INVENTIONS
PLASTIC

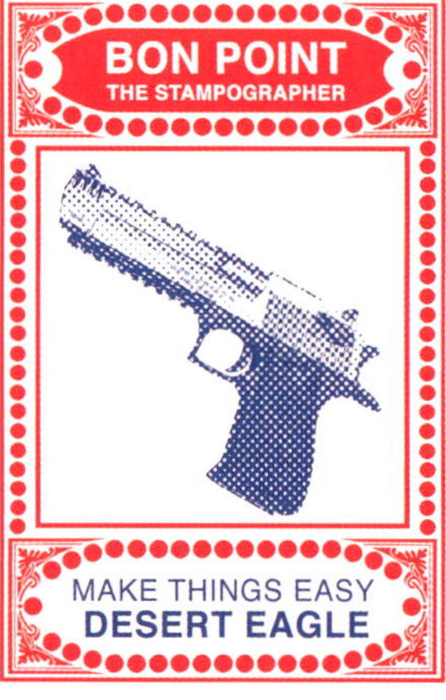
BON POINT
THE STAMPOGRAPHER
MAKE THINGS EASY
DESERT EAGLE

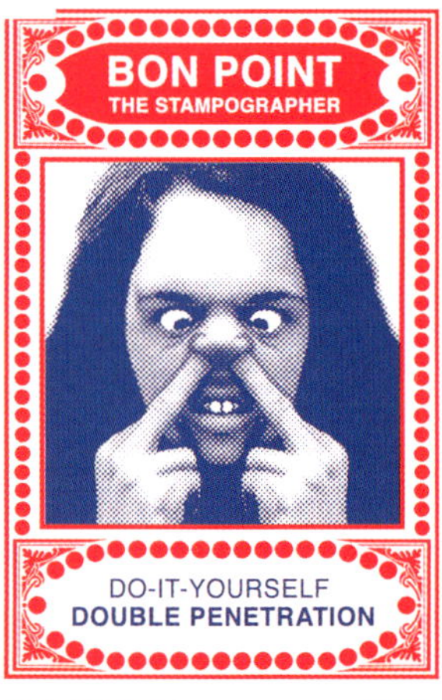
BON POINT
THE STAMPOGRAPHER
DO-IT-YOURSELF
DOUBLE PENETRATION

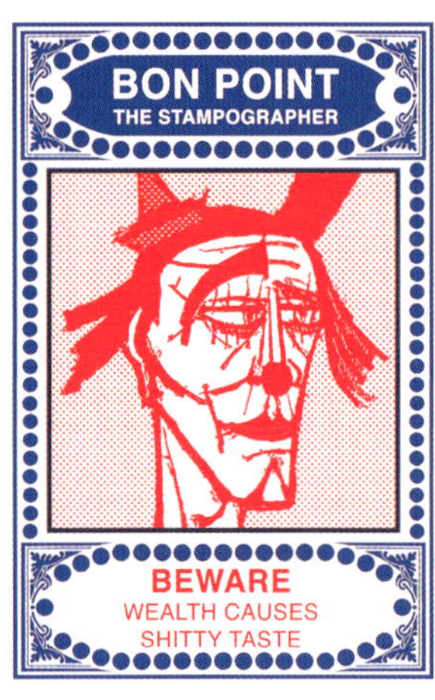
BON POINT
THE STAMPOGRAPHER
BEWARE
WEALTH CAUSES
SHITTY TASTE

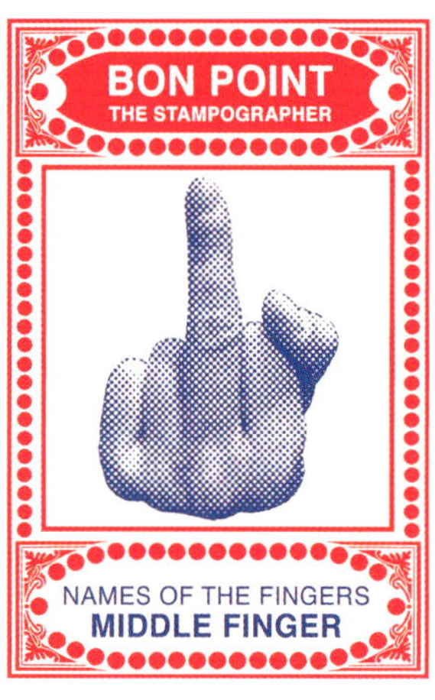
BON POINT
THE STAMPOGRAPHER
NAMES OF THE FINGERS
MIDDLE FINGER

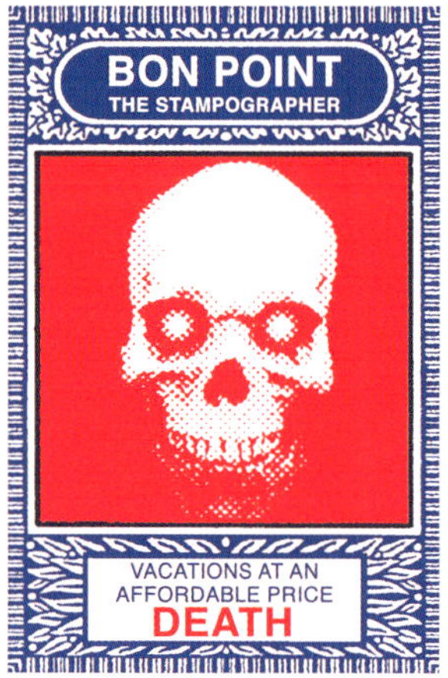
BON POINT
THE STAMPOGRAPHER
VACATIONS AT AN
AFFORDABLE PRICE
DEATH

BON POINT
THE STAMPOGRAPHER
THE ORGASM OVER TIME
1925

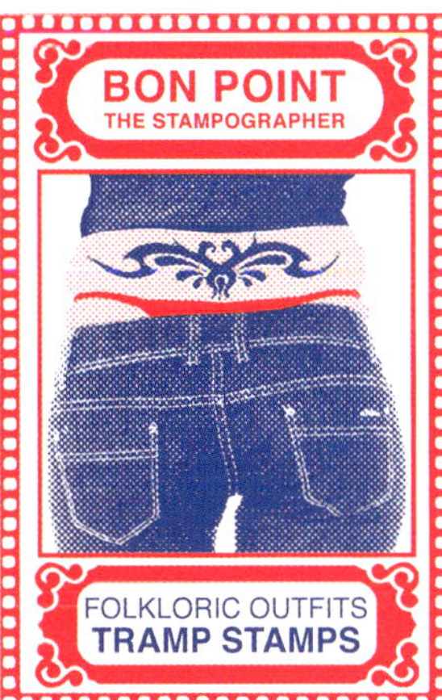
BON POINT
THE STAMPOGRAPHER
FOLKLORIC OUTFITS
TRAMP STAMPS

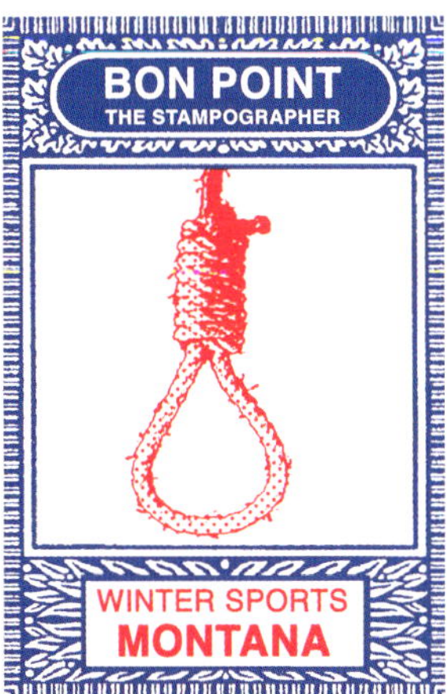
BON POINT
THE STAMPOGRAPHER
WINTER SPORTS
MONTANA

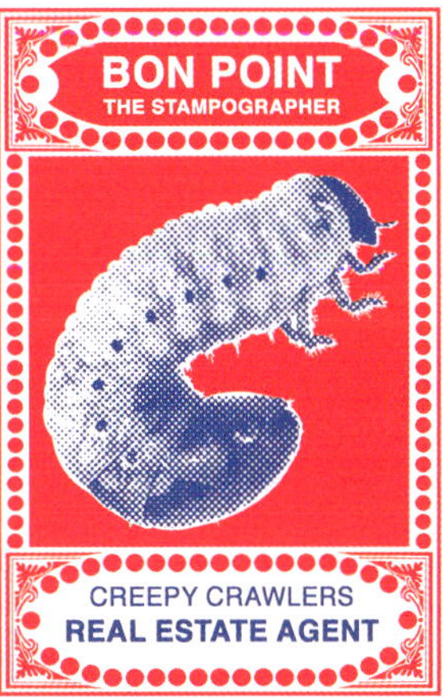
BON POINT
THE STAMPOGRAPHER
CREEPY CRAWLERS
REAL ESTATE AGENT

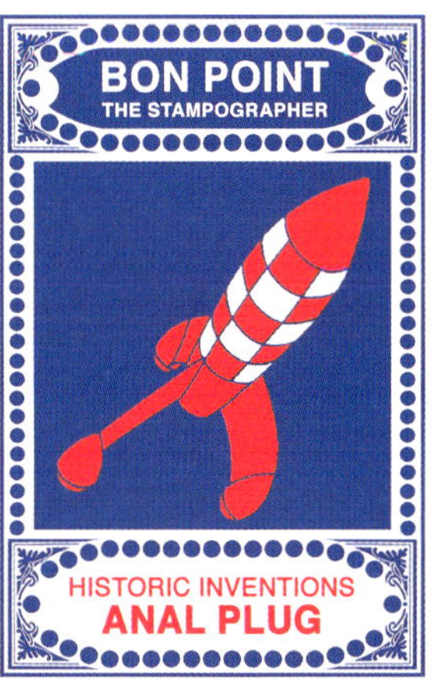
BON POINT
THE STAMPOGRAPHER
HISTORIC INVENTIONS
ANAL PLUG

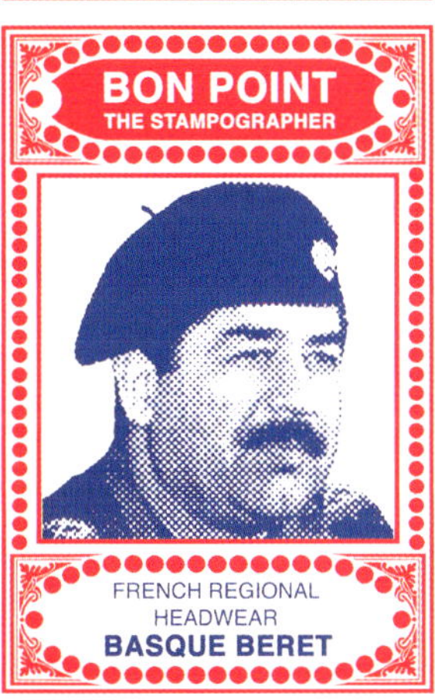
BON POINT
THE STAMPOGRAPHER
FRENCH REGIONAL HEADWEAR
BASQUE BERET

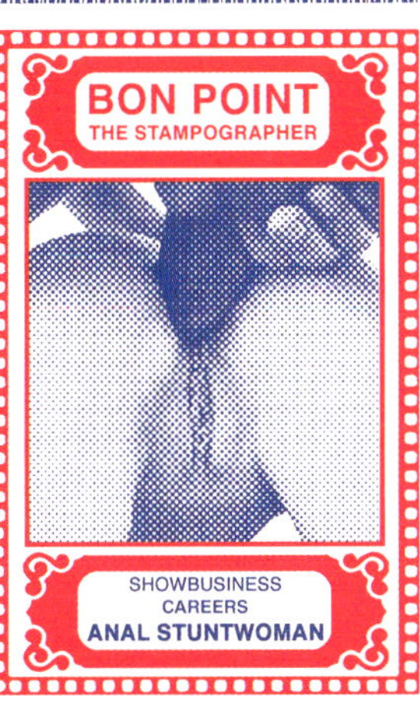
BON POINT
THE STAMPOGRAPHER
SHOWBUSINESS CAREERS
ANAL STUNTWOMAN

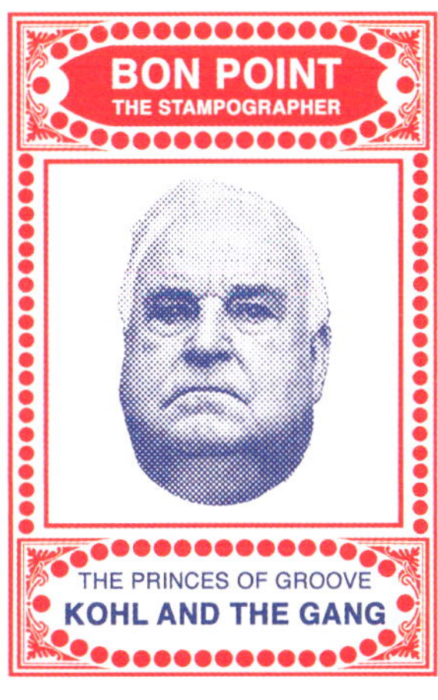
BON POINT
THE STAMPOGRAPHER
THE PRINCES OF GROOVE
KOHL AND THE GANG

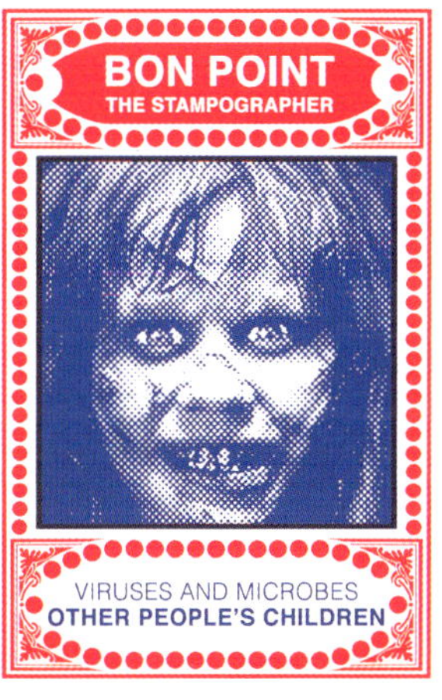
BON POINT
THE STAMPOGRAPHER
VIRUSES AND MICROBES
OTHER PEOPLE'S CHILDREN

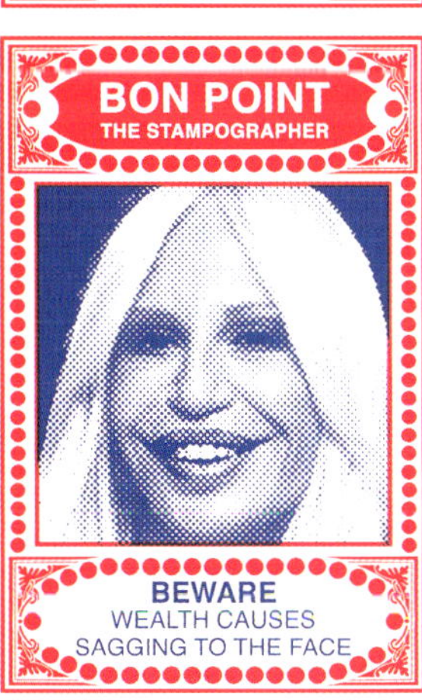
BON POINT
THE STAMPOGRAPHER
BEWARE
WEALTH CAUSES
SAGGING TO THE FACE

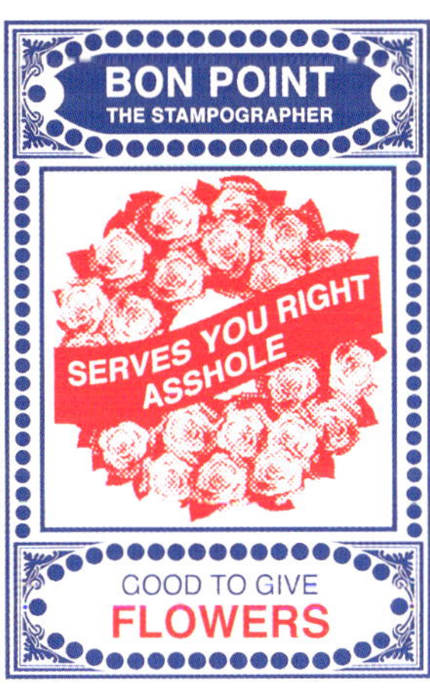
BON POINT
THE STAMPOGRAPHER
SERVES YOU RIGHT
ASSHOLE
GOOD TO GIVE
FLOWERS

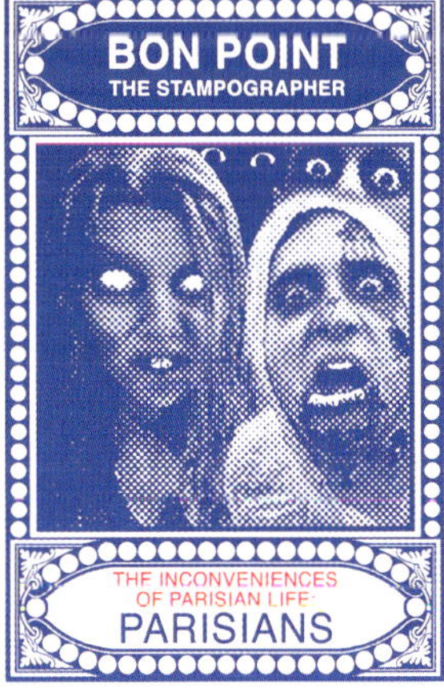
BON POINT
THE STAMPOGRAPHER
THE INCONVENIENCES
OF PARISIAN LIFE
PARISIANS

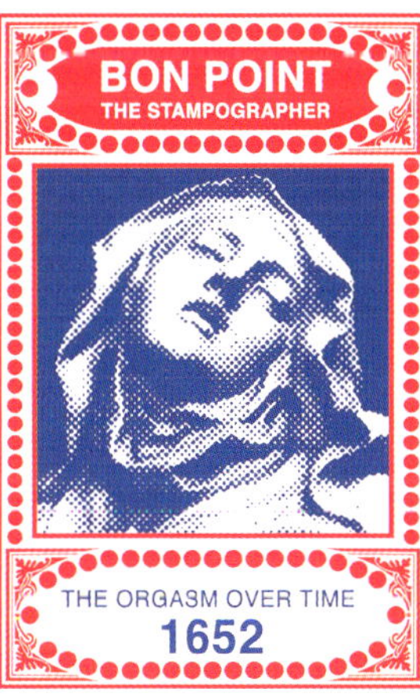
BON POINT
THE STAMPOGRAPHER
THE ORGASM OVER TIME
1652

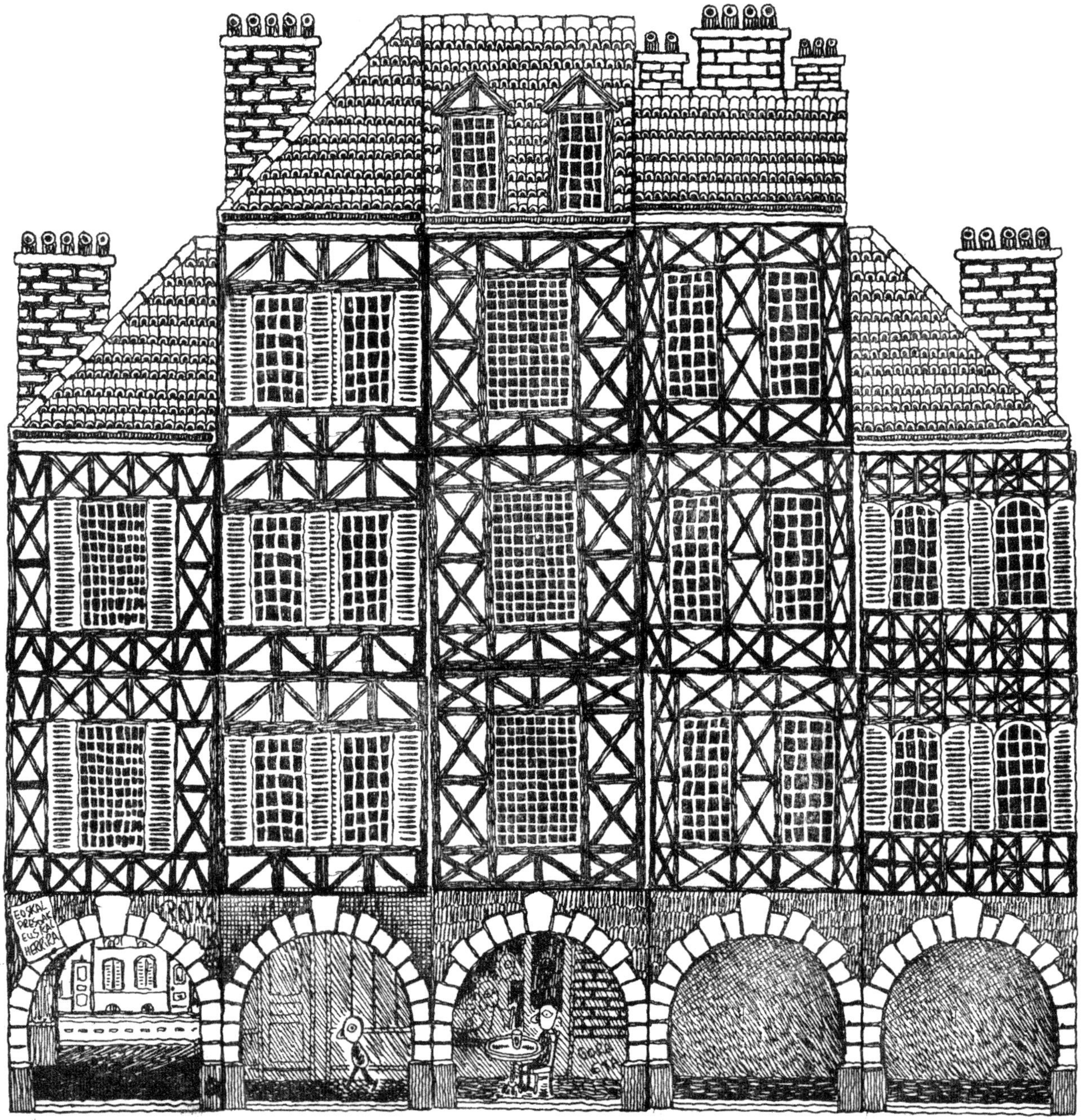

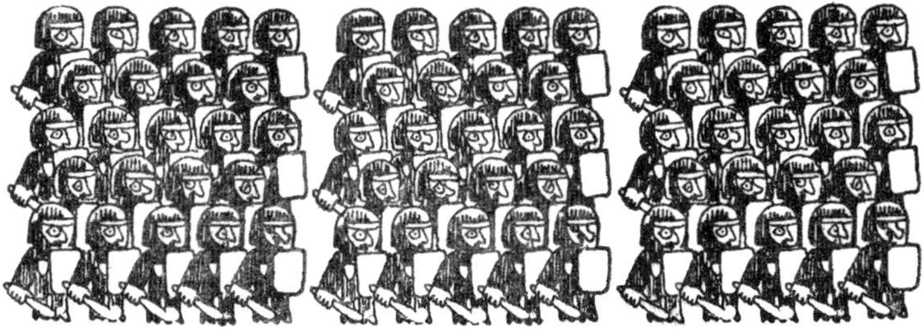

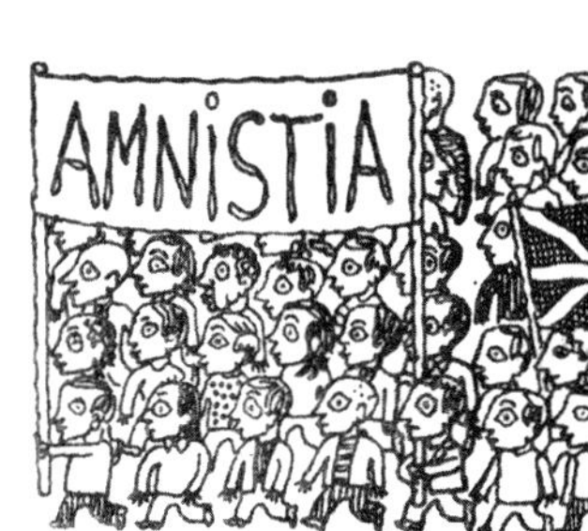
AMNISTIA

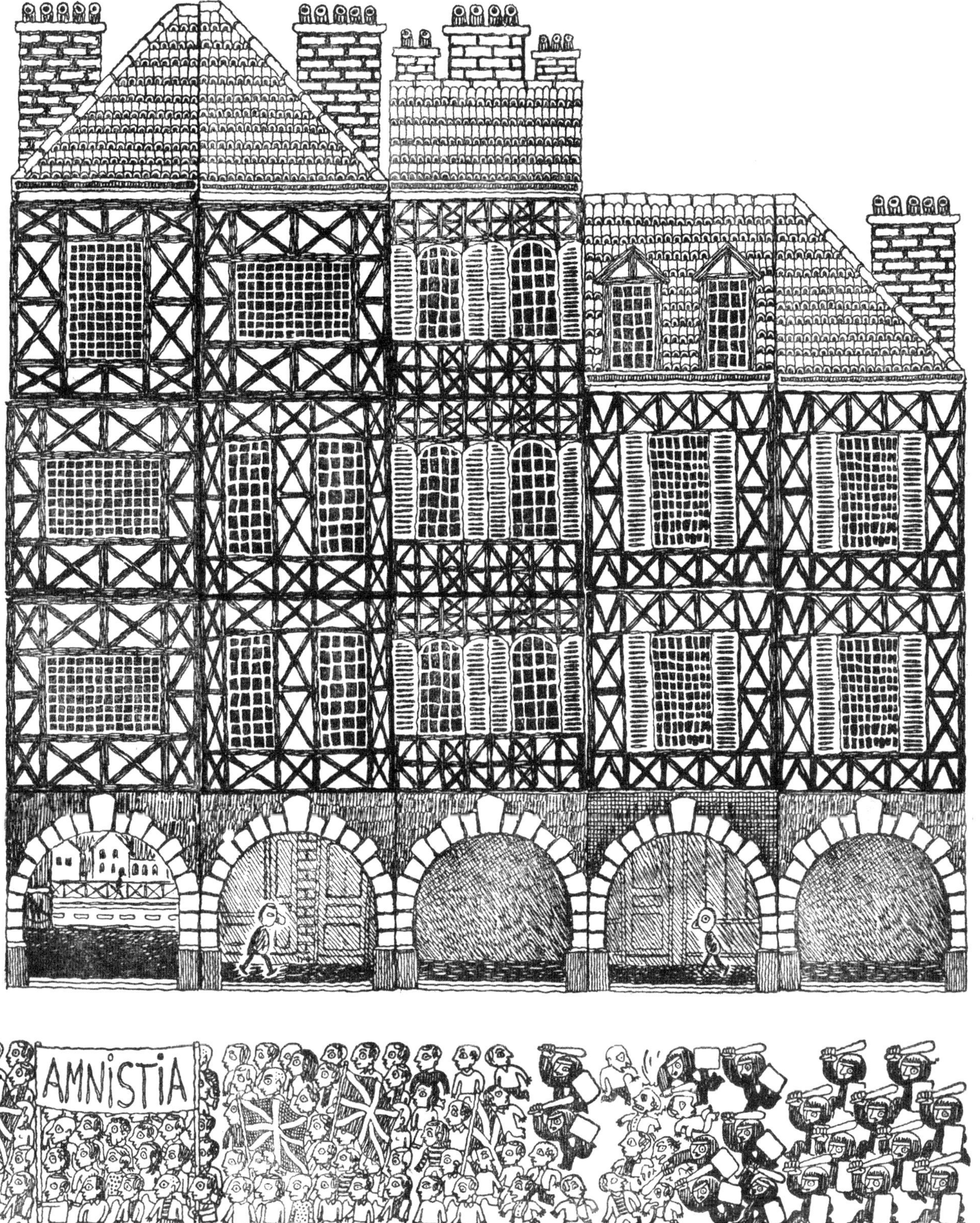
AMNISTIA

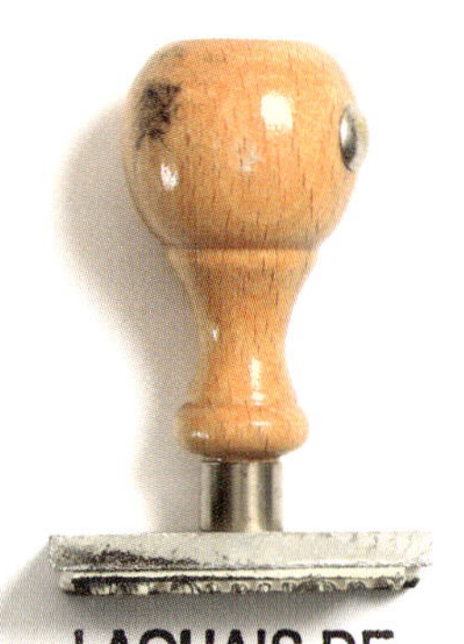

LAQUAIS DE
LA PRESSE
BOURGEOISE

Bourgeois press flunky

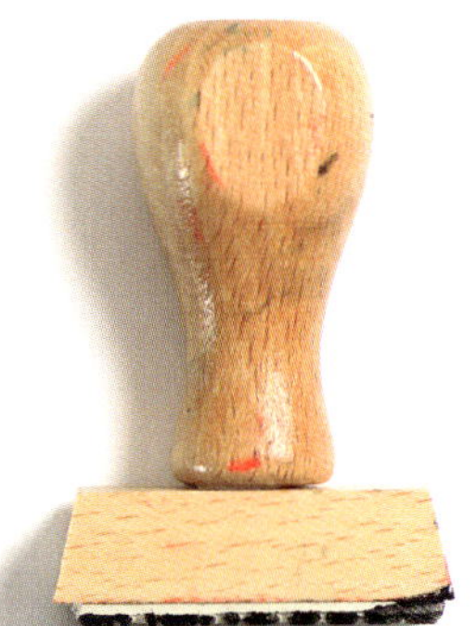

FOSSOYEUR
DE LA
RÉVOLUTION

Grave digger of the revolution

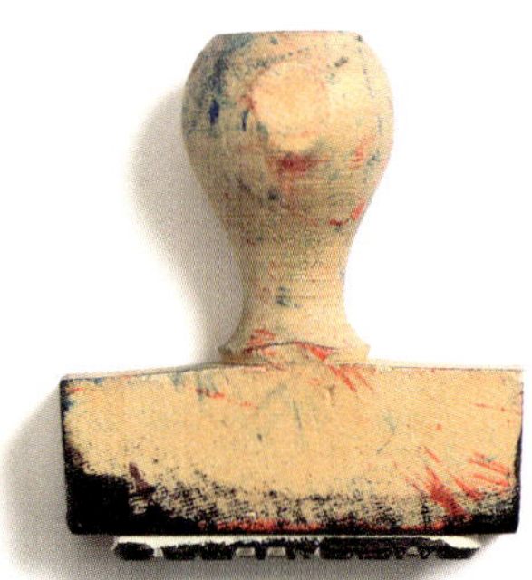

GUERILLERO
DE CANAPÉ

Couch guerilla

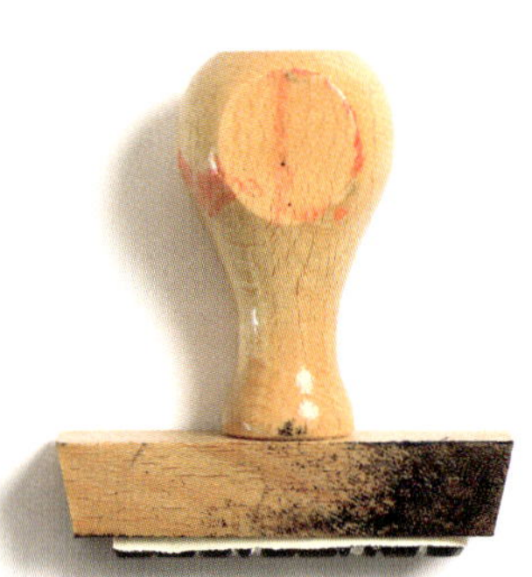

CENTRISTE

centrist

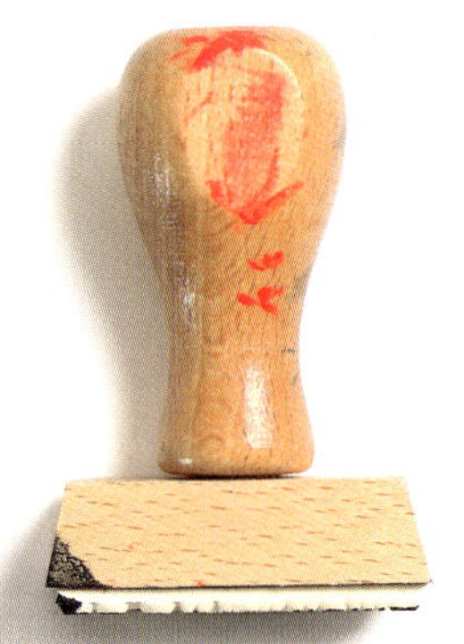

BIFTECKARD
STALINIEN

Stalinist cheese steak

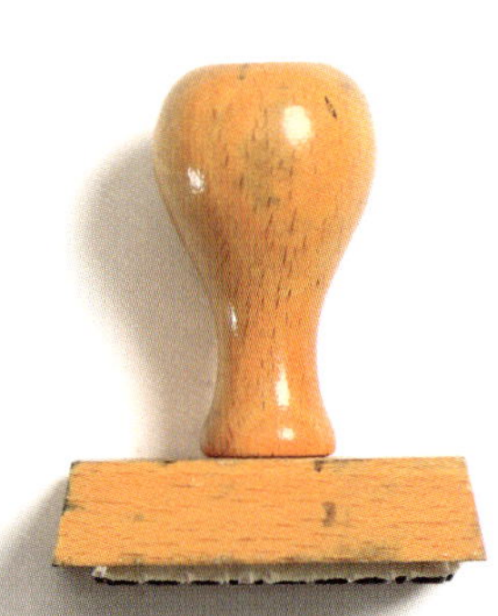

ANARCHISTE
PETIT-
BOURGEOIS

petty bourgeois anarchist

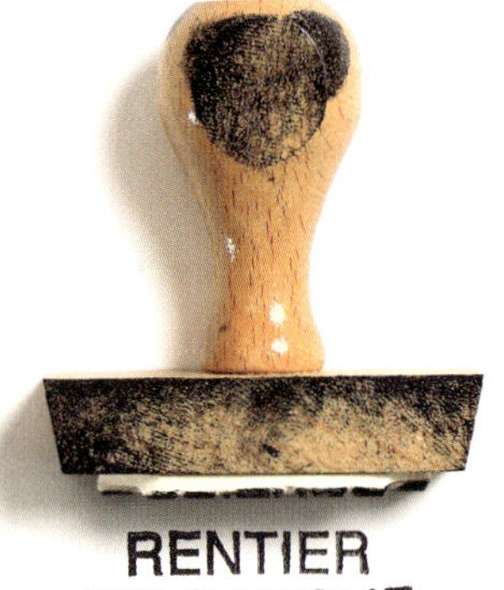

RENTIER
DE GAUCHE

leftist gentleman of leisure

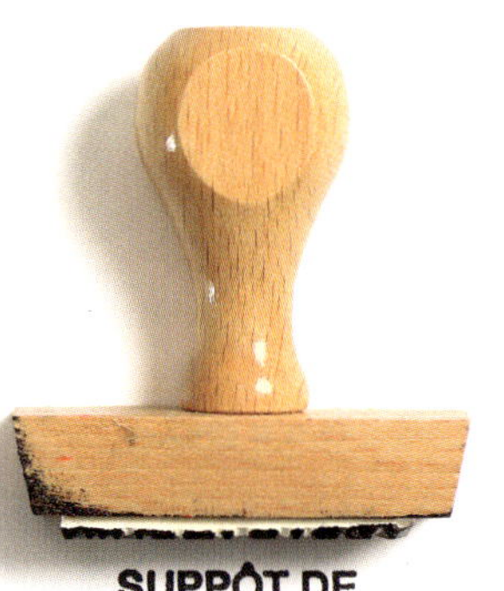

SUPPÔT DE
L'IMPÉRIALISME
NORD-AMÉRICAIN

Henchman of north-american imperialism

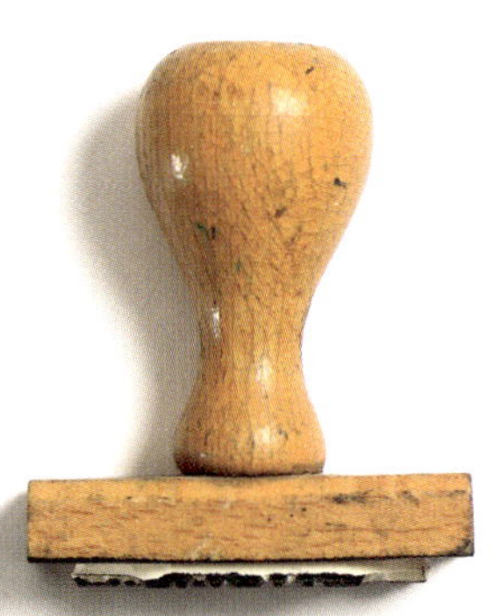

ARRIVISTE
JAUNE

Scab upstart

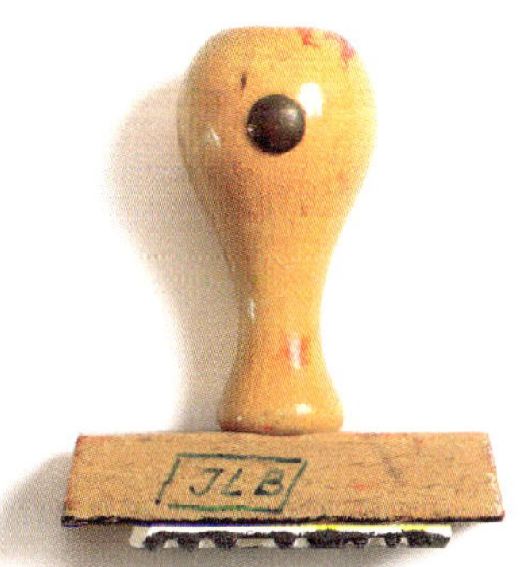

MA CAC PE TINE

I shit on you

MANCA MI CURU

eat my ass

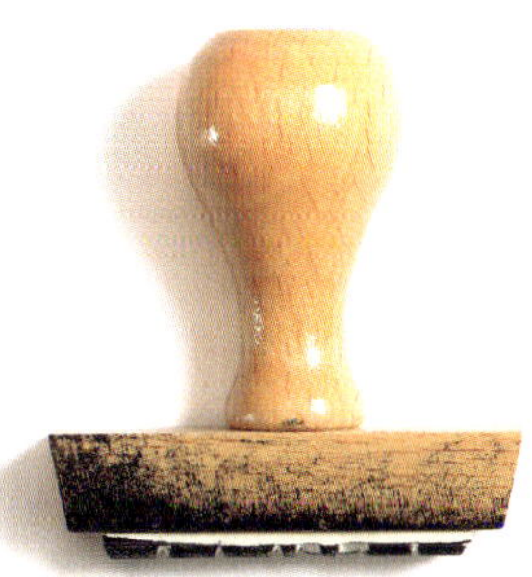

DU-TE ÎN PIZDA MATII

Go back inside your mother's cunt

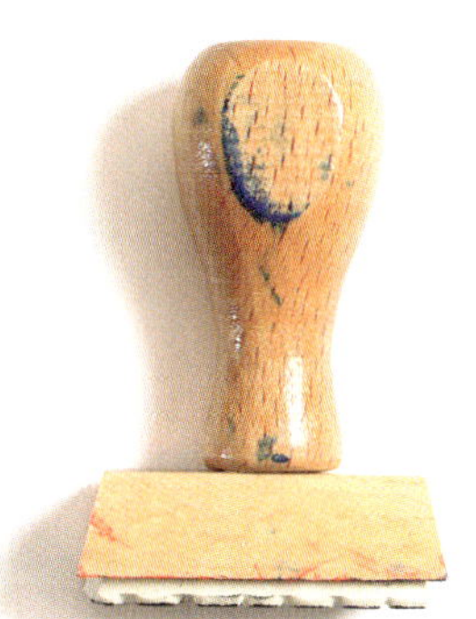

PROST CA GARDU

dumb as a post

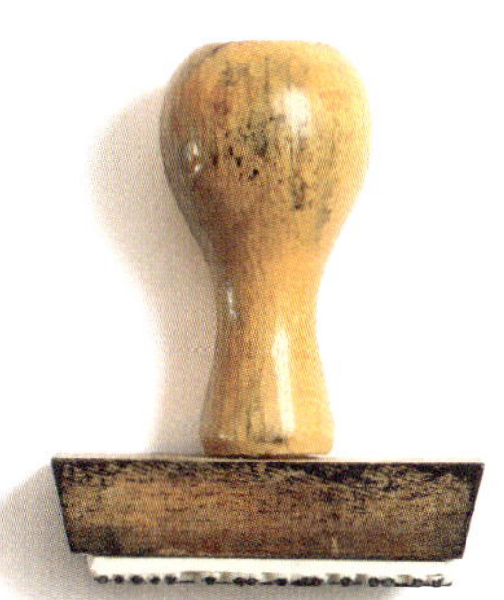

CACAT ÎMPRASTIAT

Flying shit-pile

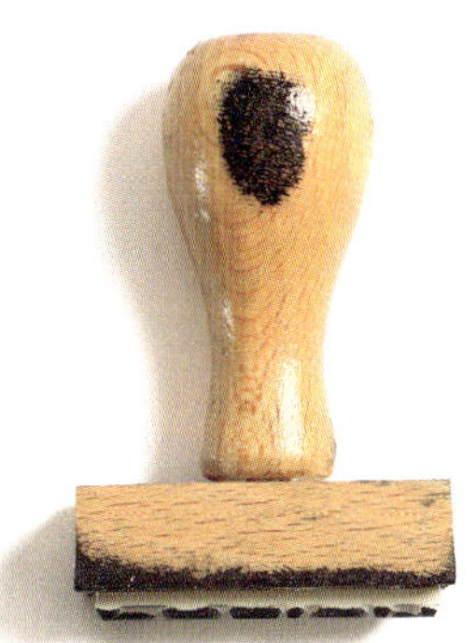

TE FUT IN GURA

I fuck you in the mouth

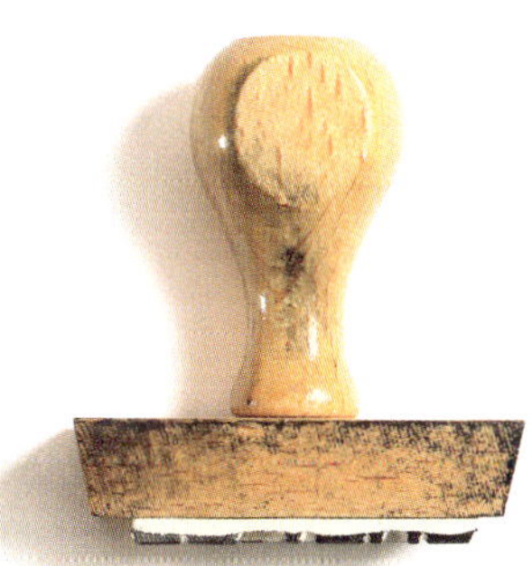

FUTA-TE BECU

Get fucked in the ass by a lightbulb

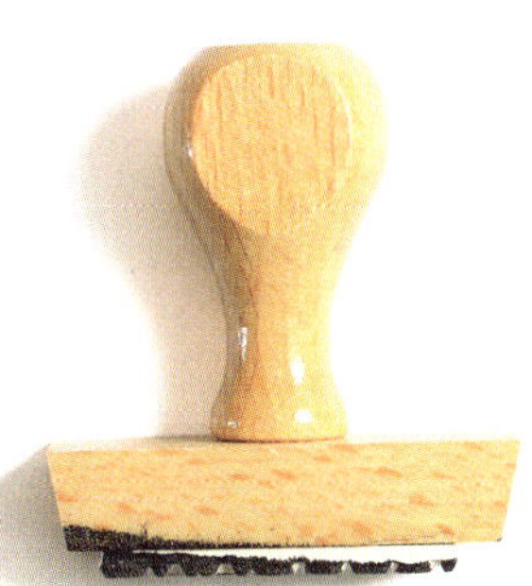

RUPA-SI DUMNEZEU PULA IN TINE

May God break His dick inside you

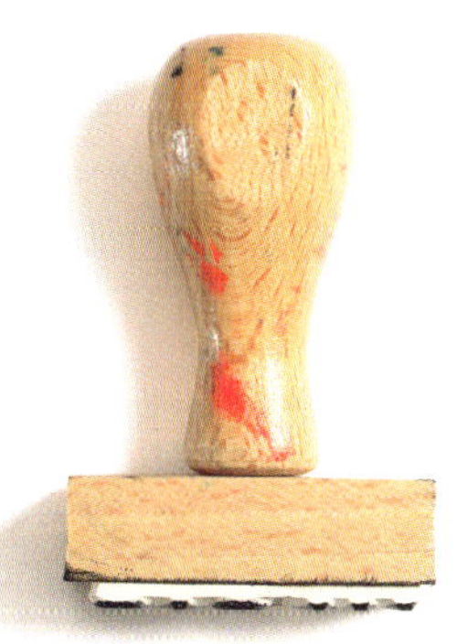

SCROAFA DRACULUI

Devil's sow

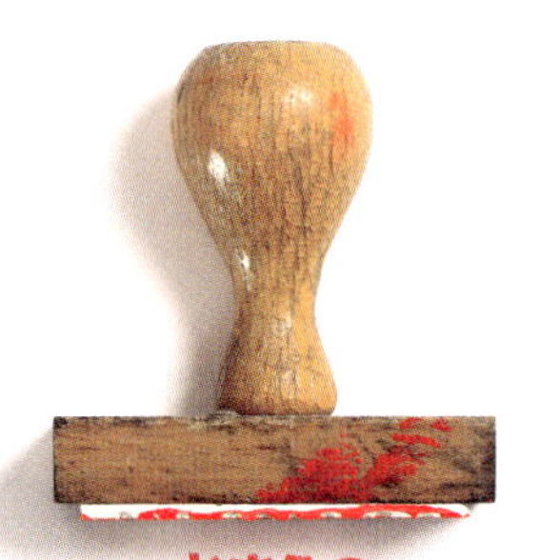

おまえの
かあちゃんでべそ

I saw the inside of your mother's navel

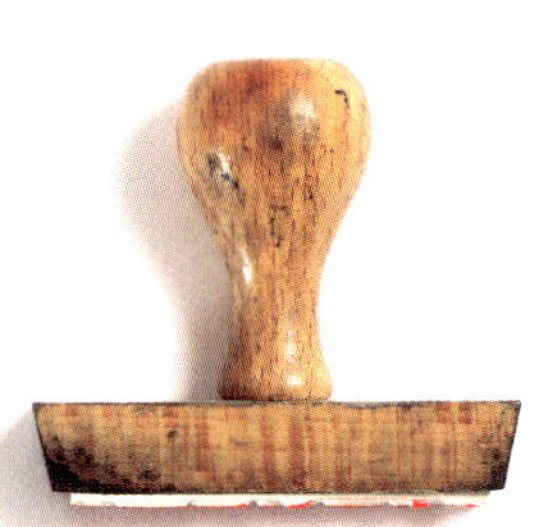

ひょっとこ野郎

Filthy octopus

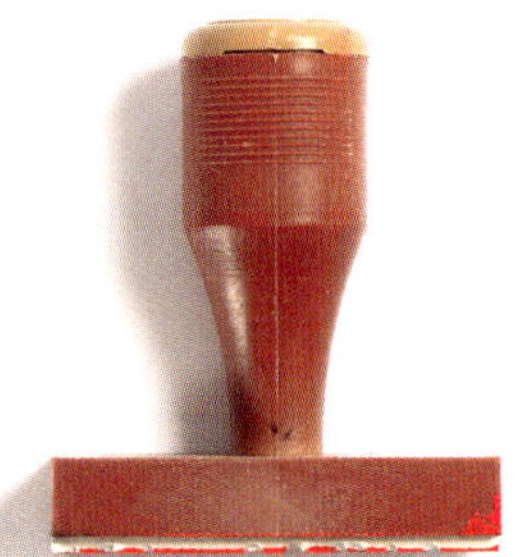

洟垂れ坊主

Snot-nosed bonze

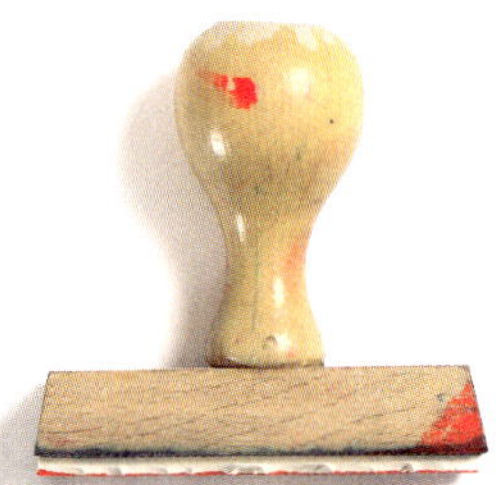

ちんかす野郎

Stinky dick

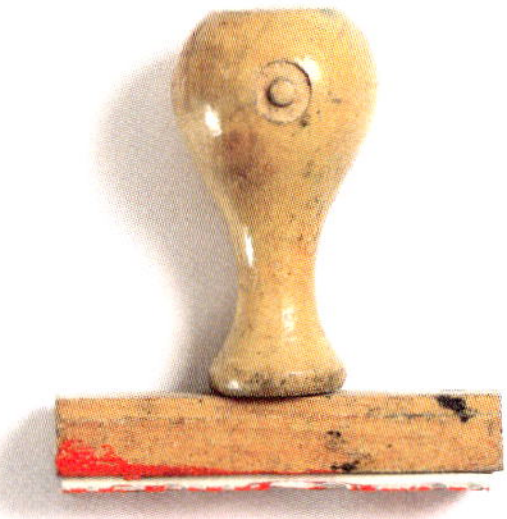

地獄へ落ちろ

go to hell

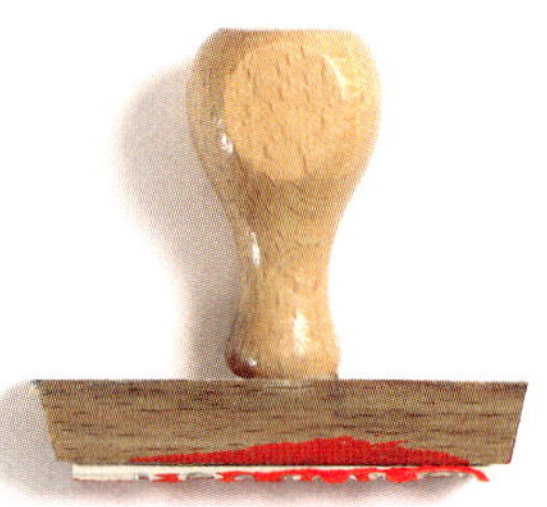

土手カボチャ

pumpkin on a riverbank

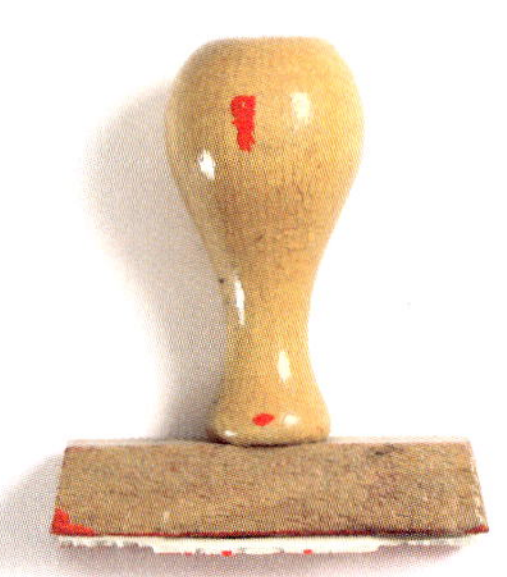

豆腐の角に
頭をぶつけて死んじまえ

Die beating your head on tofu

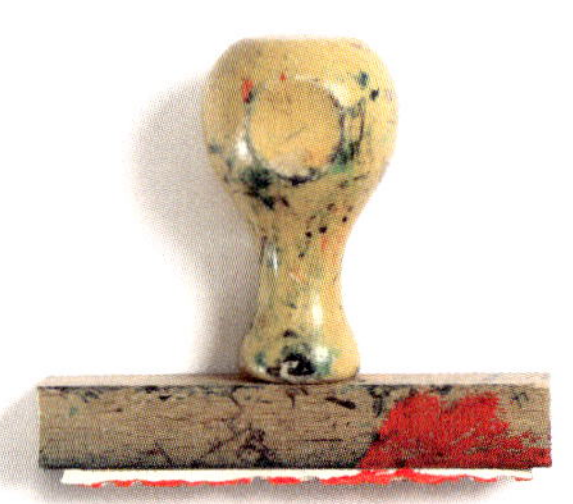

くたばり損ない

You're too dumb to die

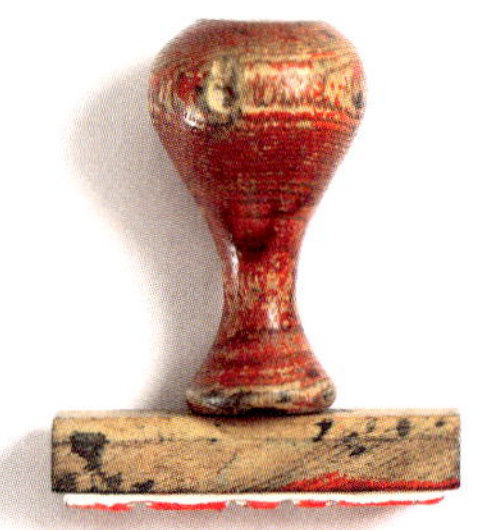

寝小便垂れ

piss ant

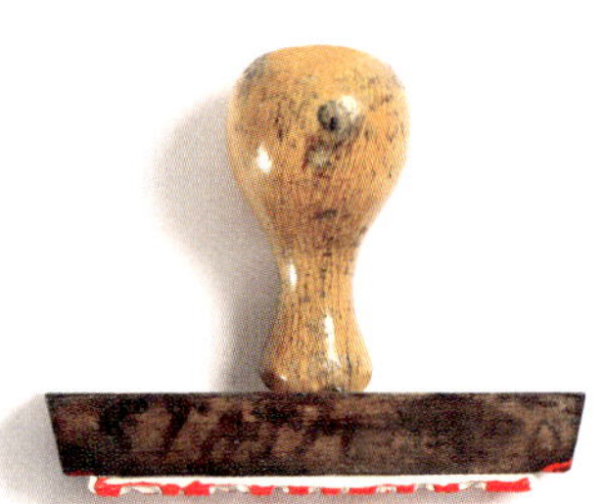

いかれぽんち

Simpleton

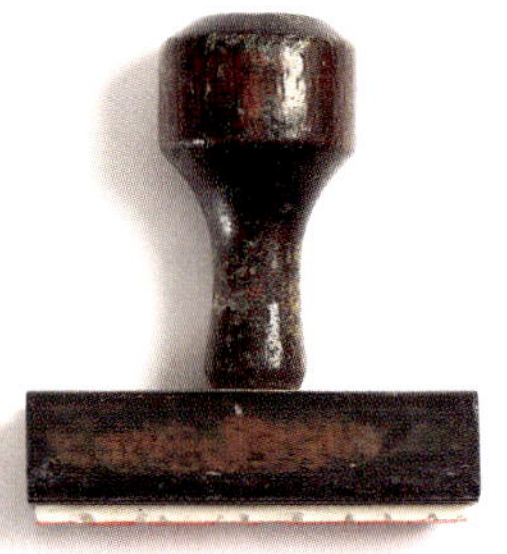

へそ噛んで死ね

Die biting your own navel

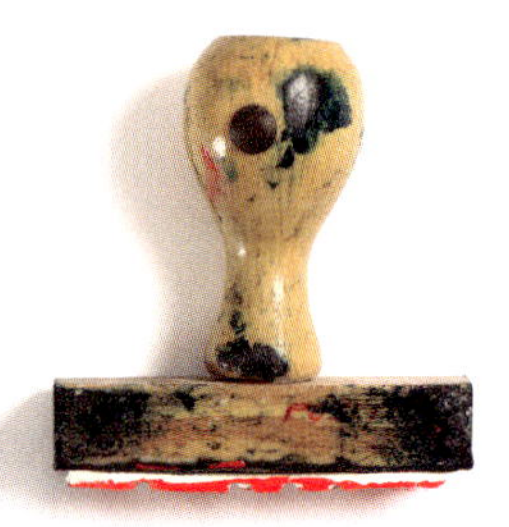

くされ餓鬼

Little disgusting ogre

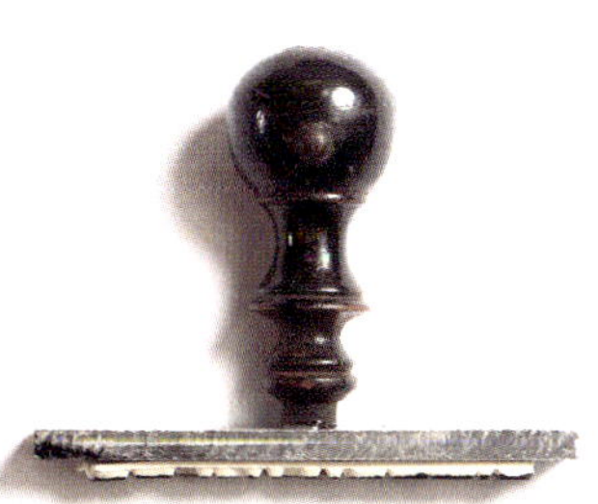

DU LAUCH

You leek

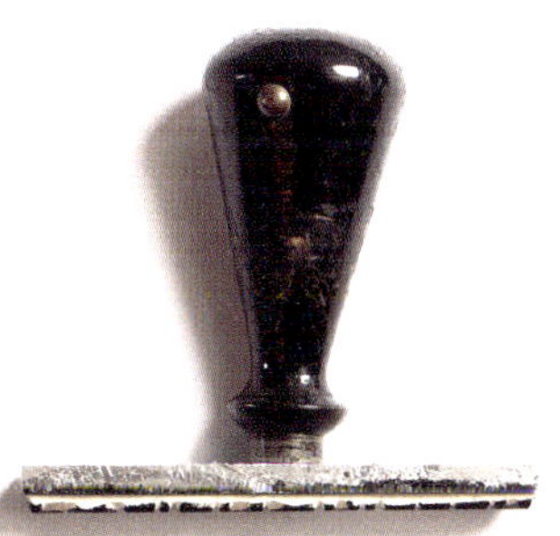

HOSENSCHEISSER

pants-shitter

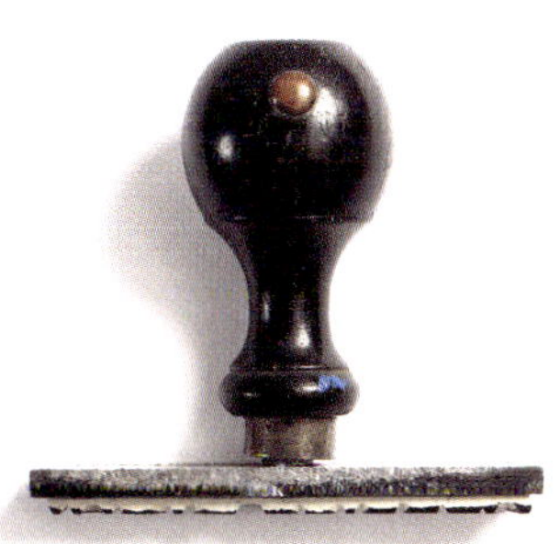

AFFENSCHWANZ

ape-dick

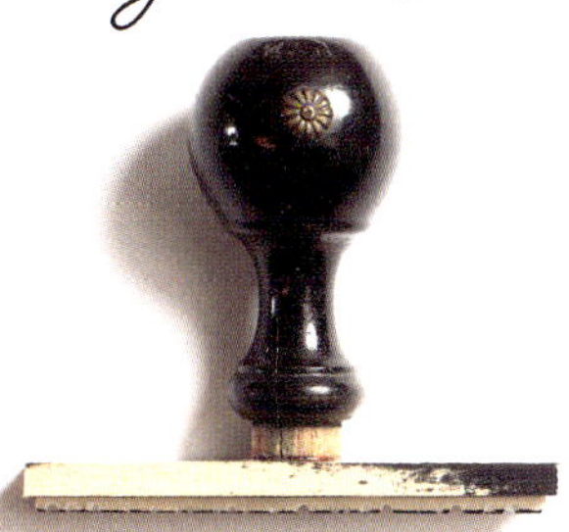

SCHWEINEPRIESTER

pig priest (bastard, traitor)

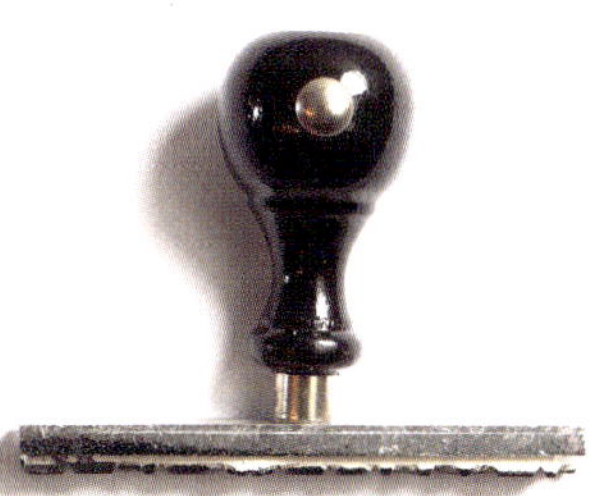

JEANSBÜGLER

you iron your jeans

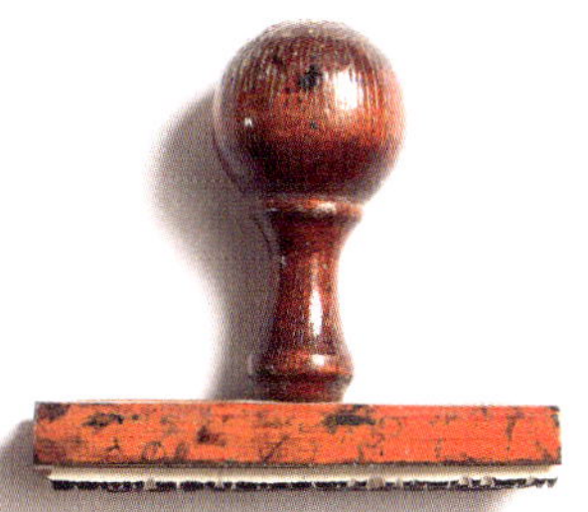

EVOLUTIONSBREMSE

Evolution brake

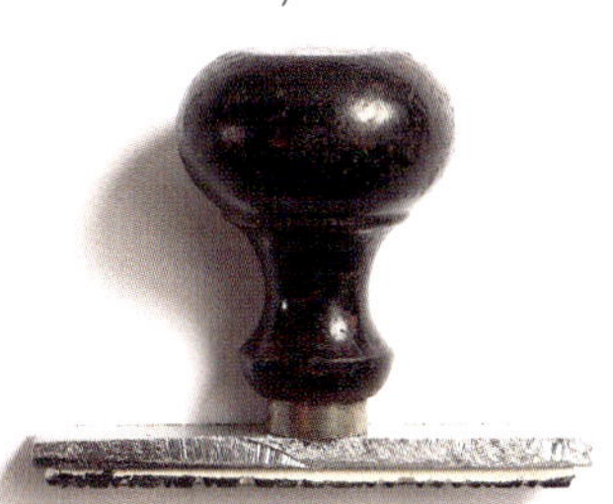

ARSCH MIT OHREN

ass with ears

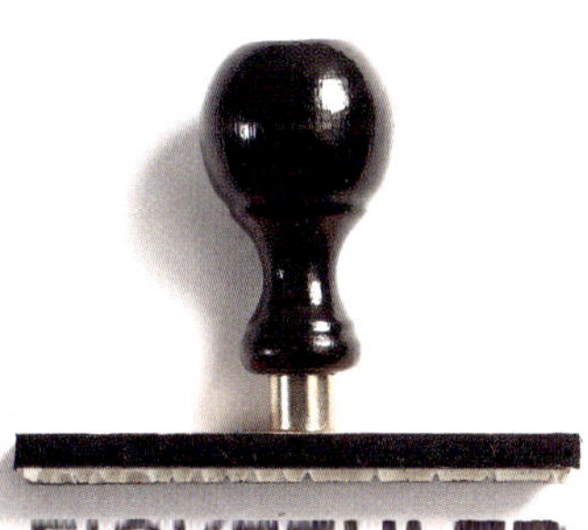

FICKFEHLER

Fuck mistake

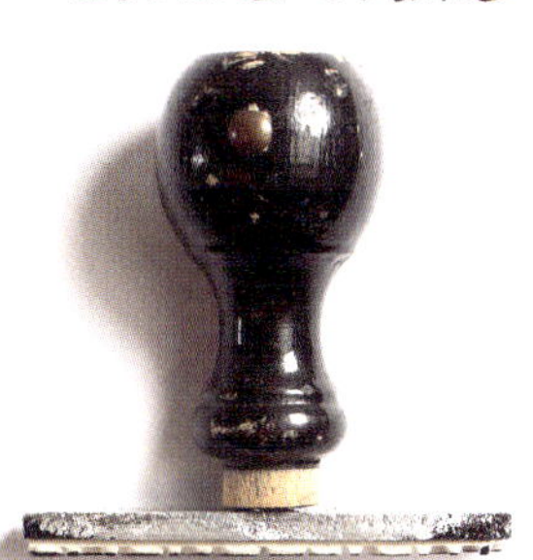

LUSTMOLCH

Sex-salamander

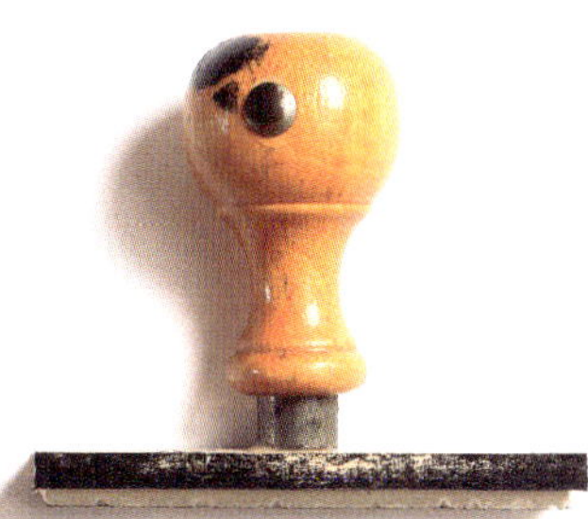

HACKFRESSE

meatface

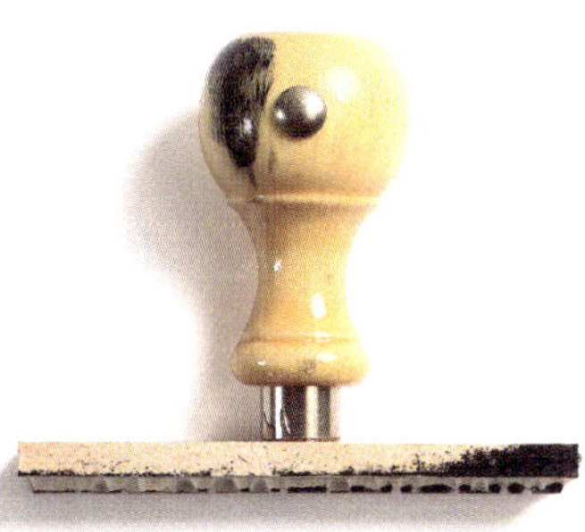

EINZELLER

Single-cell organism

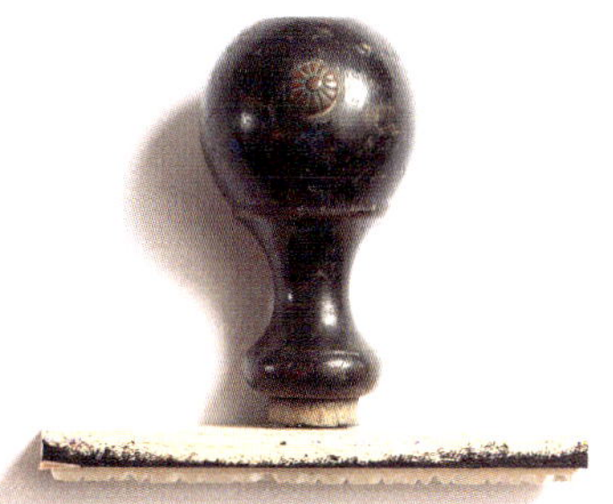

DU ARSCHGEFICKTES SUPPENHUHN

You're the chicken (for dinner) that got fucked in the ass

DEATH AWAITS

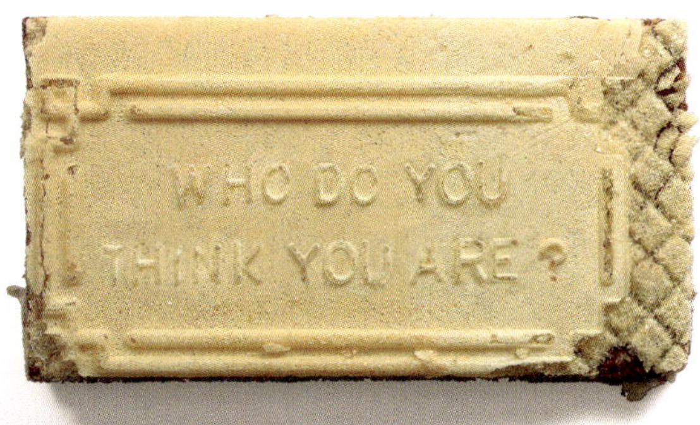
WHO DO YOU
THINK YOU ARE ?

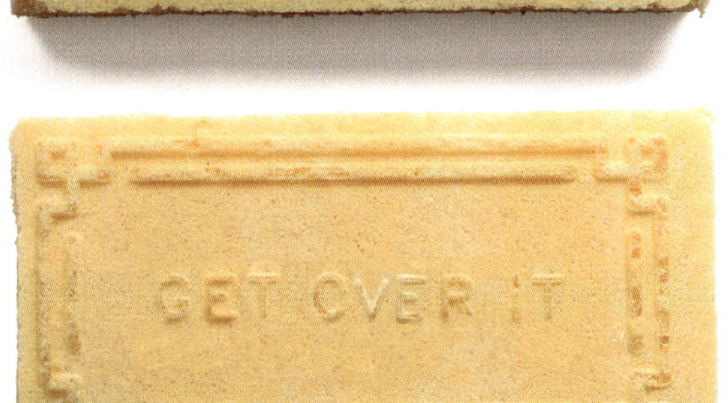
GET OVER IT

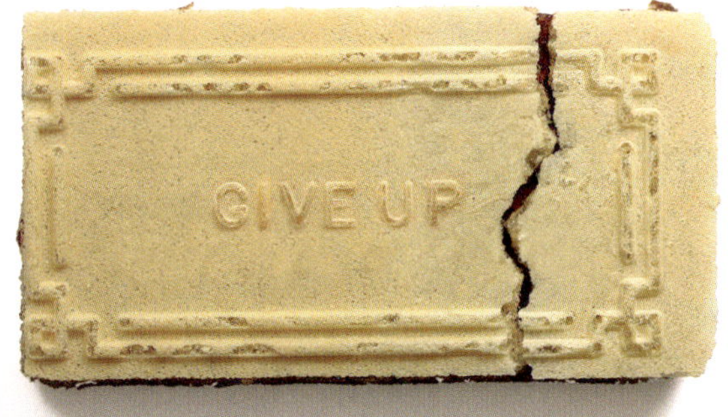
GIVE UP

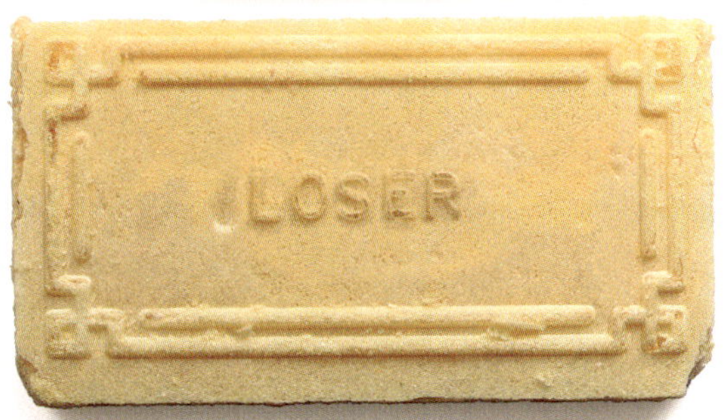
LOSER

YOU'RE
PITIFULL

YOU SUCK

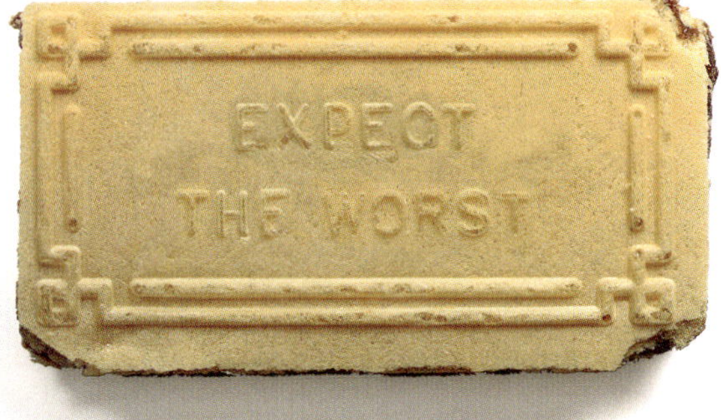
EXPECT
THE WORST

STOP
DREAMING
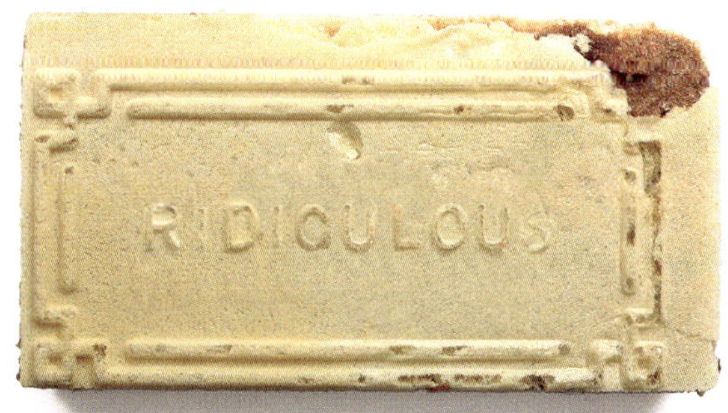
RIDICULOUS

YOUR LIFE
IS A FAILURE
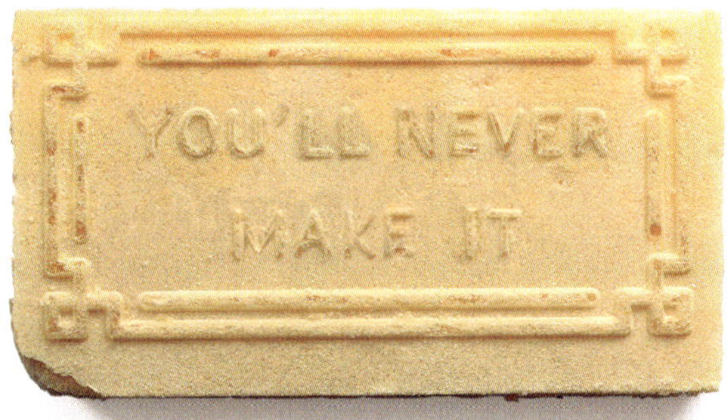
YOU'LL NEVER
MAKE IT
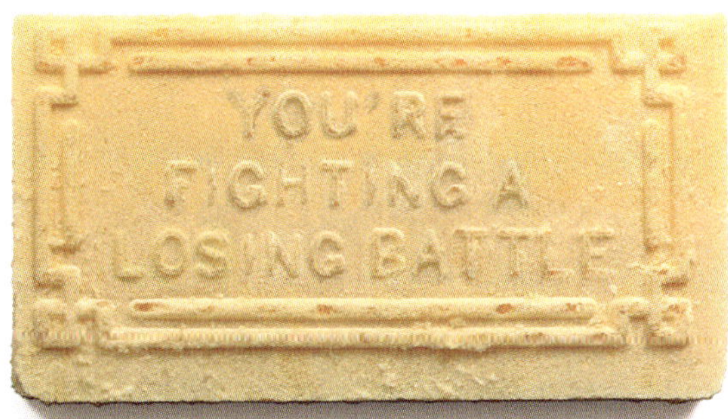
YOU'RE
FIGHTING A
LOSING BATTLE
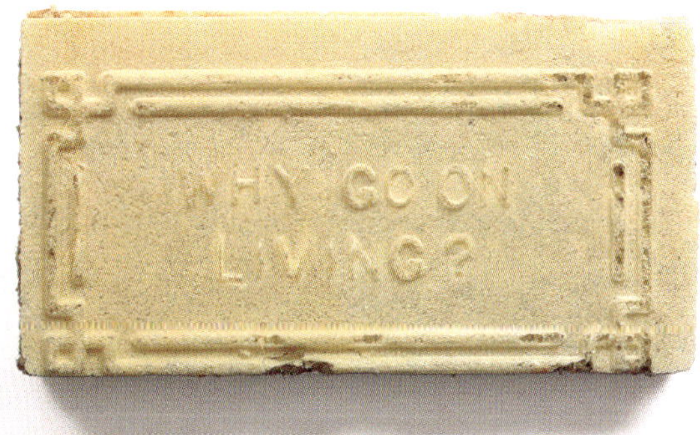
WHY GO ON
LIVING?
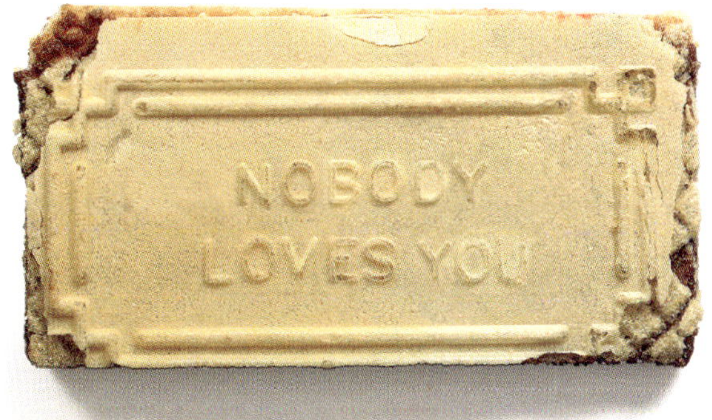
NOBODY
LOVES YOU
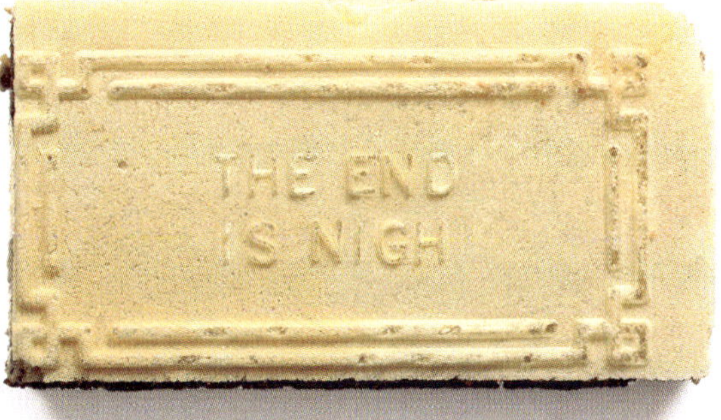
THE END
IS NIGH

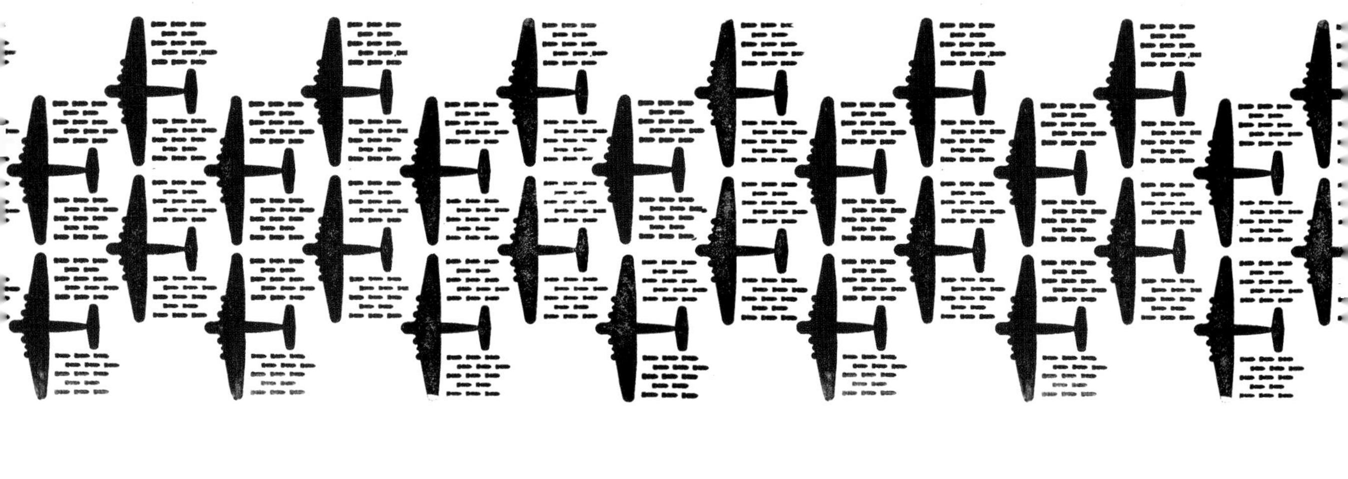

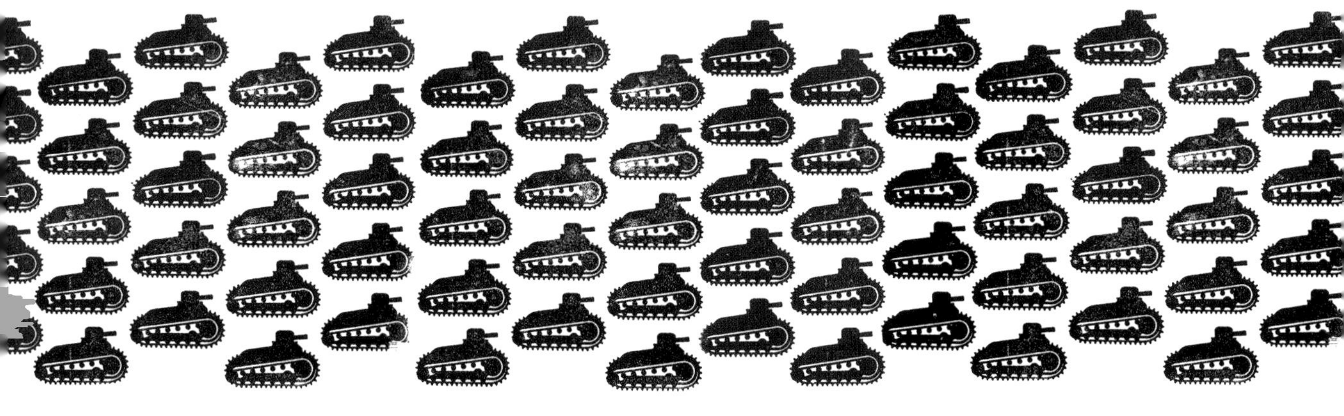

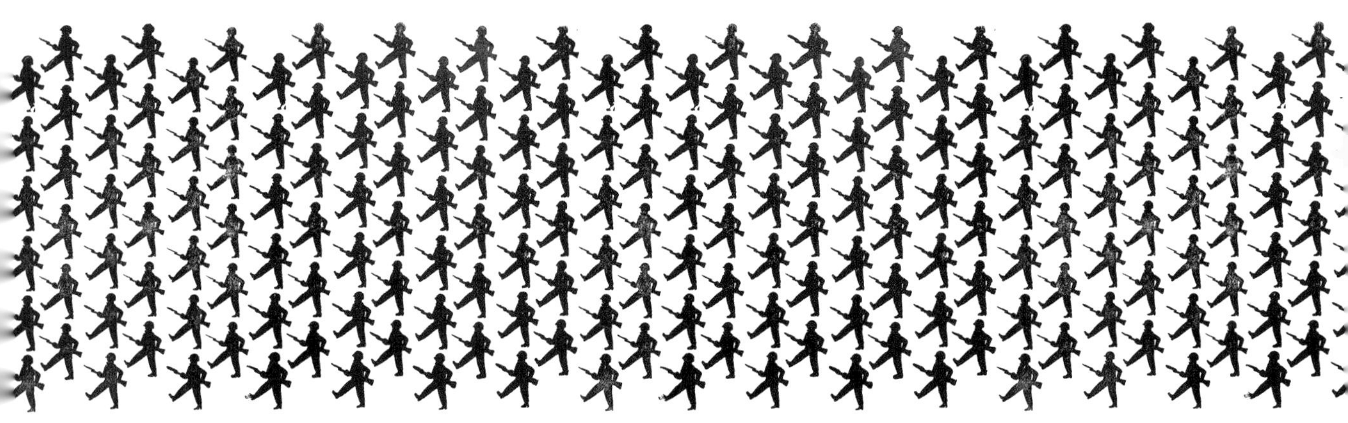

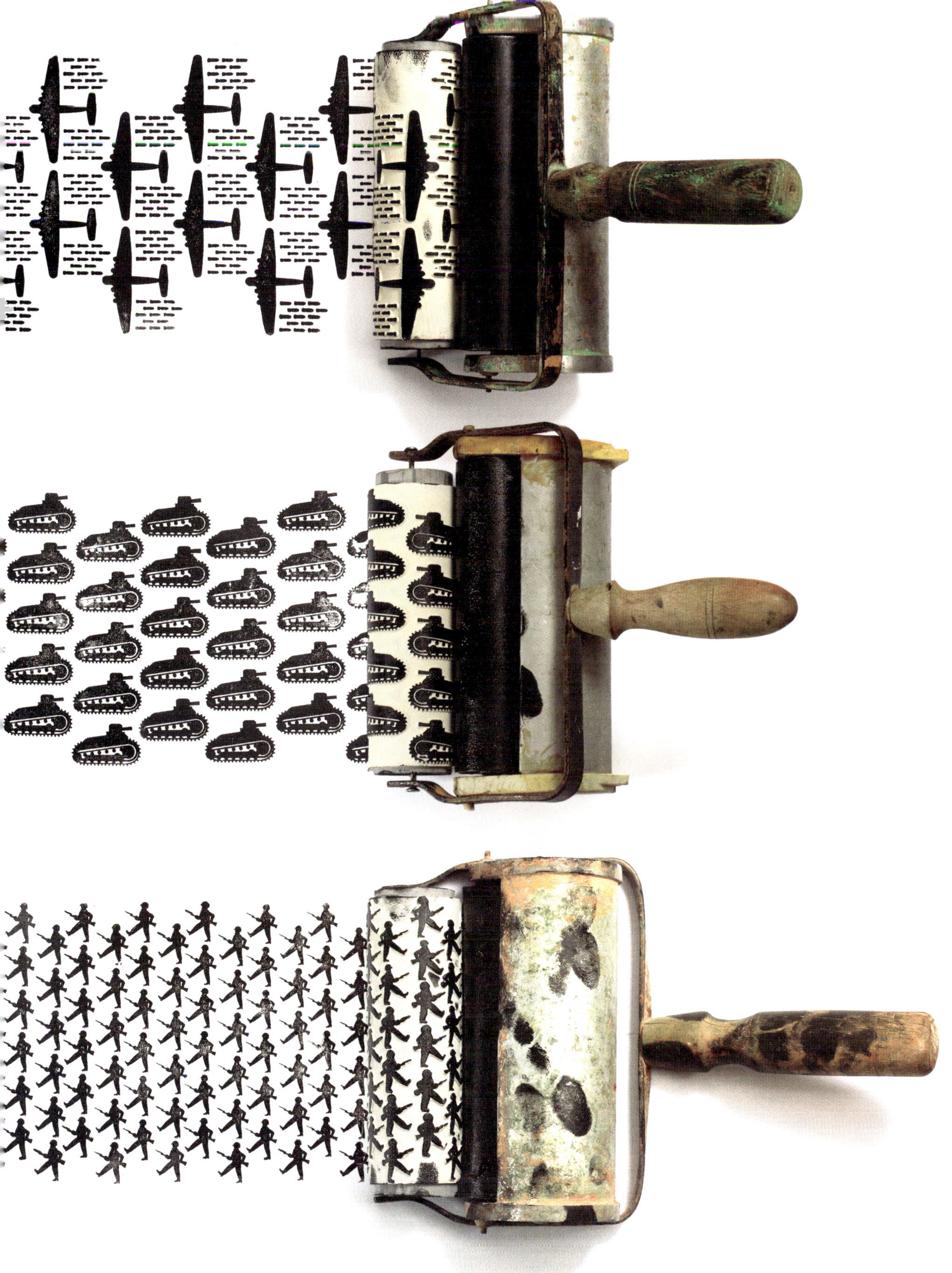

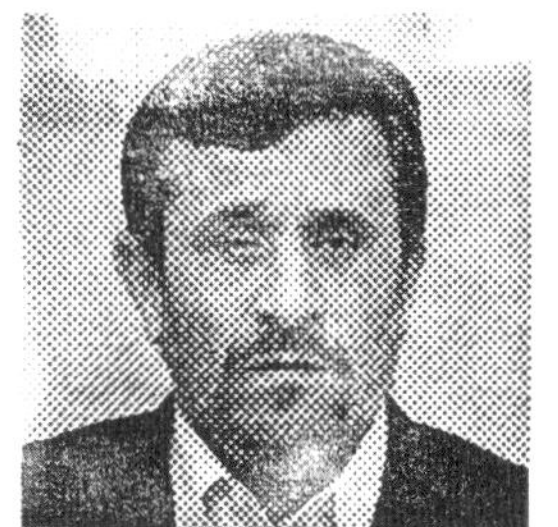
FREDERIC AHMADINEJAD

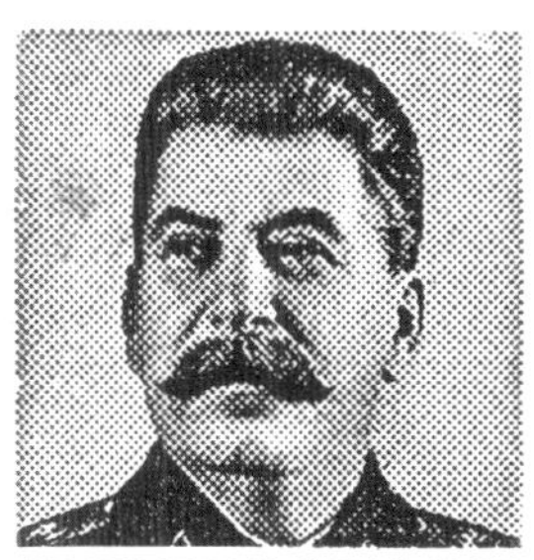
FREDERIC STALINE

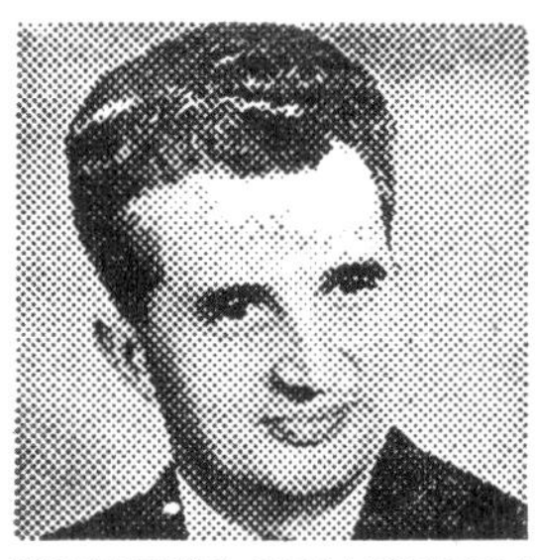
FREDERIC CEAUCESCU

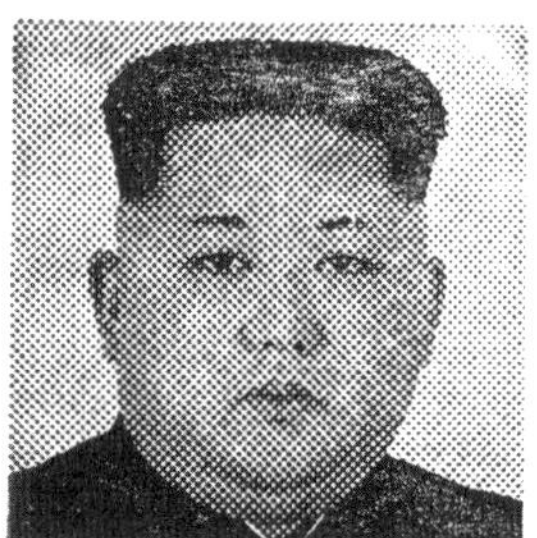
FREDERIC JONG-UN

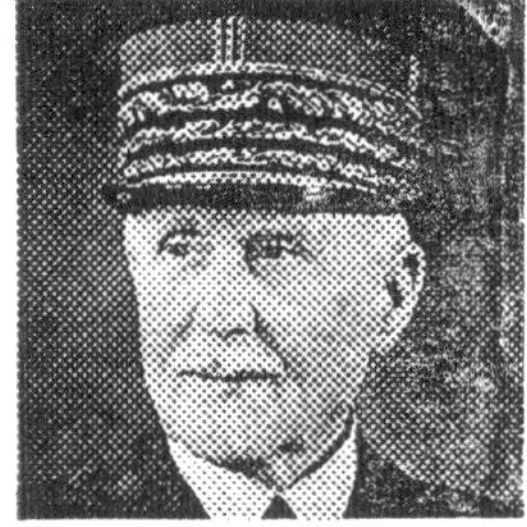
FREDERIC PÉTAIN

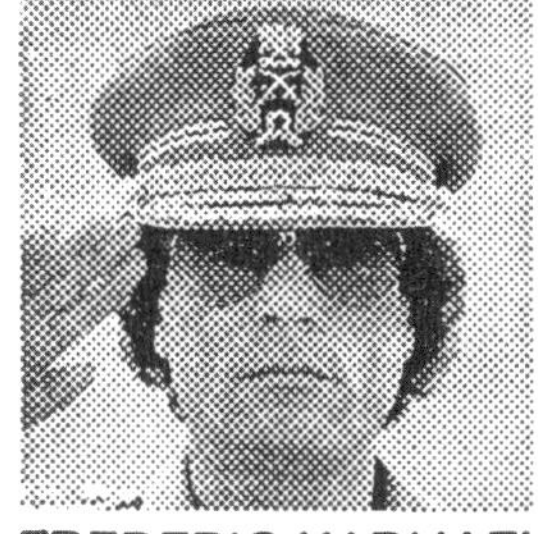
FREDERIC KADHAFI

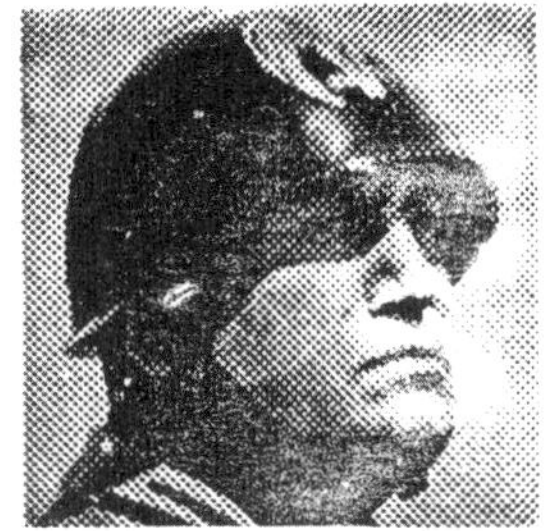
FREDERIC MUSSOLINI

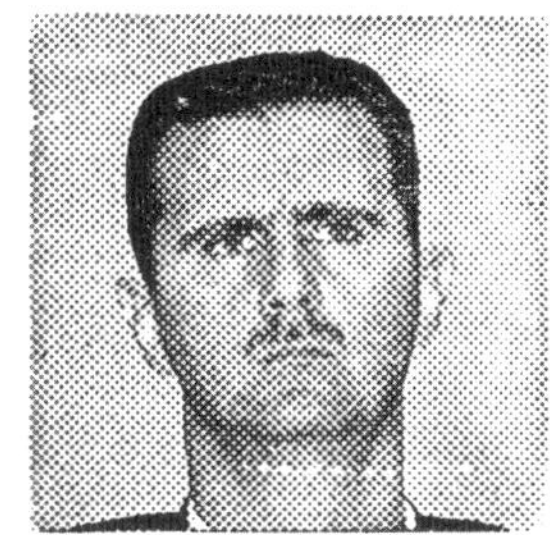
FREDERIC EL-ASSAD

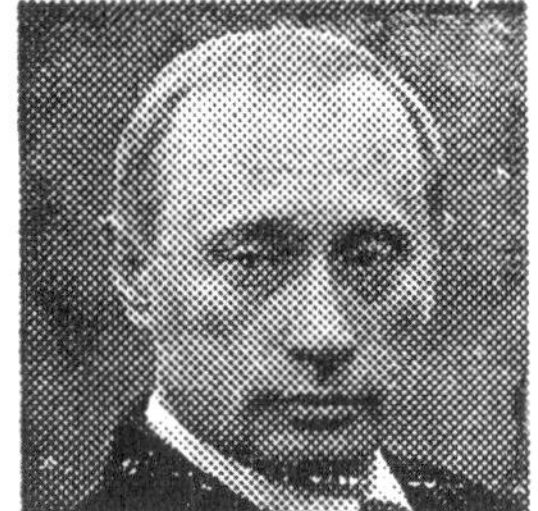
FREDERIC POUTINE

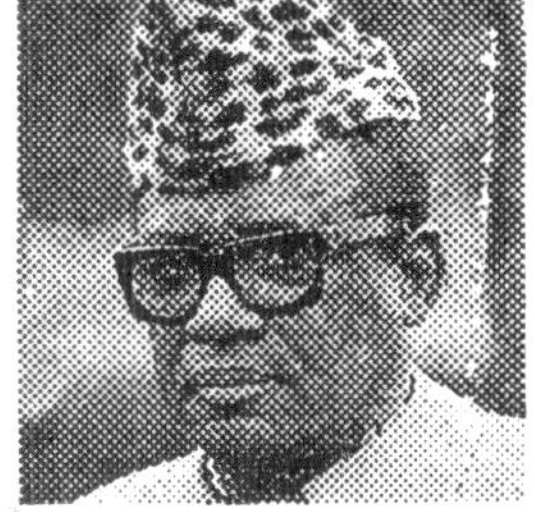
FREDERIC MOBUTU

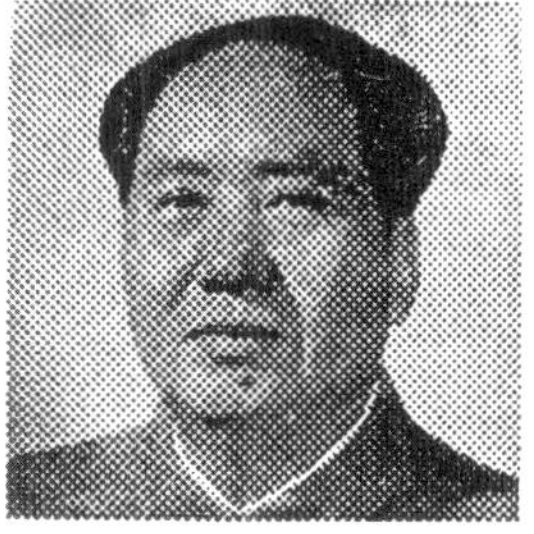
FREDERIC ZEDONG

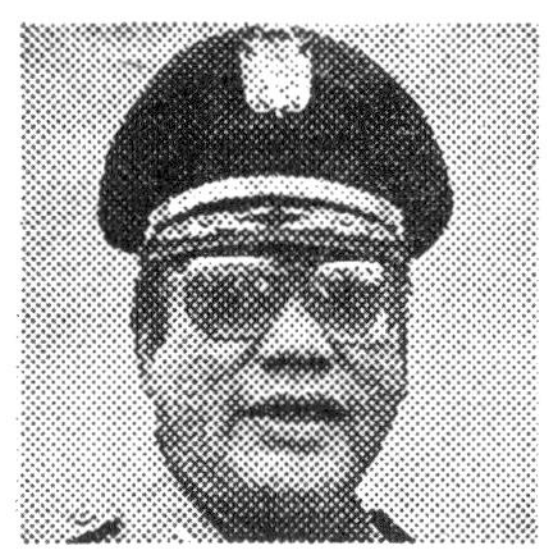
FREDERIC NORIEGA

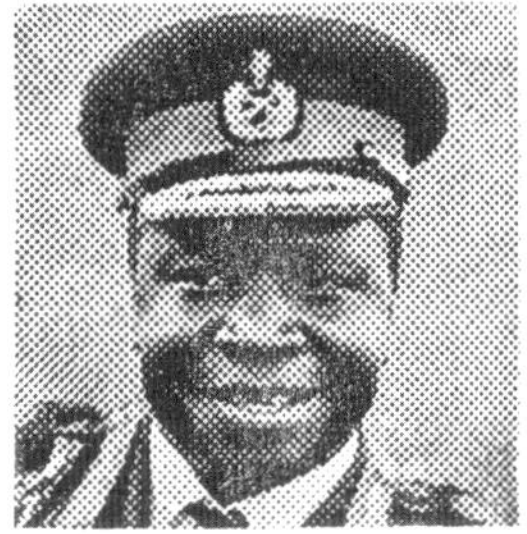
FREDERIC AMIN DADA

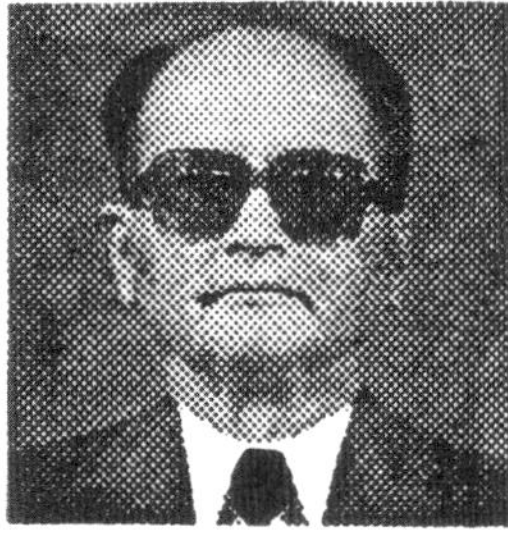
FREDERIC JARUZELSKI

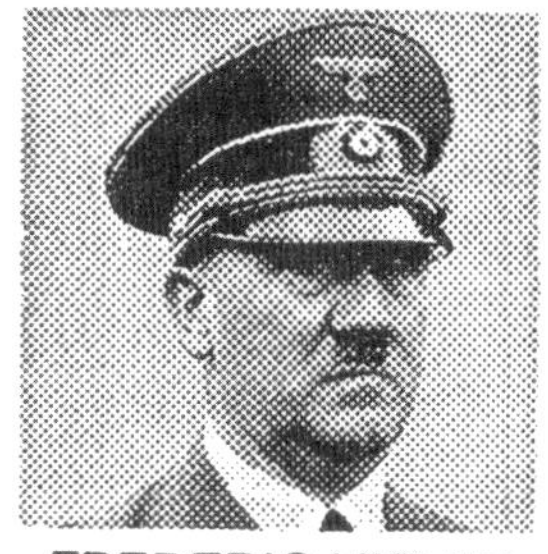
FREDERIC HITLER

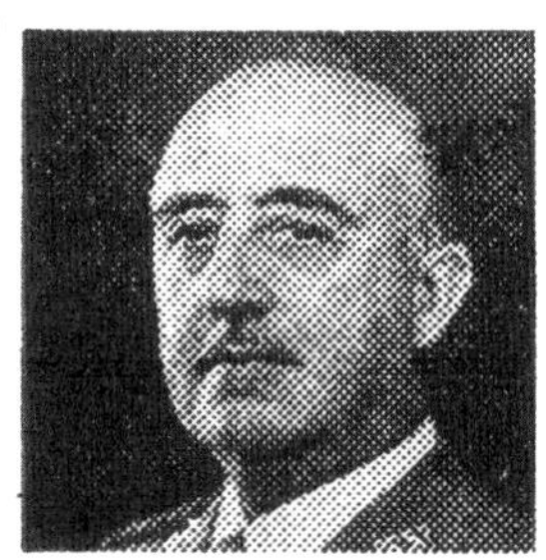
FREDERIC FRANCO

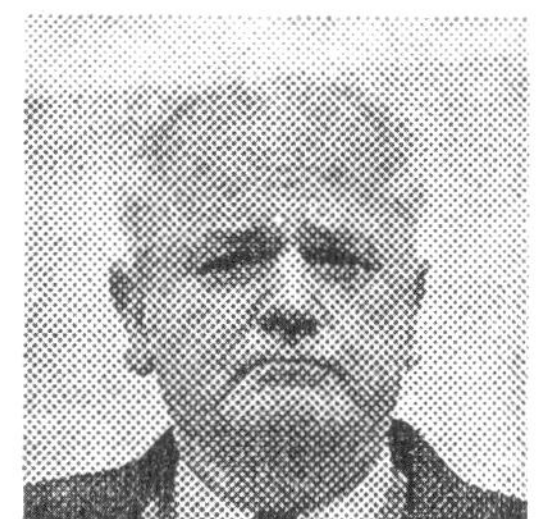
FREDERIC MILOSEVIC

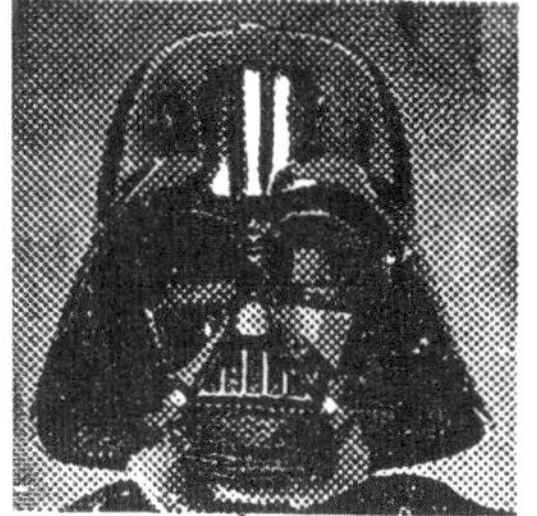
FREDERIC VADER

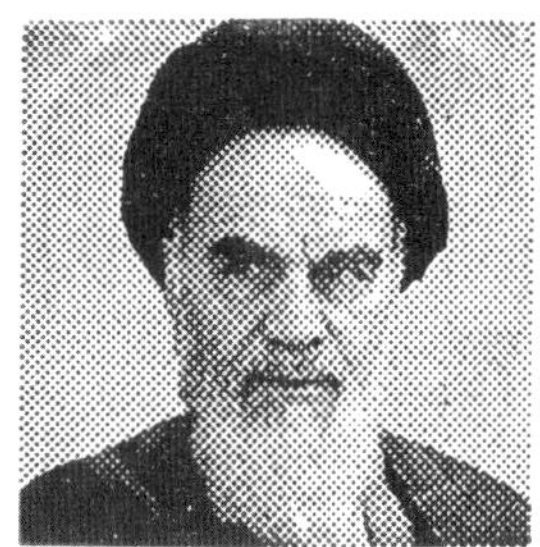
THE AYATOLLAH FREDERIC

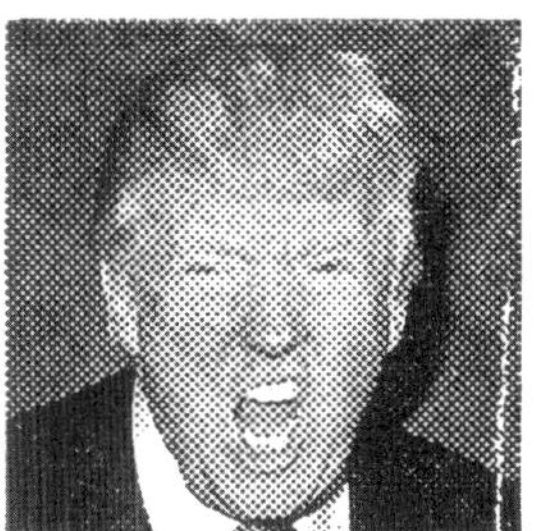
FREDERIC TRUMP

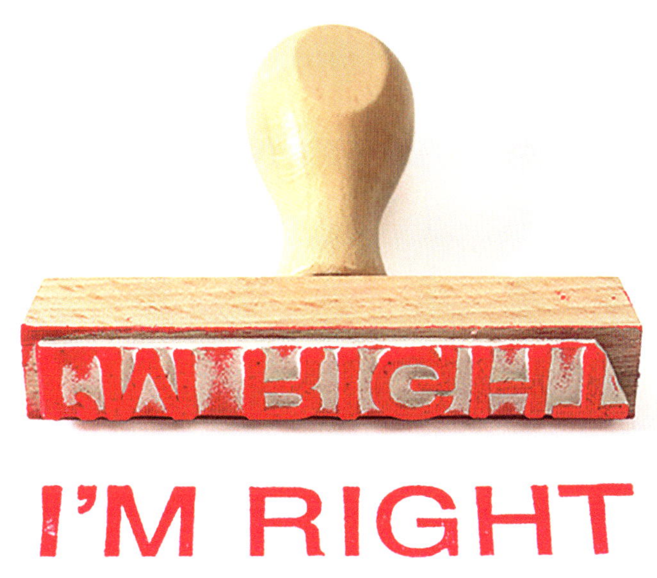
I'M RIGHT

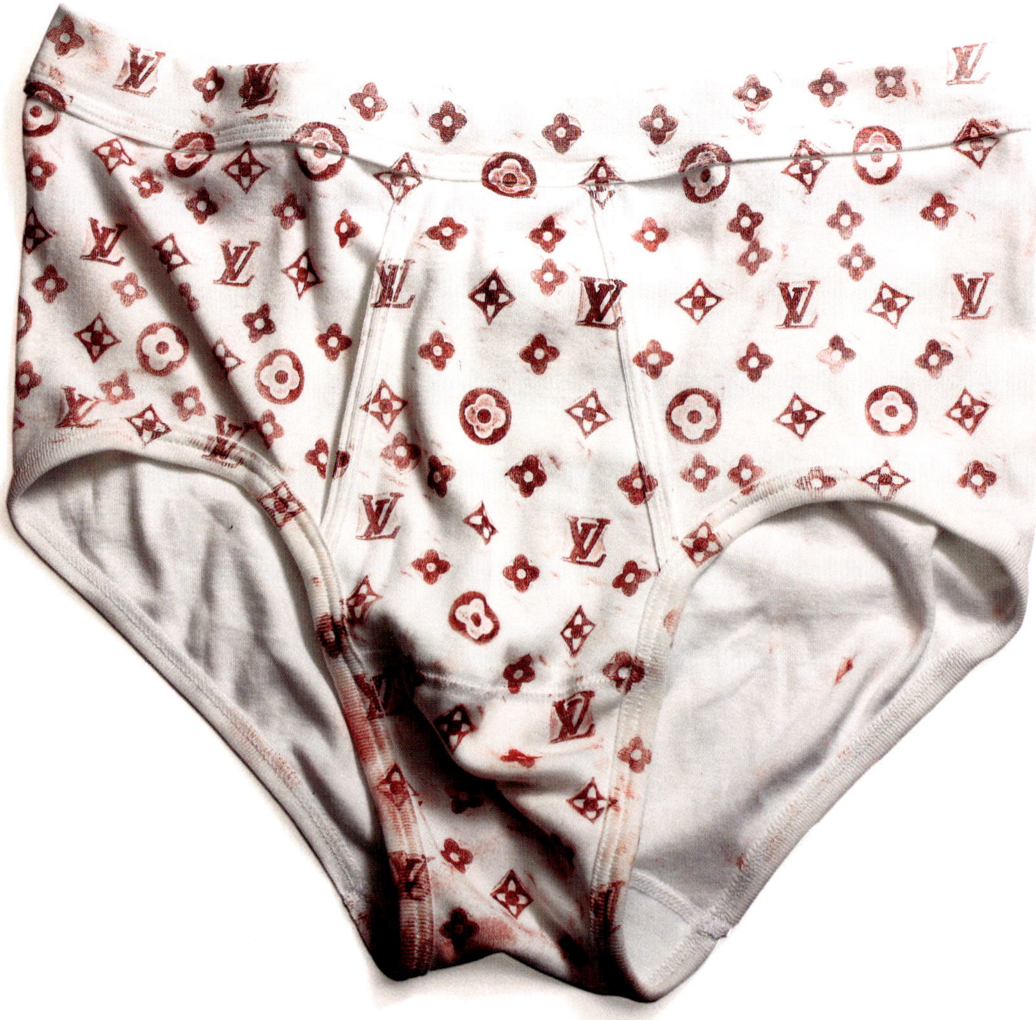

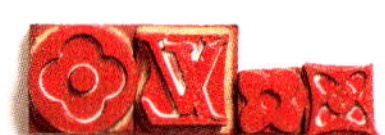

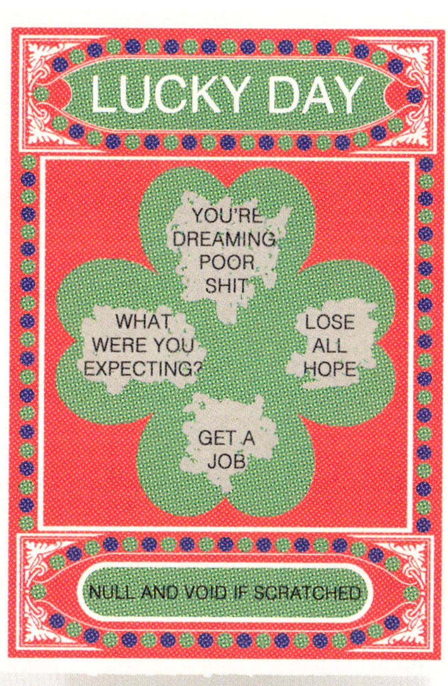
LUCKY DAY
YOU'RE DREAMING POOR SHIT
WHAT WERE YOU EXPECTING?
LOSE ALL HOPE
GET A JOB
NULL AND VOID IF SCRATCHED

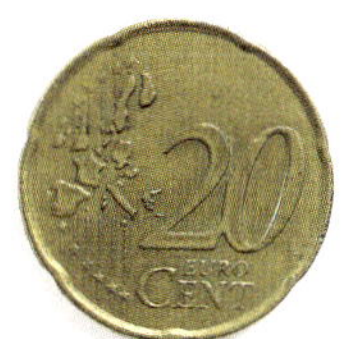
20
EURO CENT

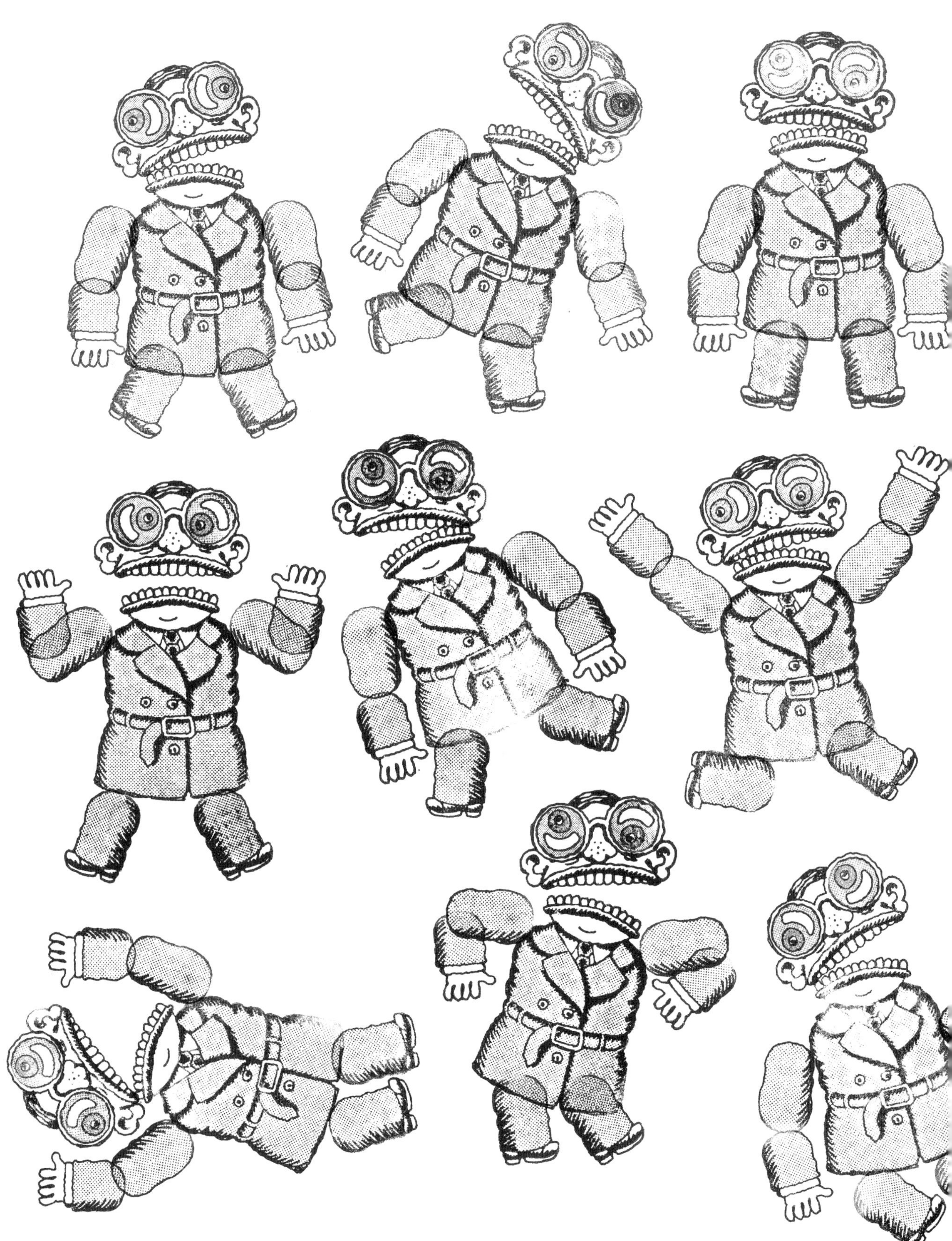

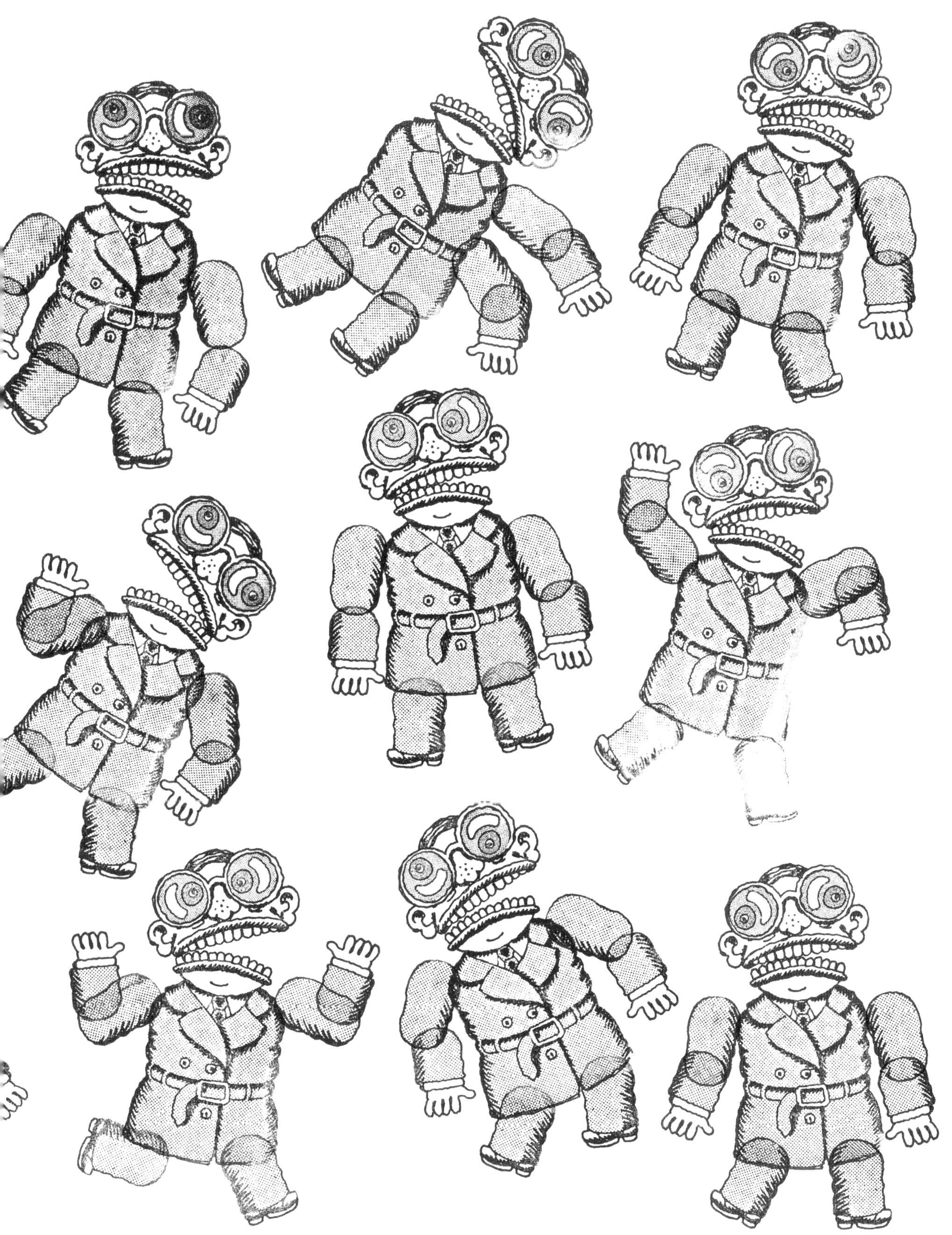

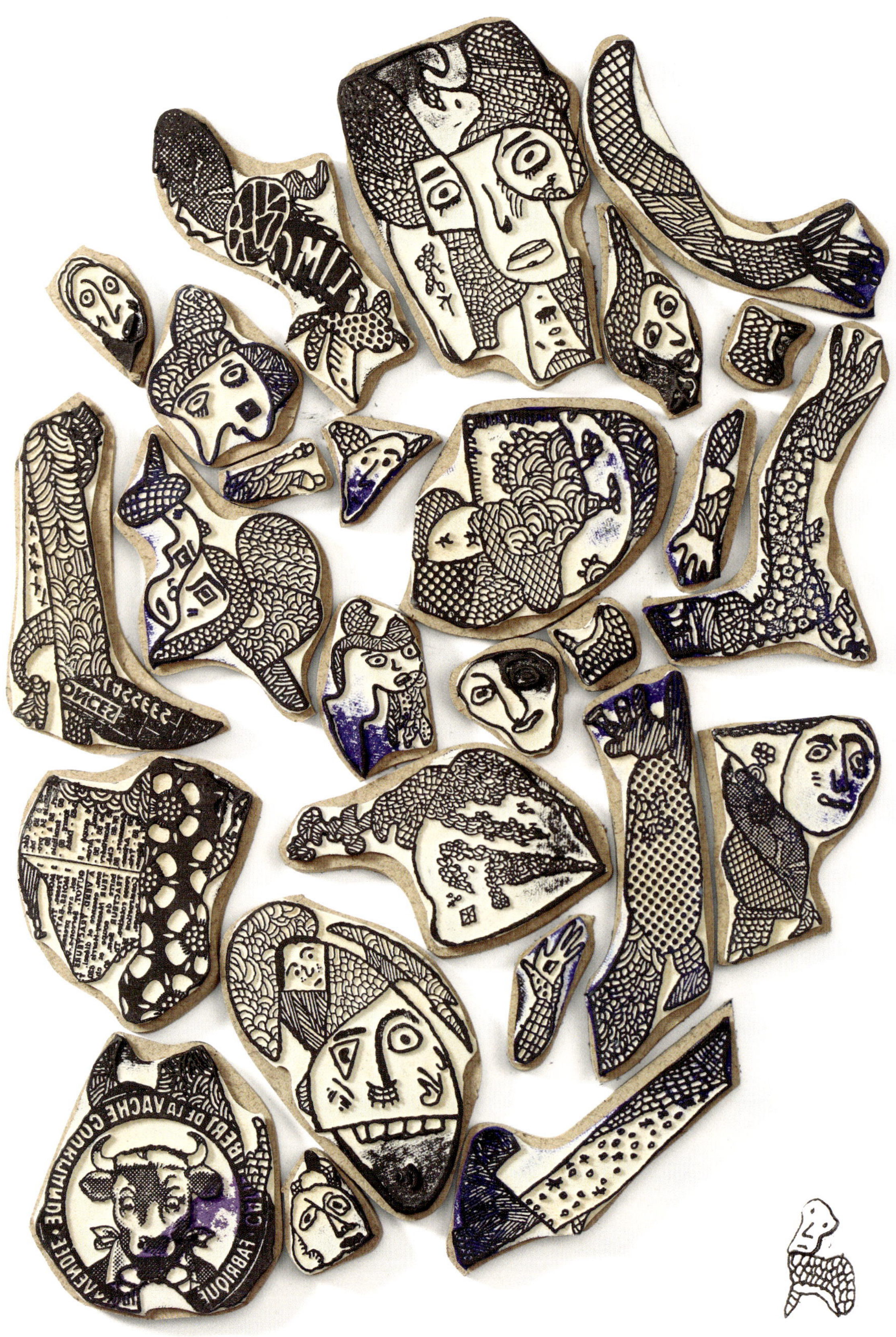

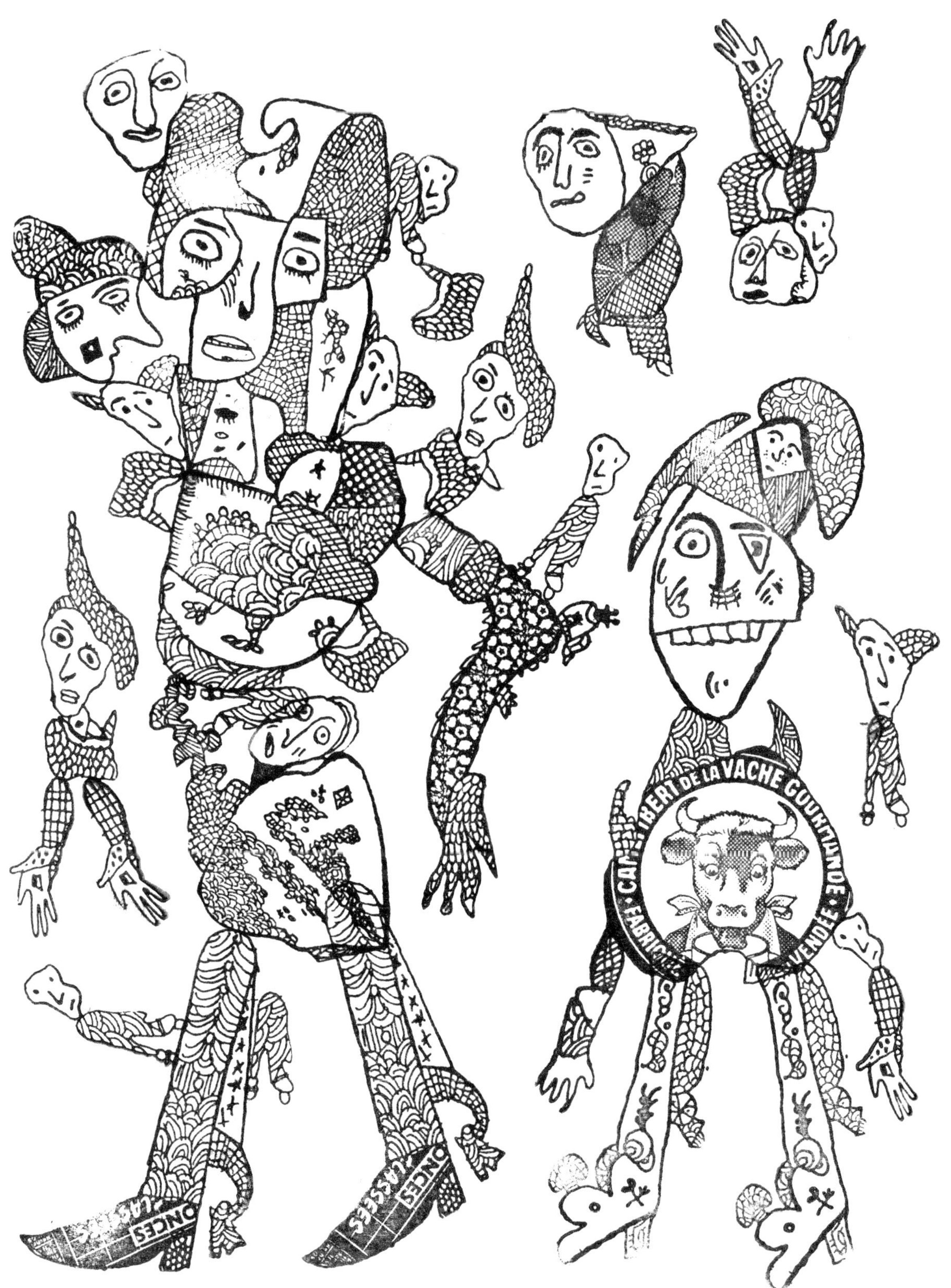
BERT DE LA VACHE
VENDÉE
ONCES
CASSÉES

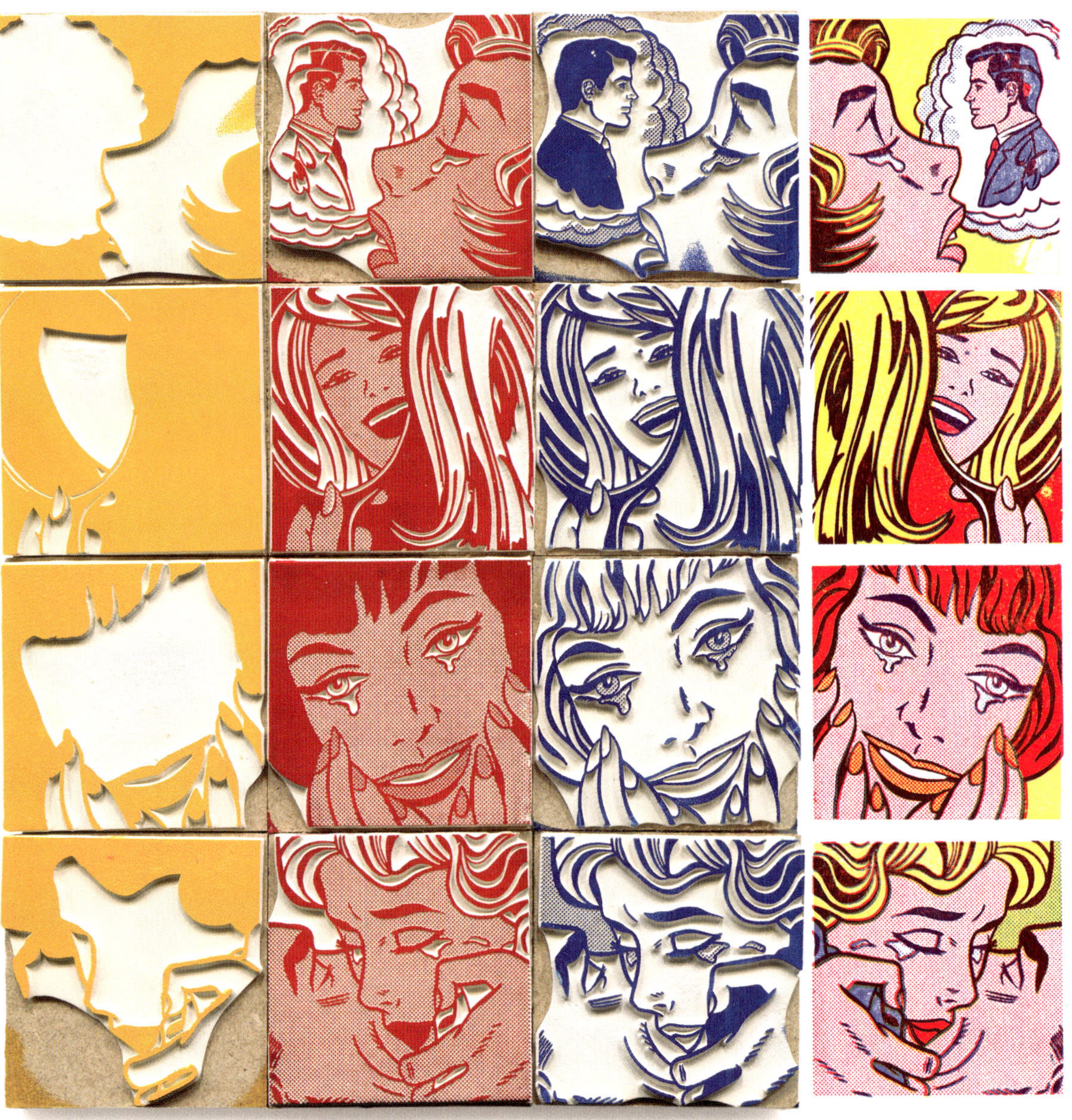

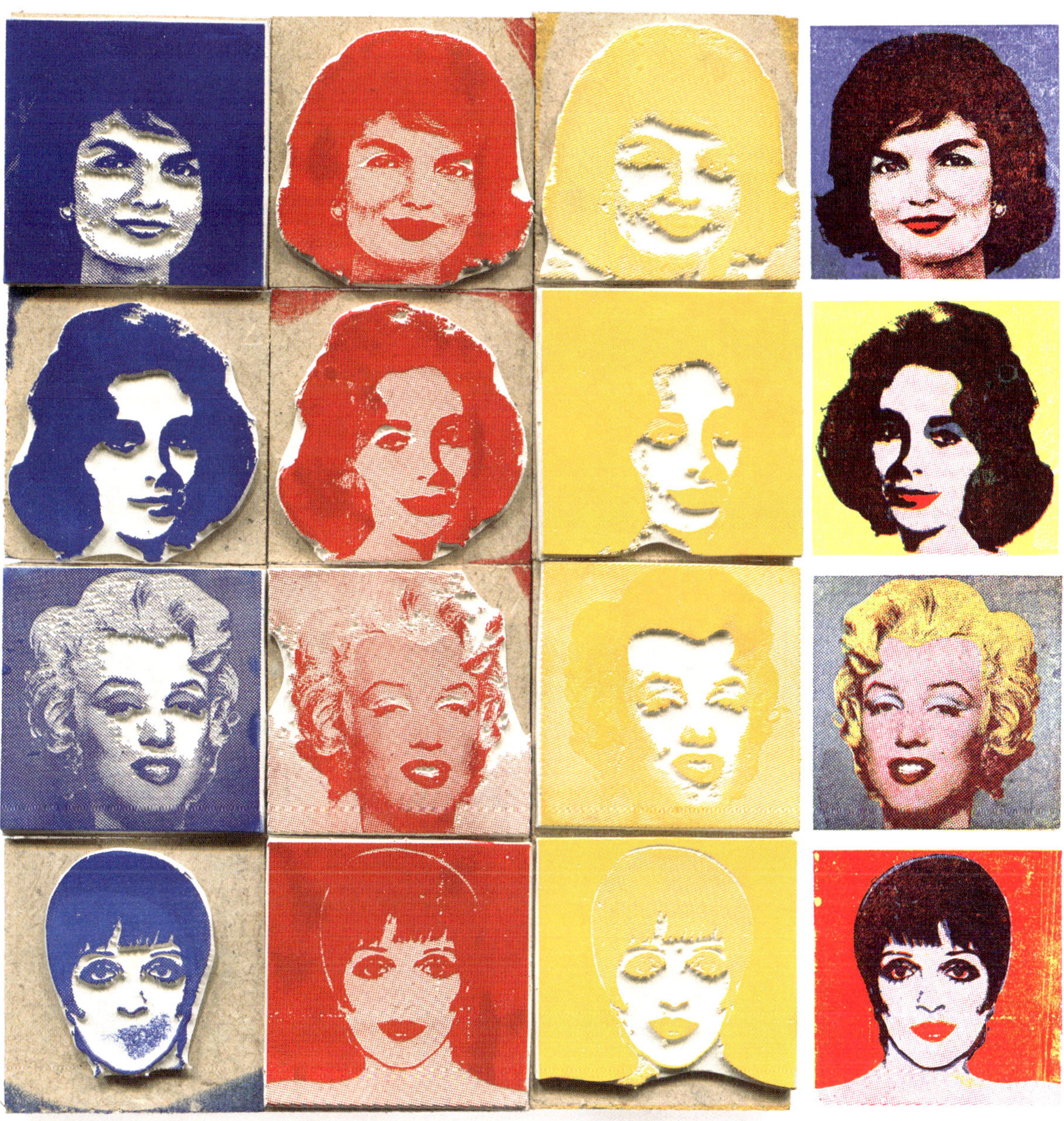

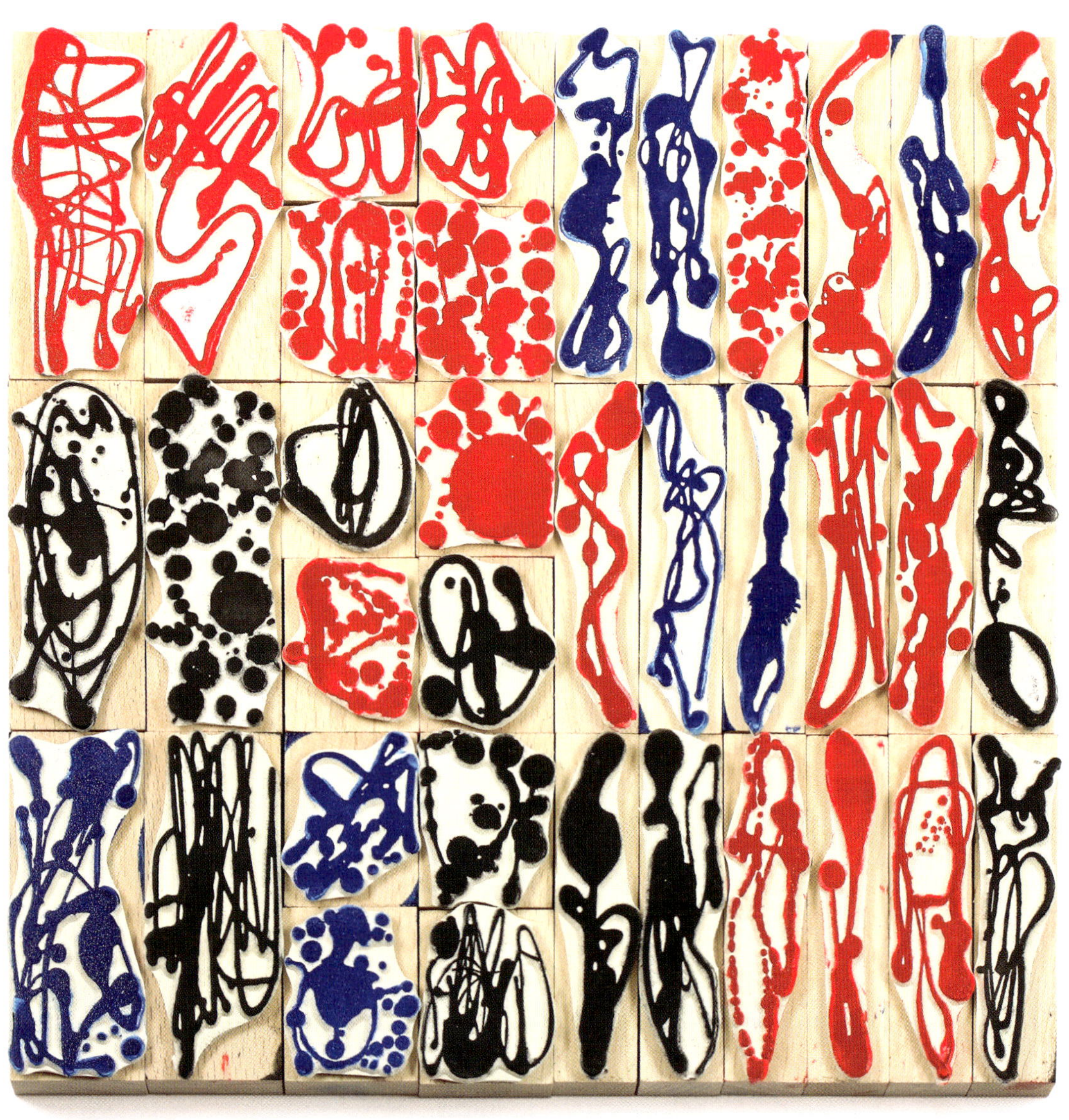

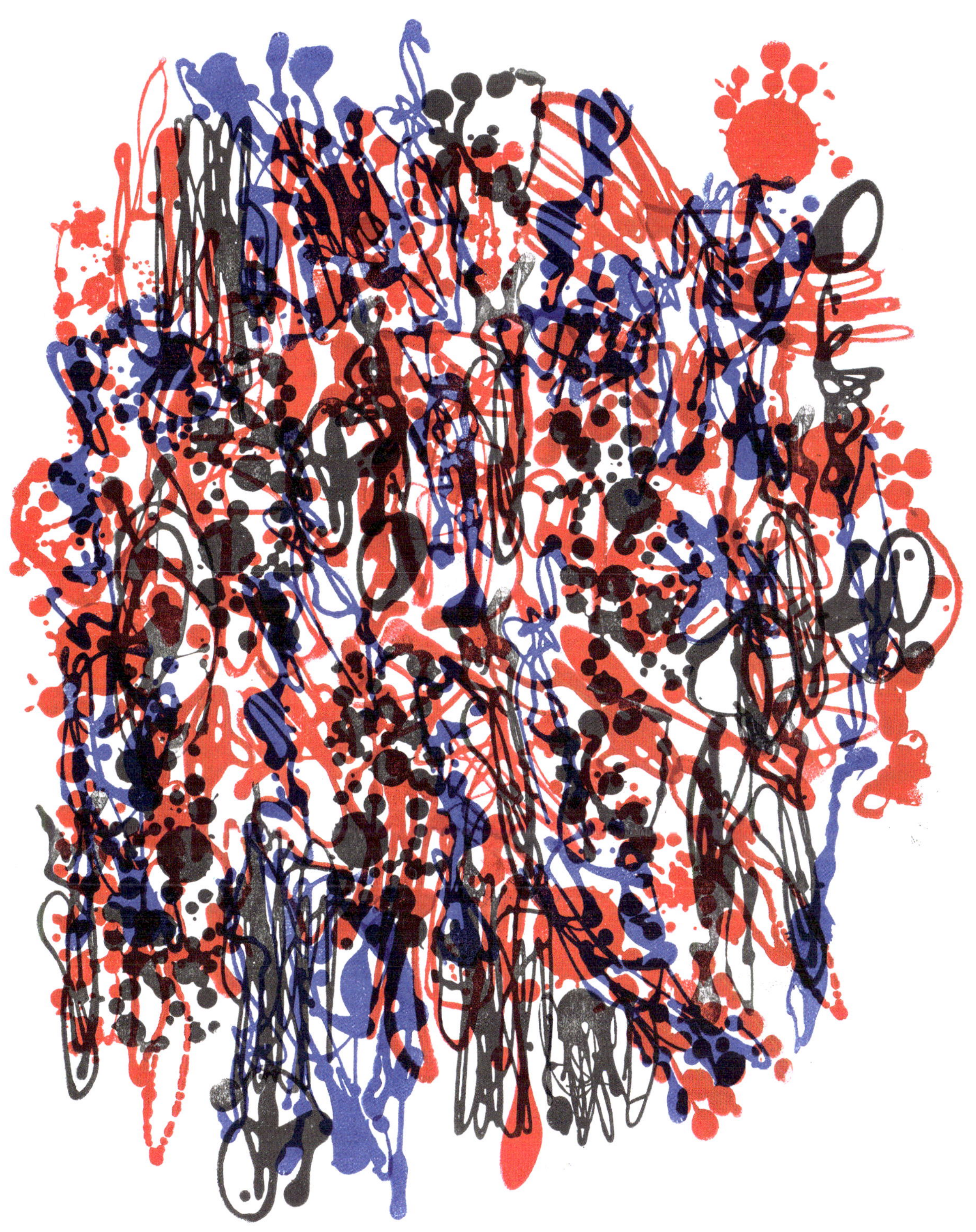

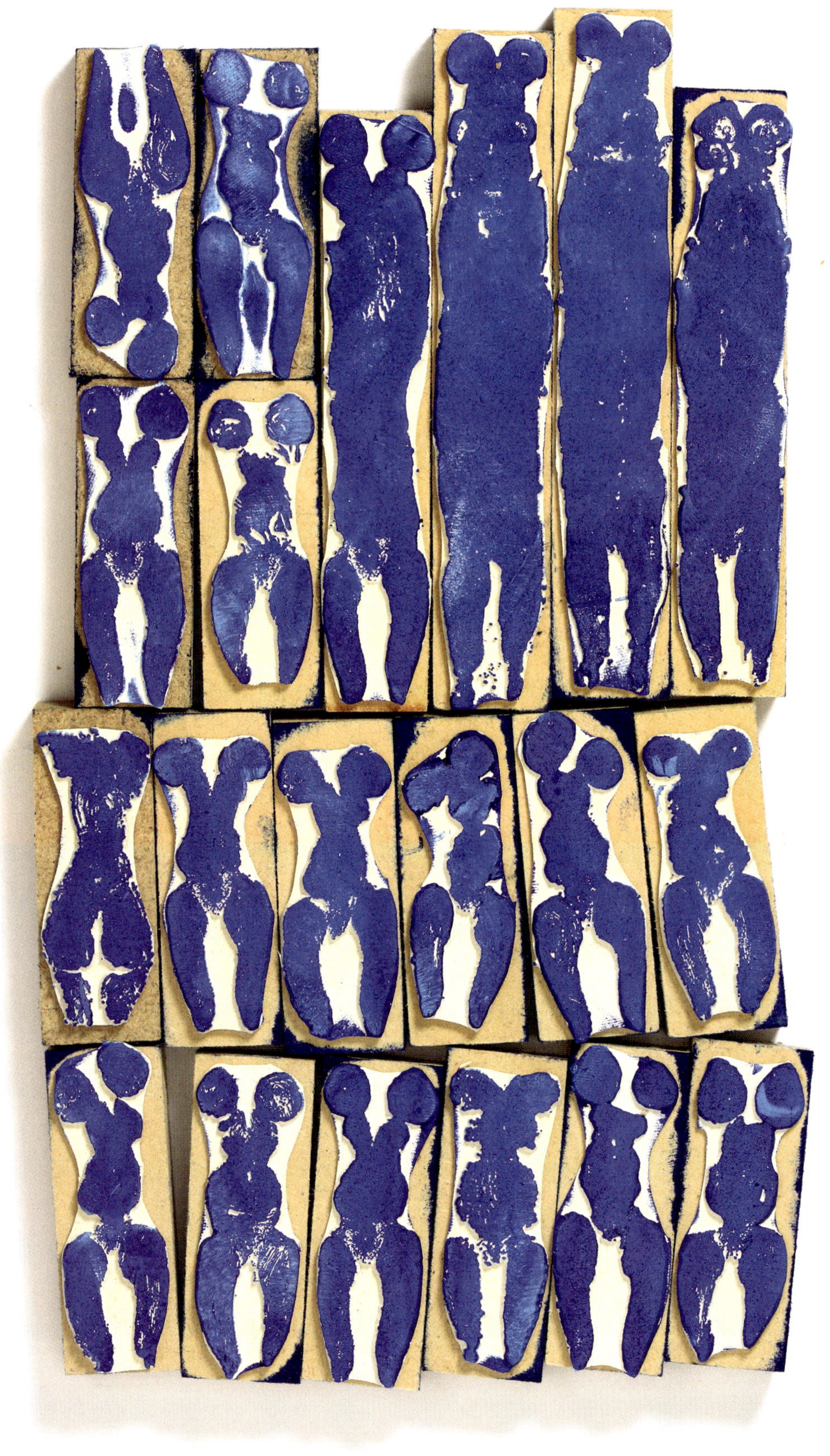

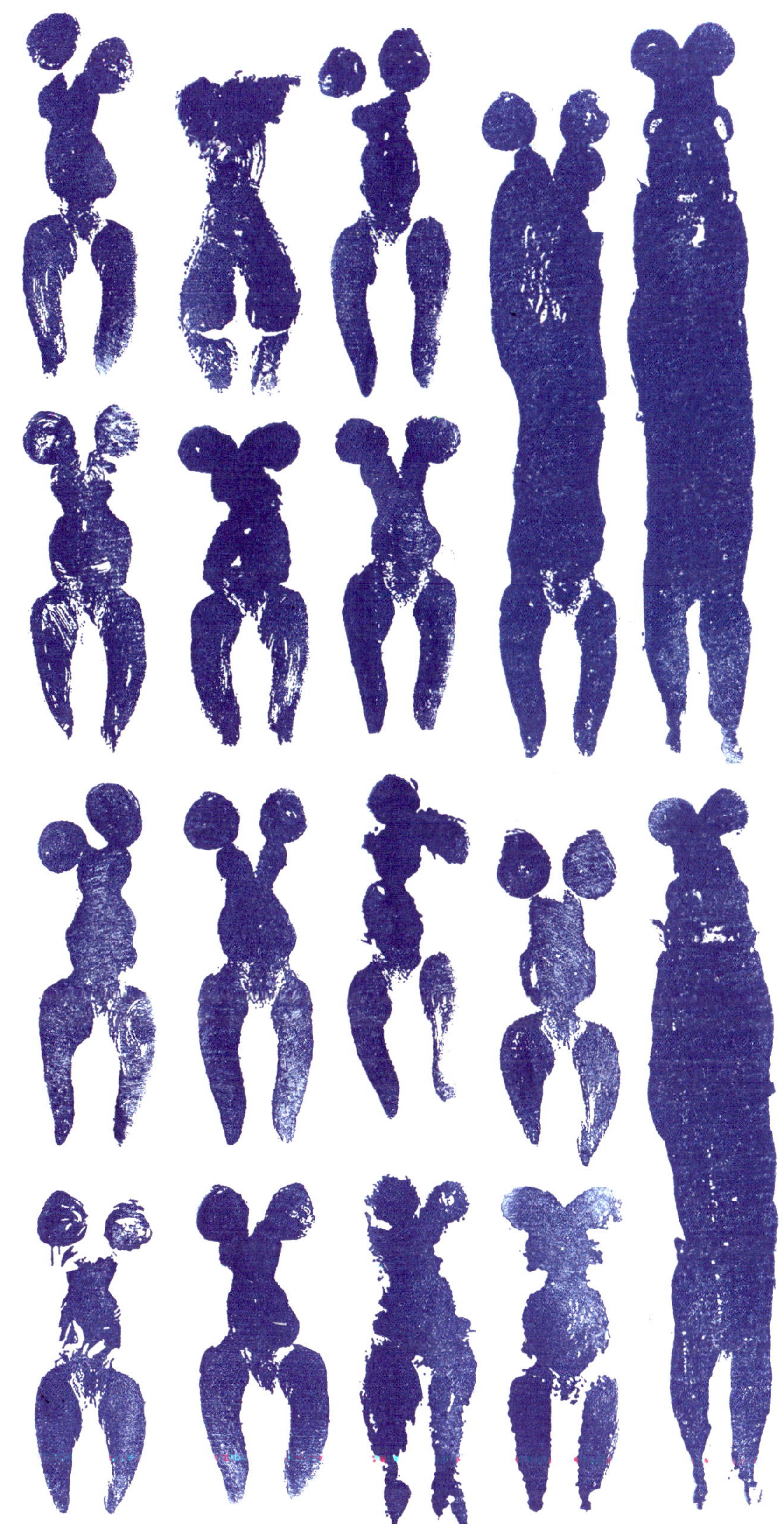

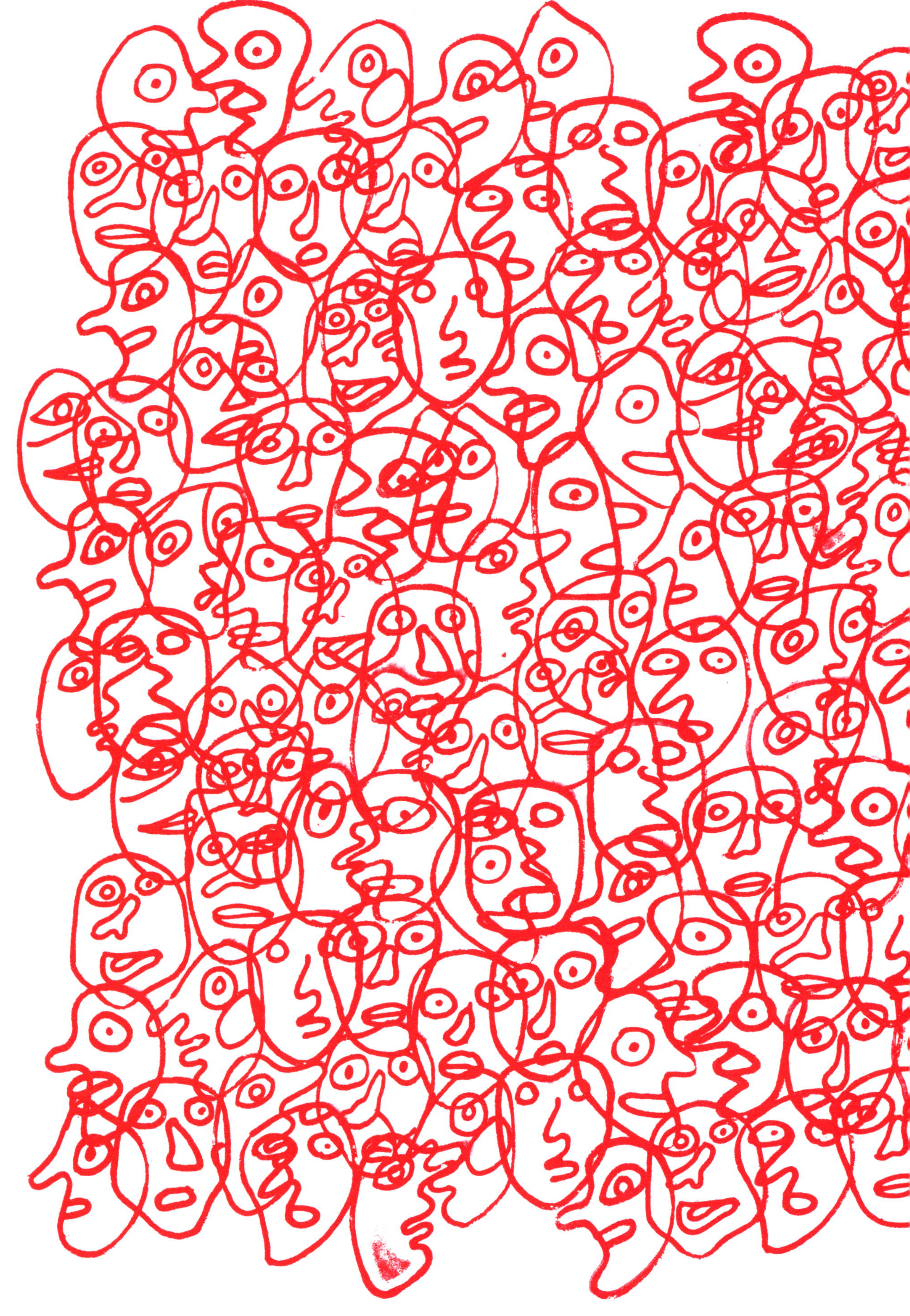

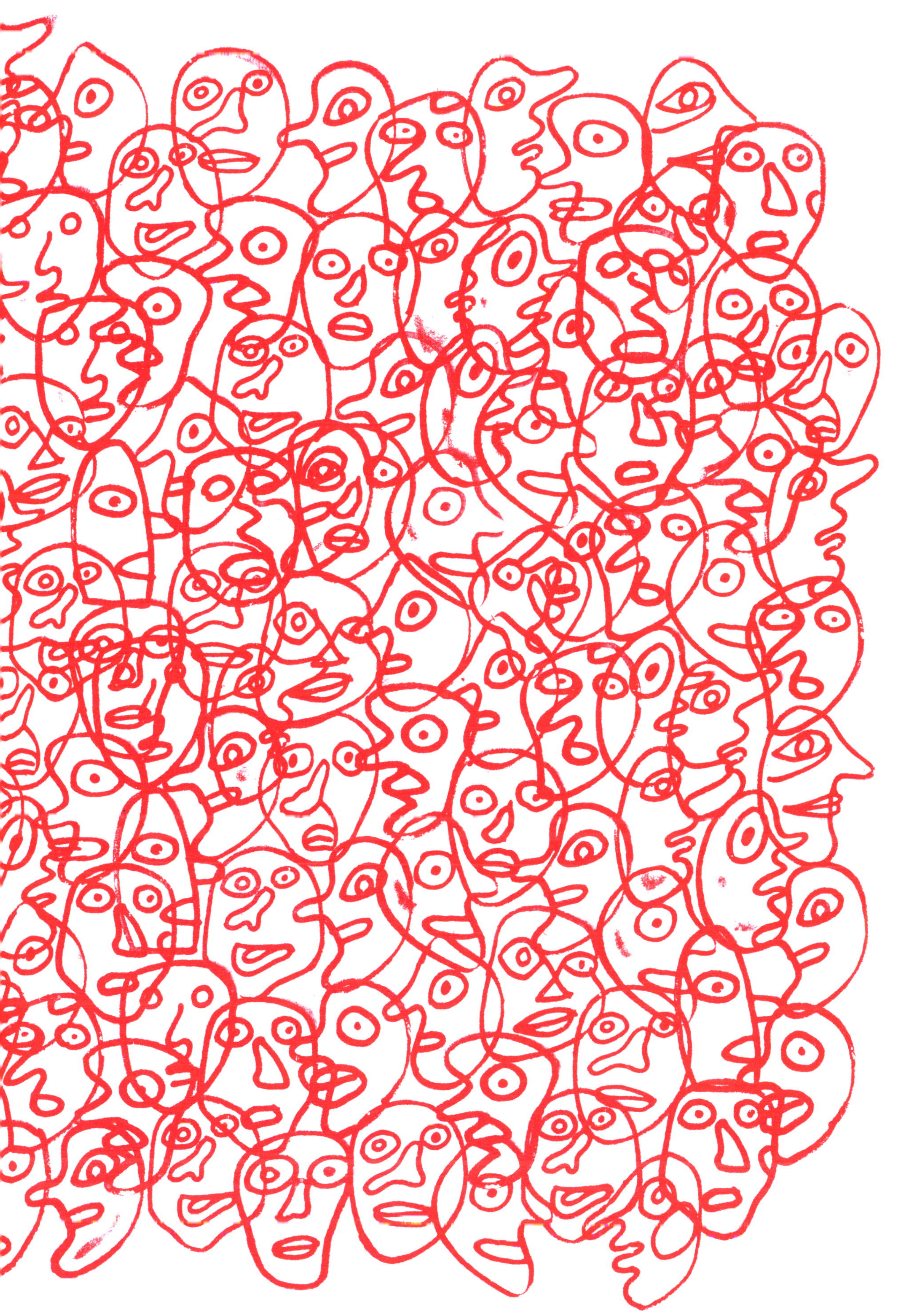

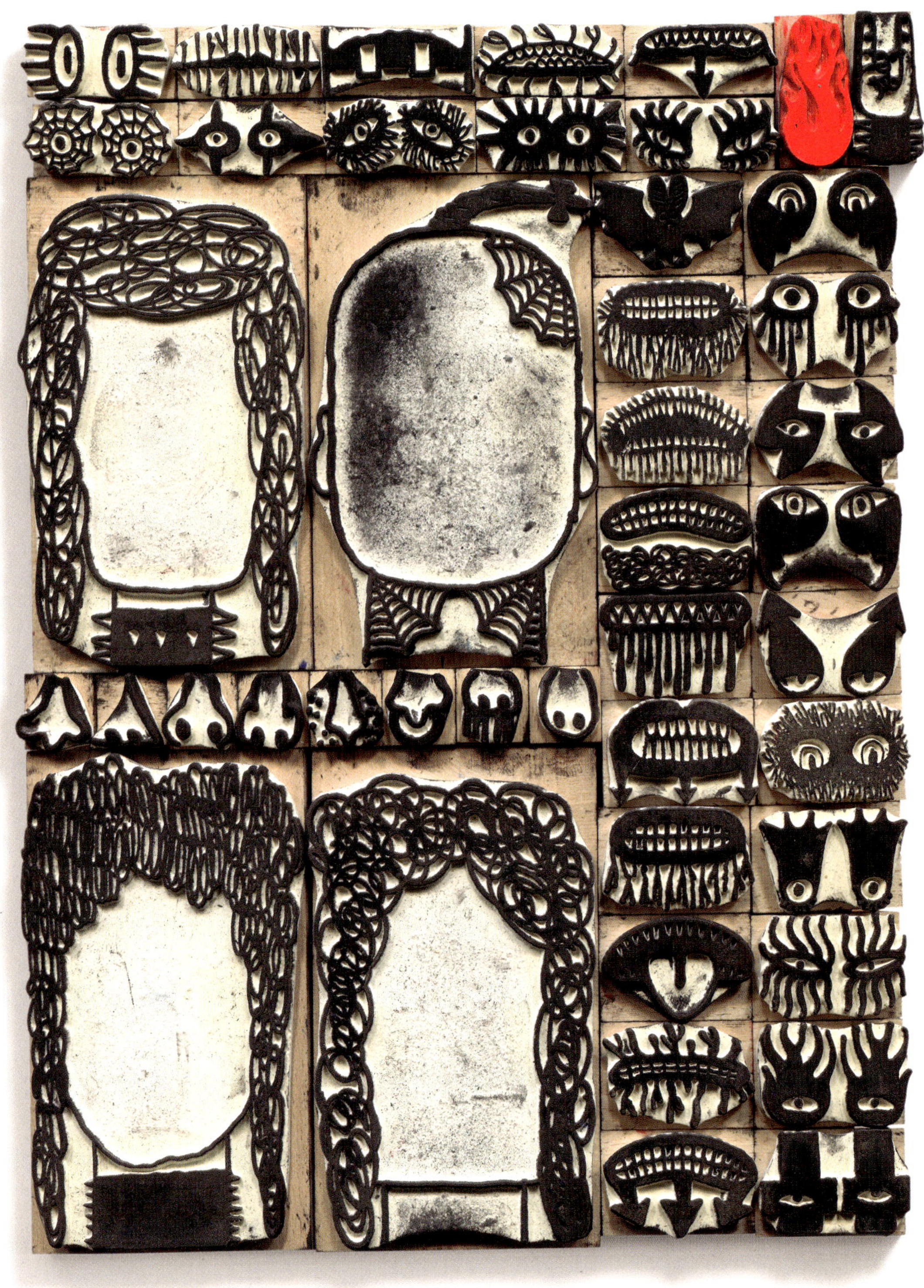

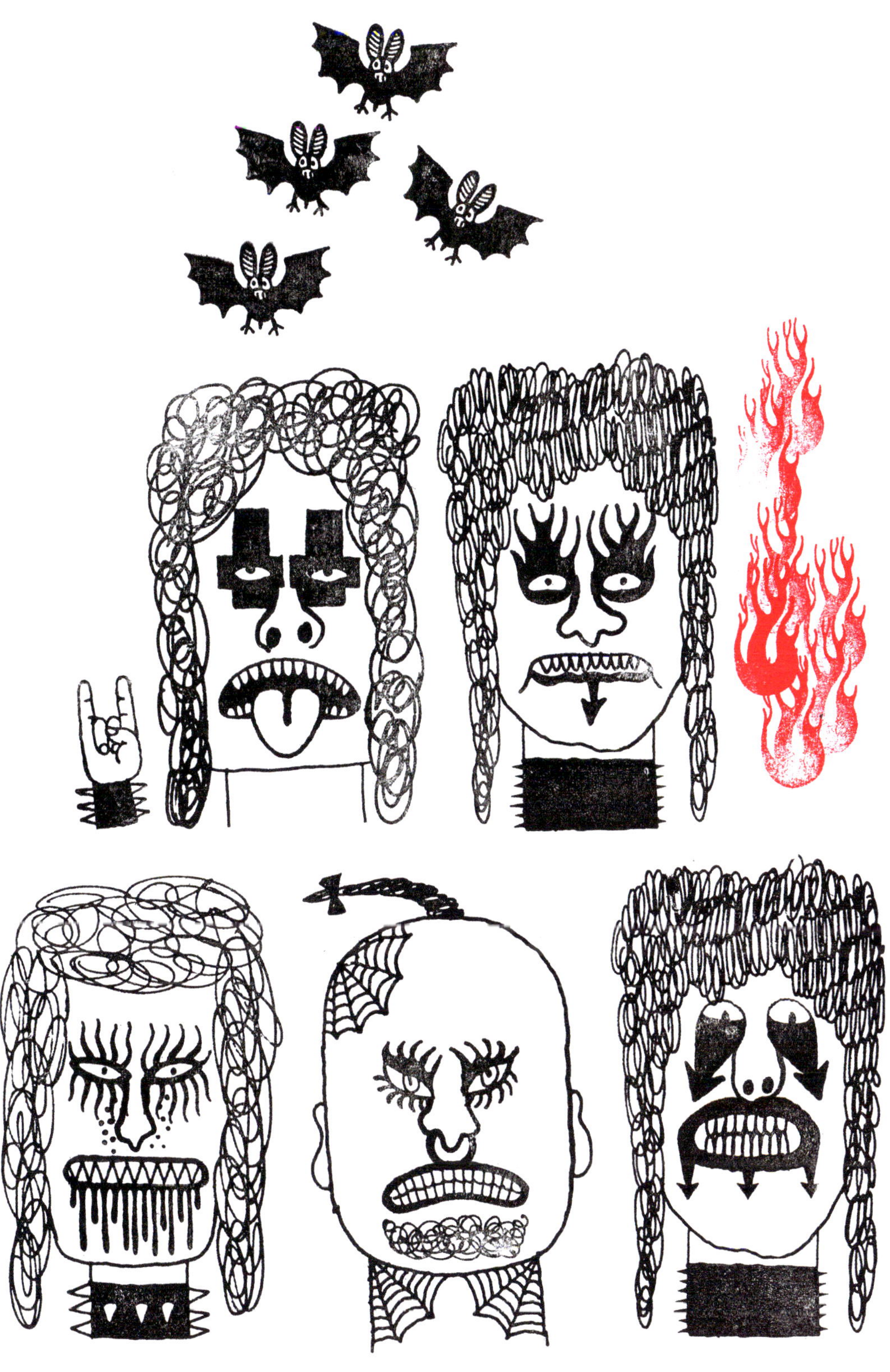

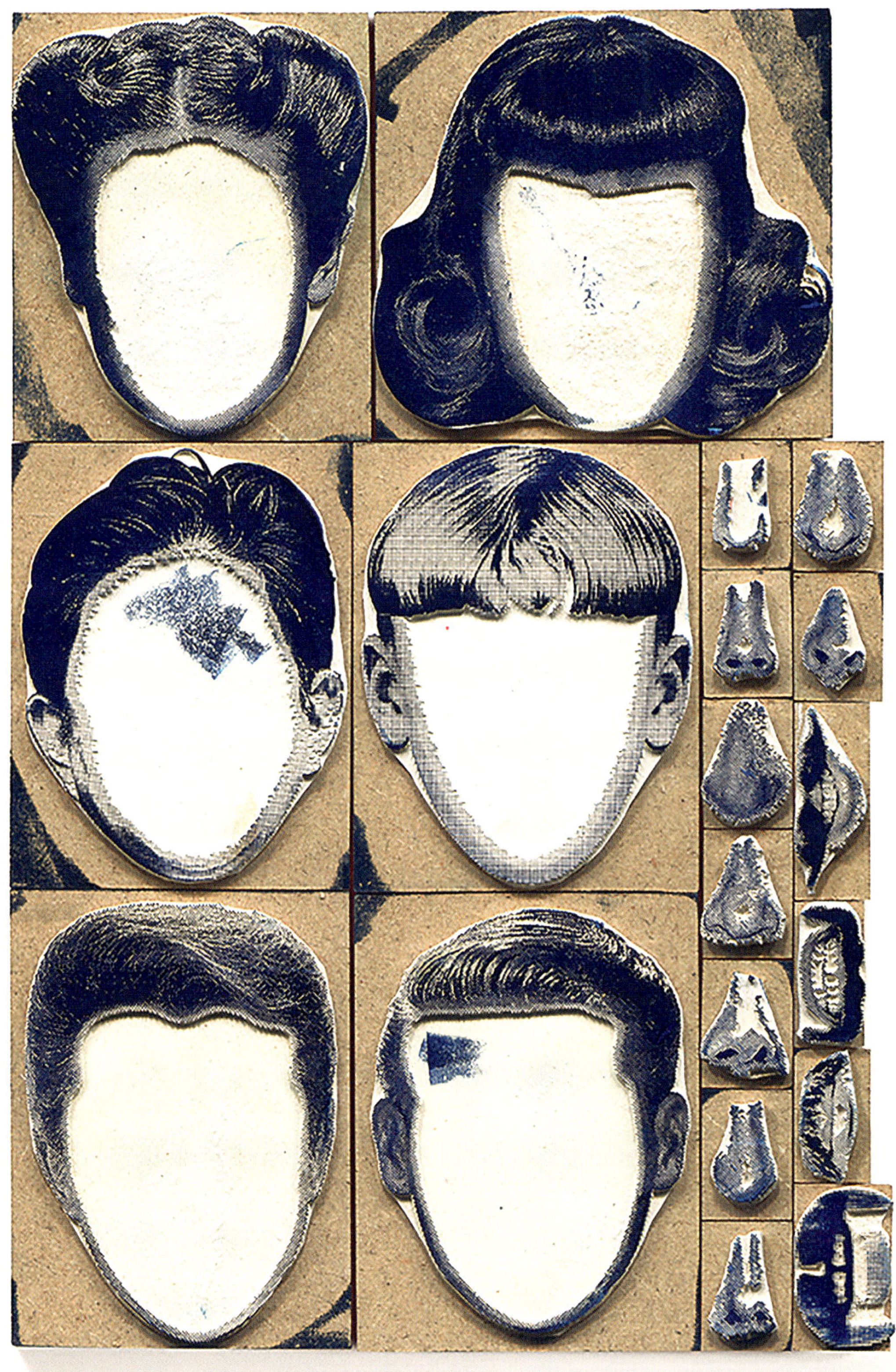

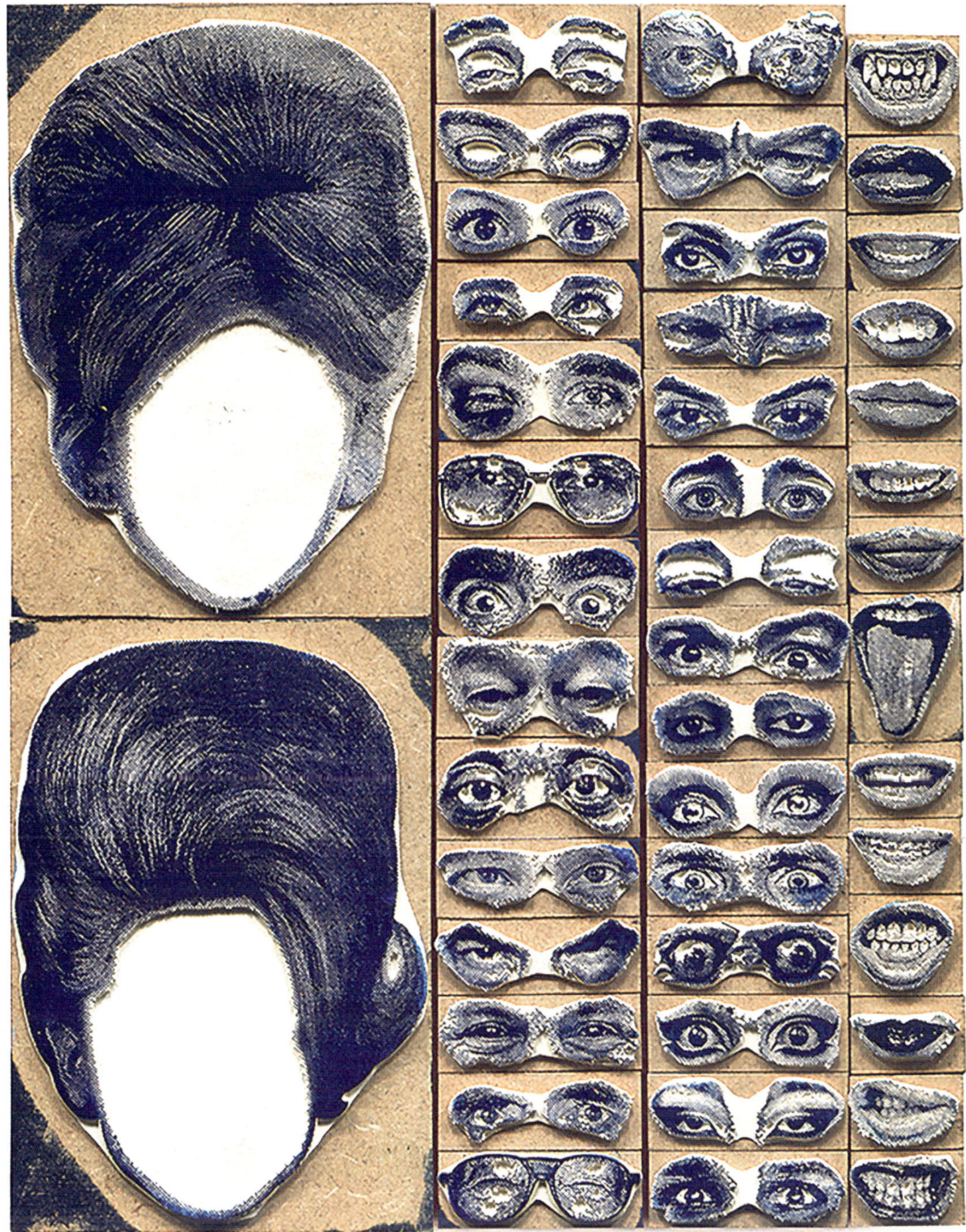

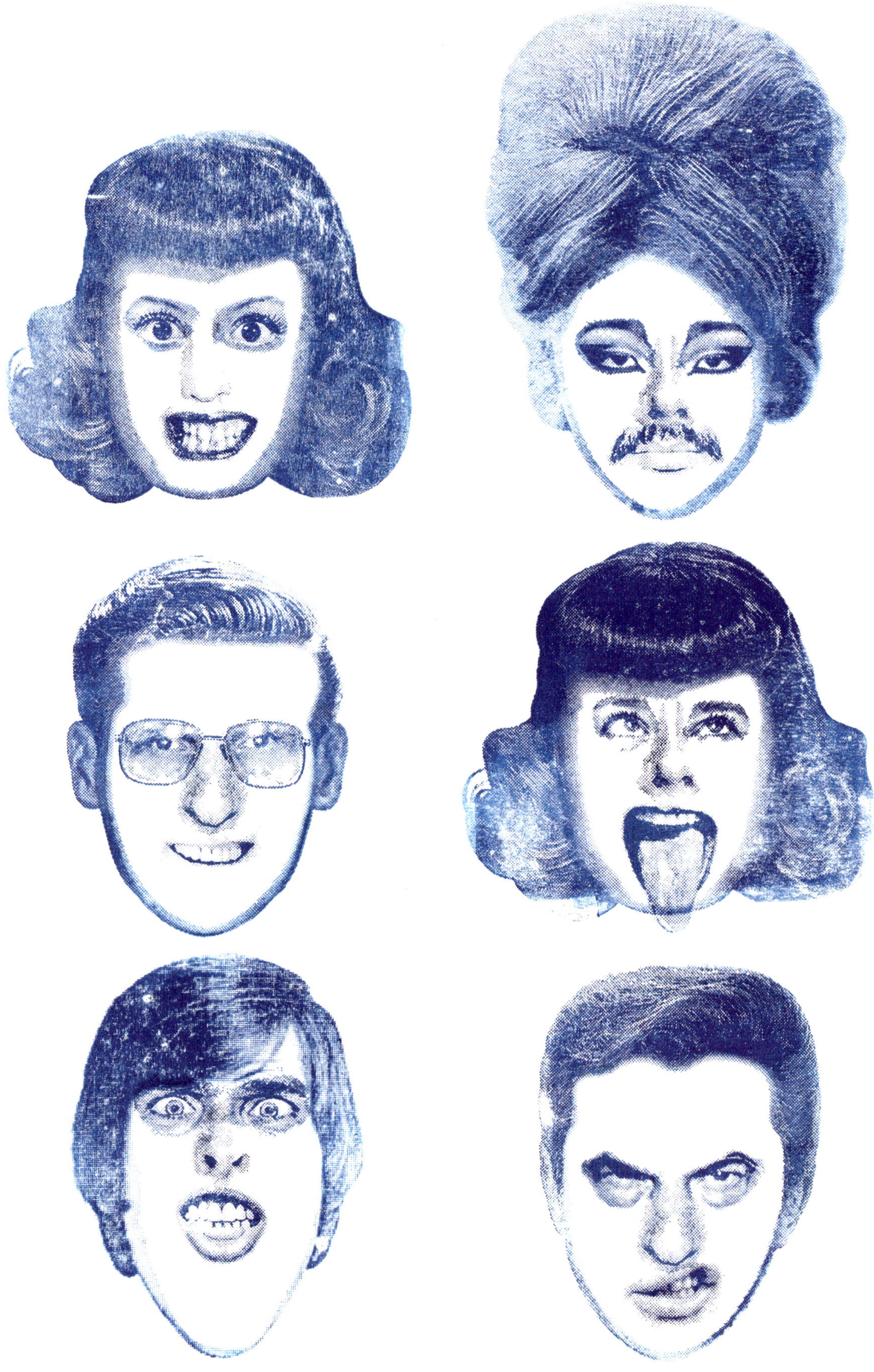

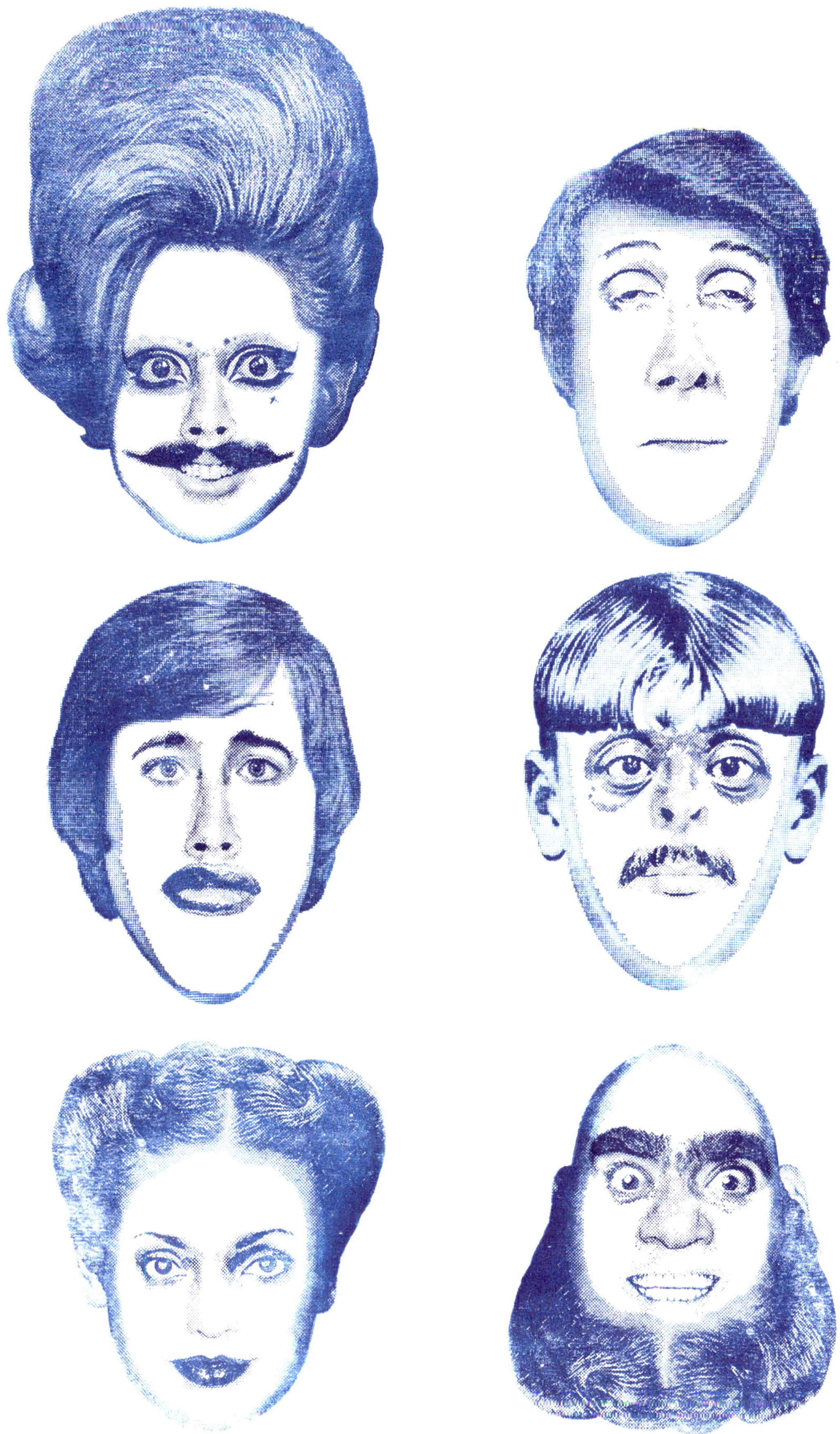

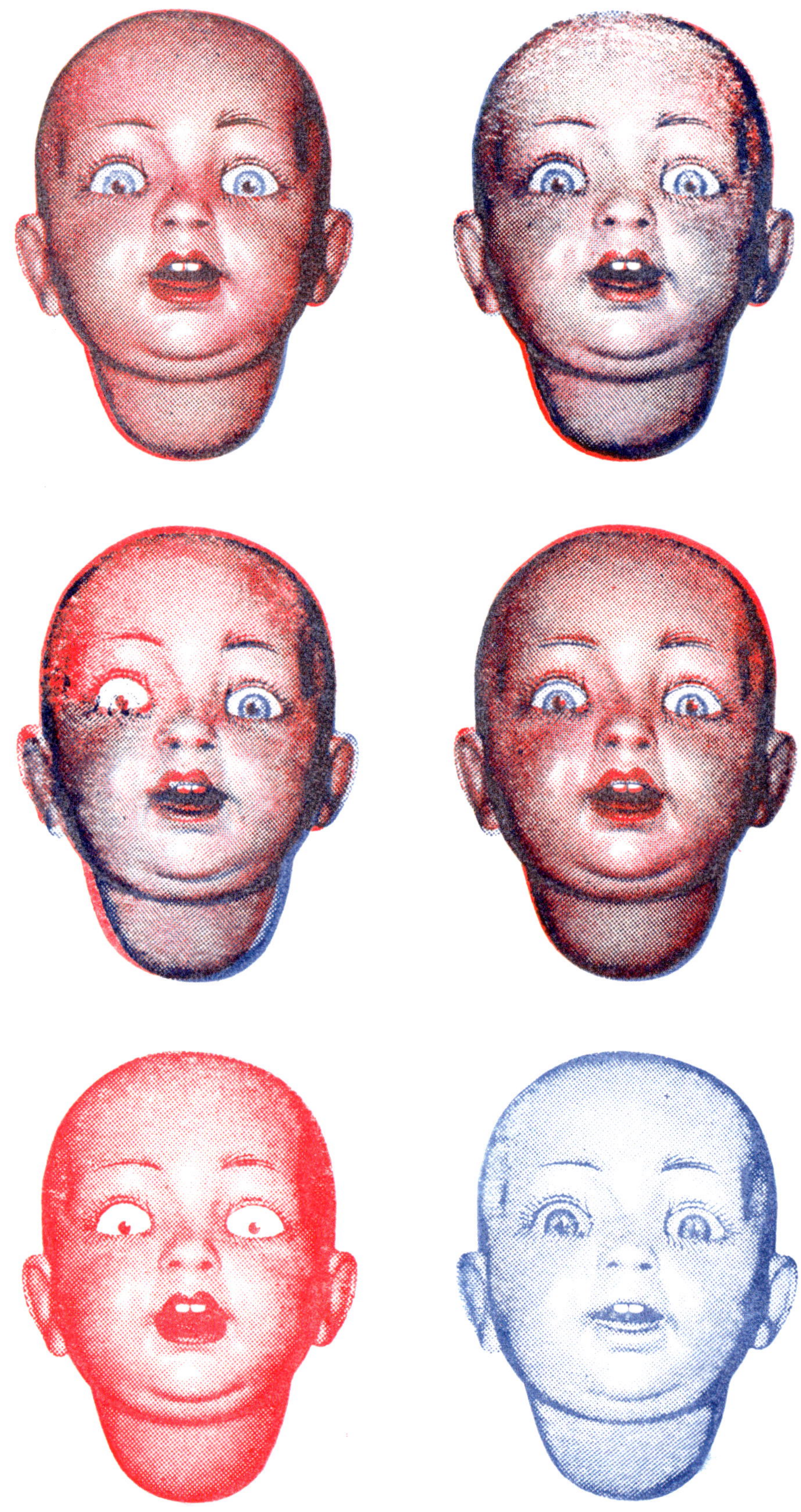

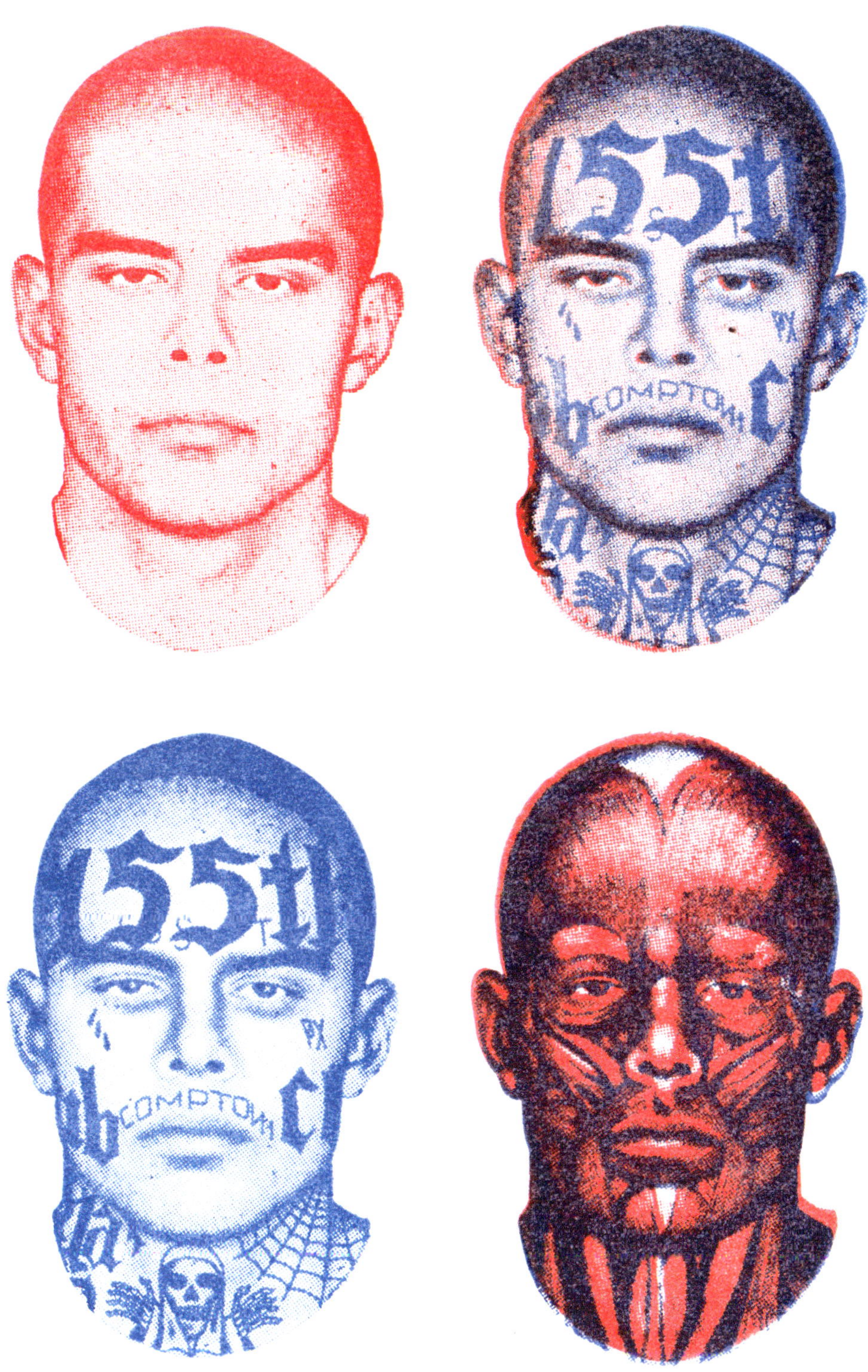
55t
COMPTON
55t
COMPTON

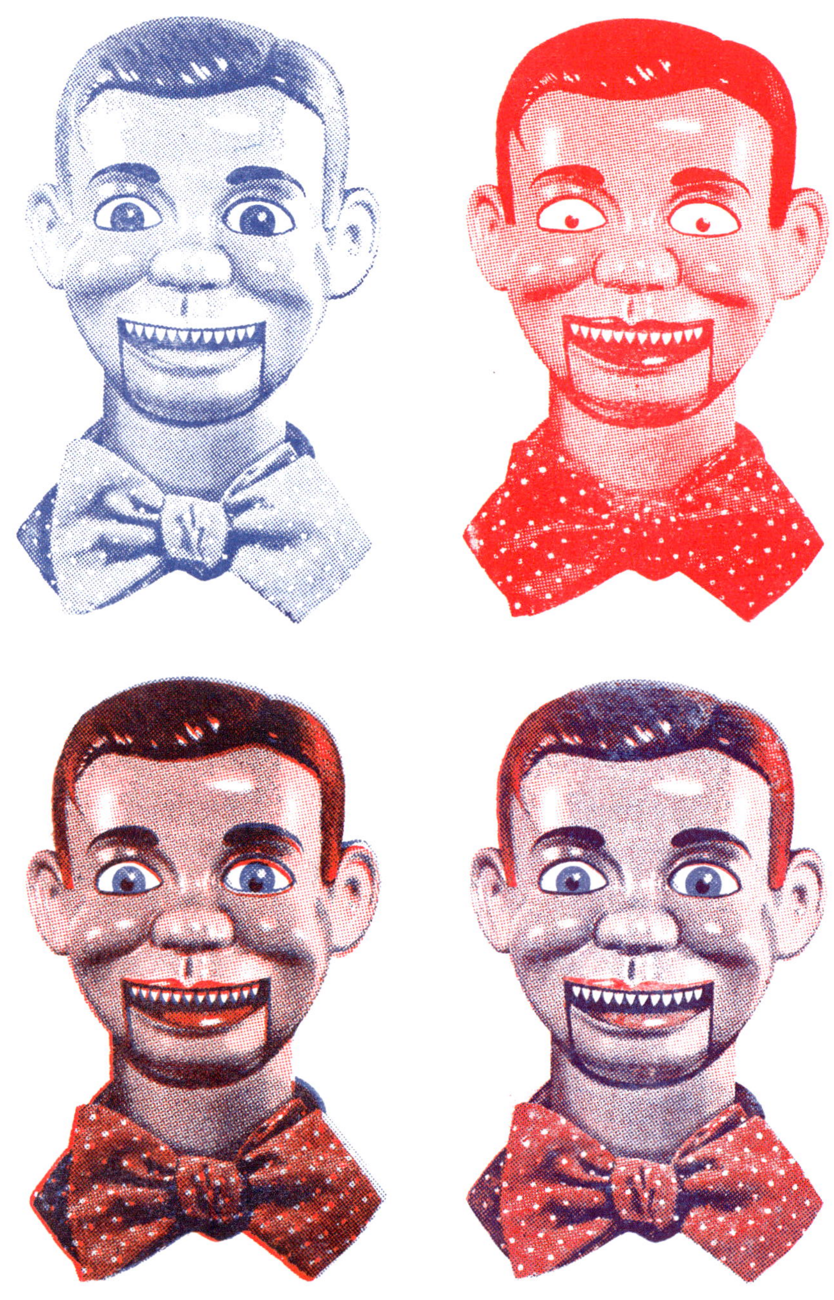

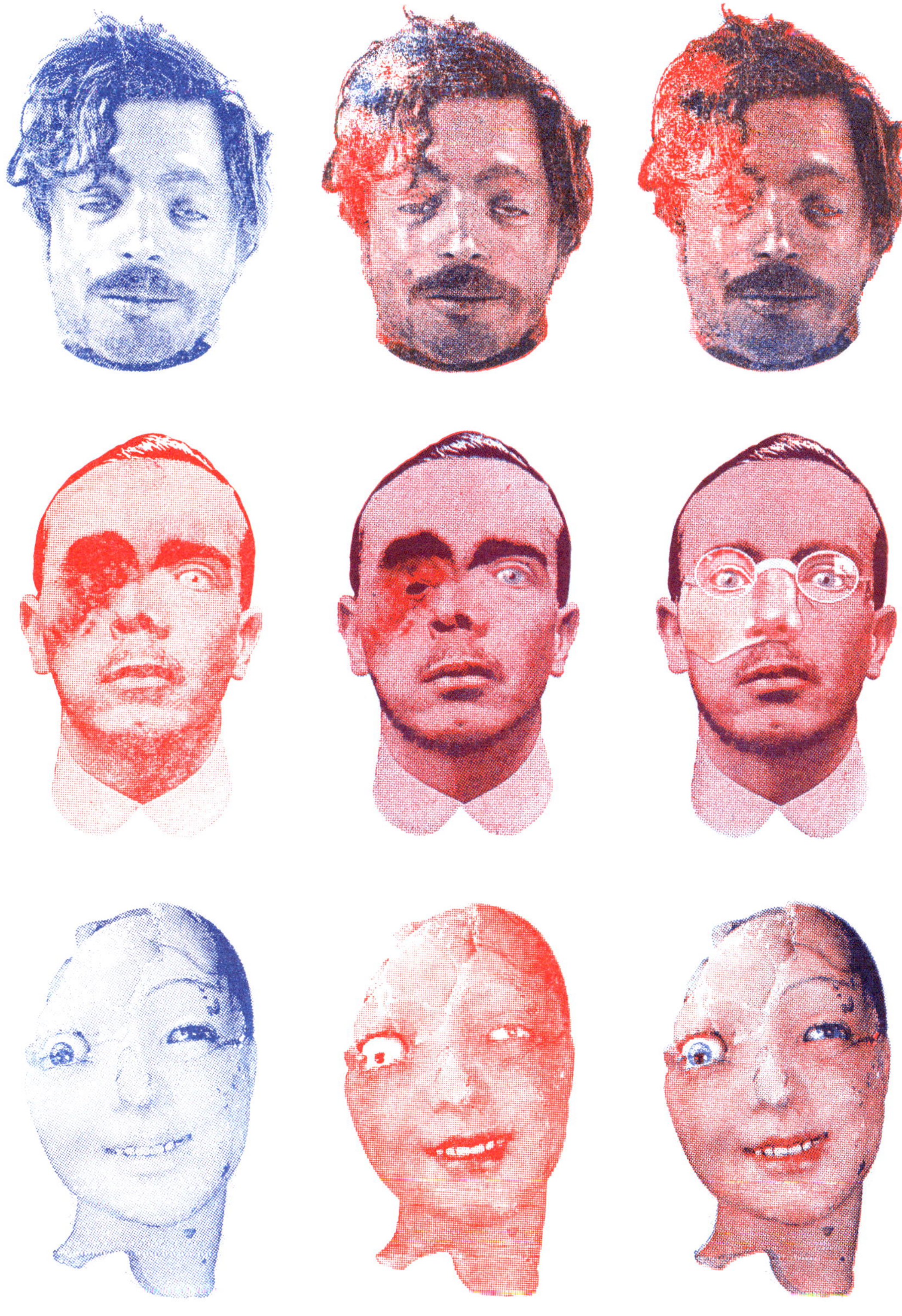

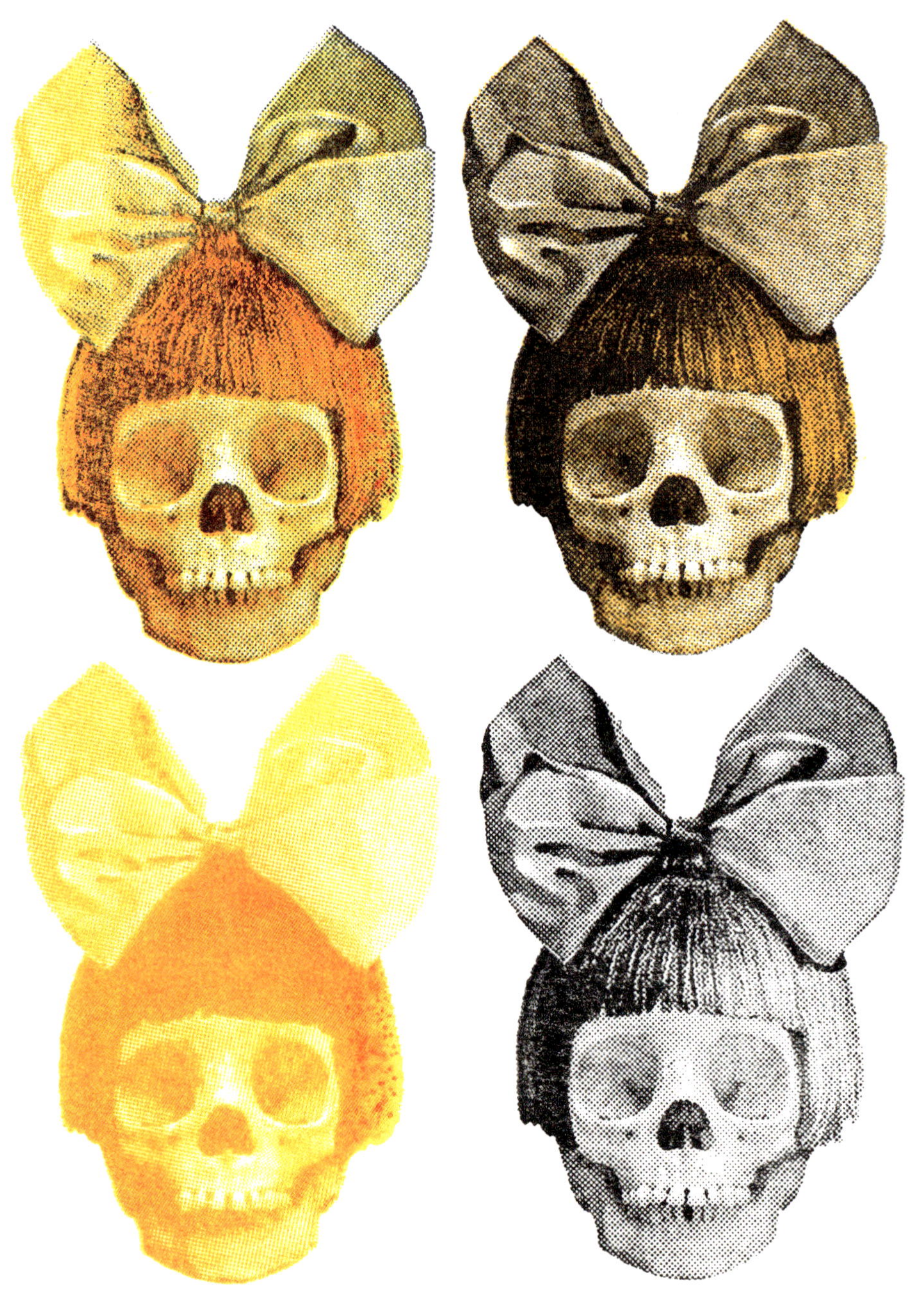

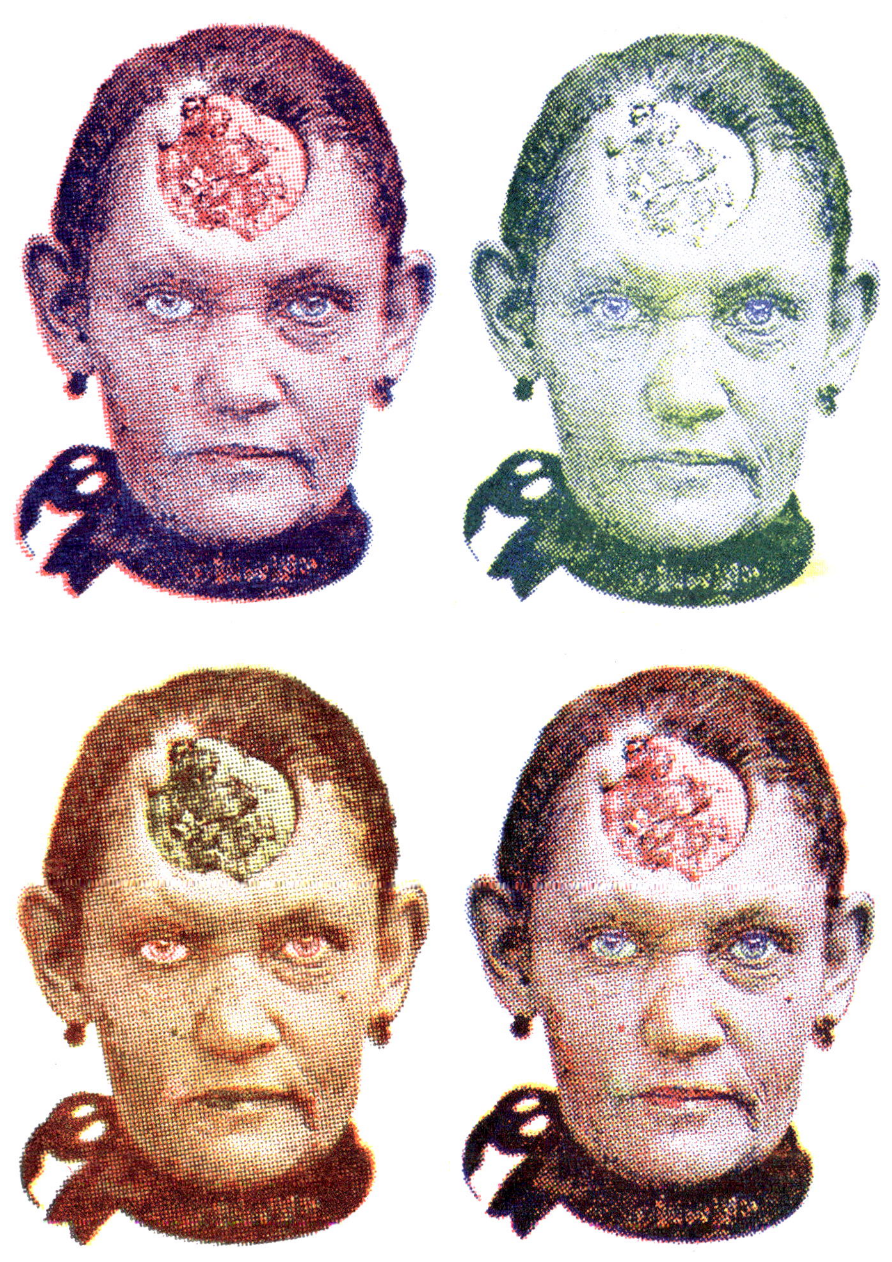

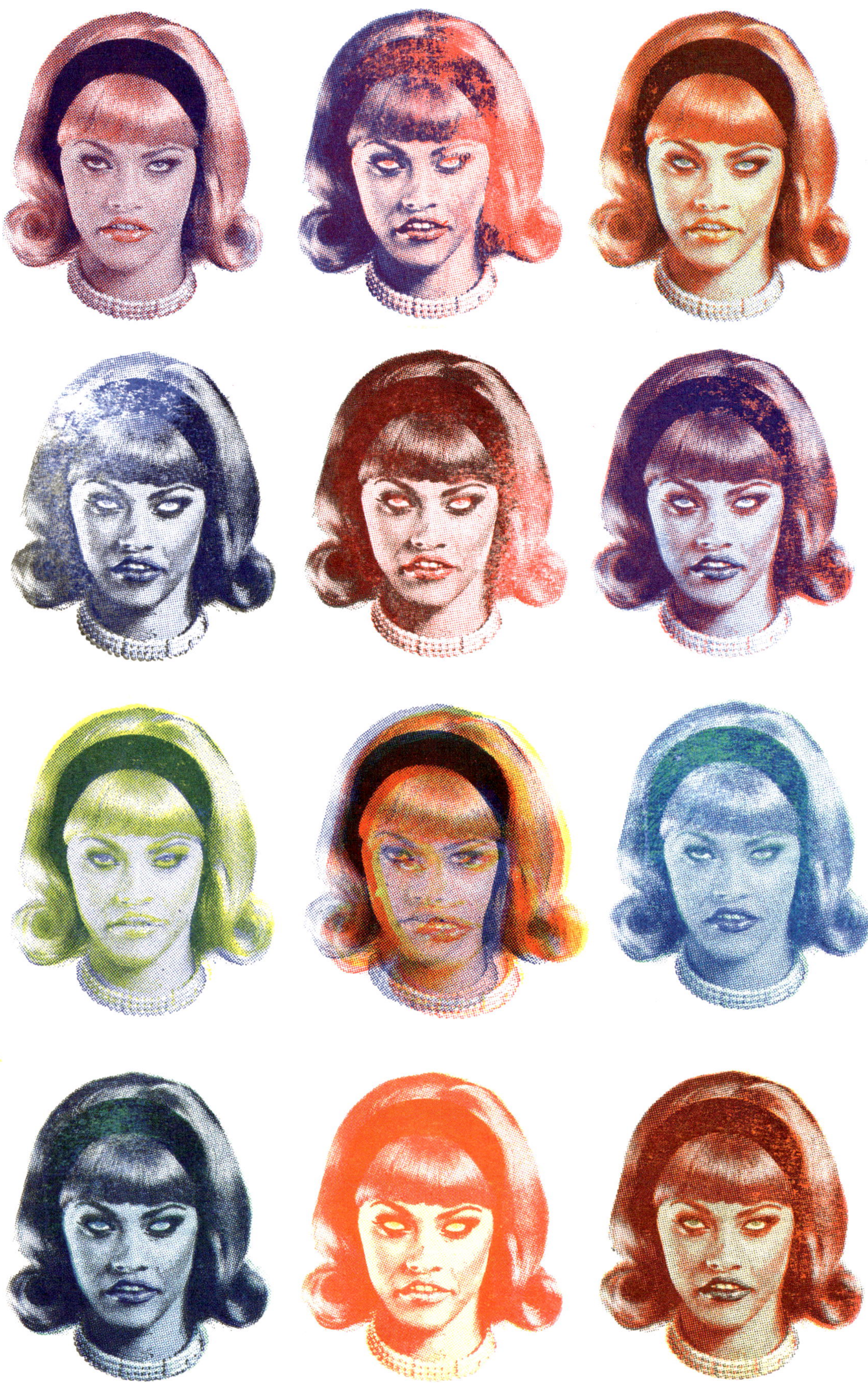

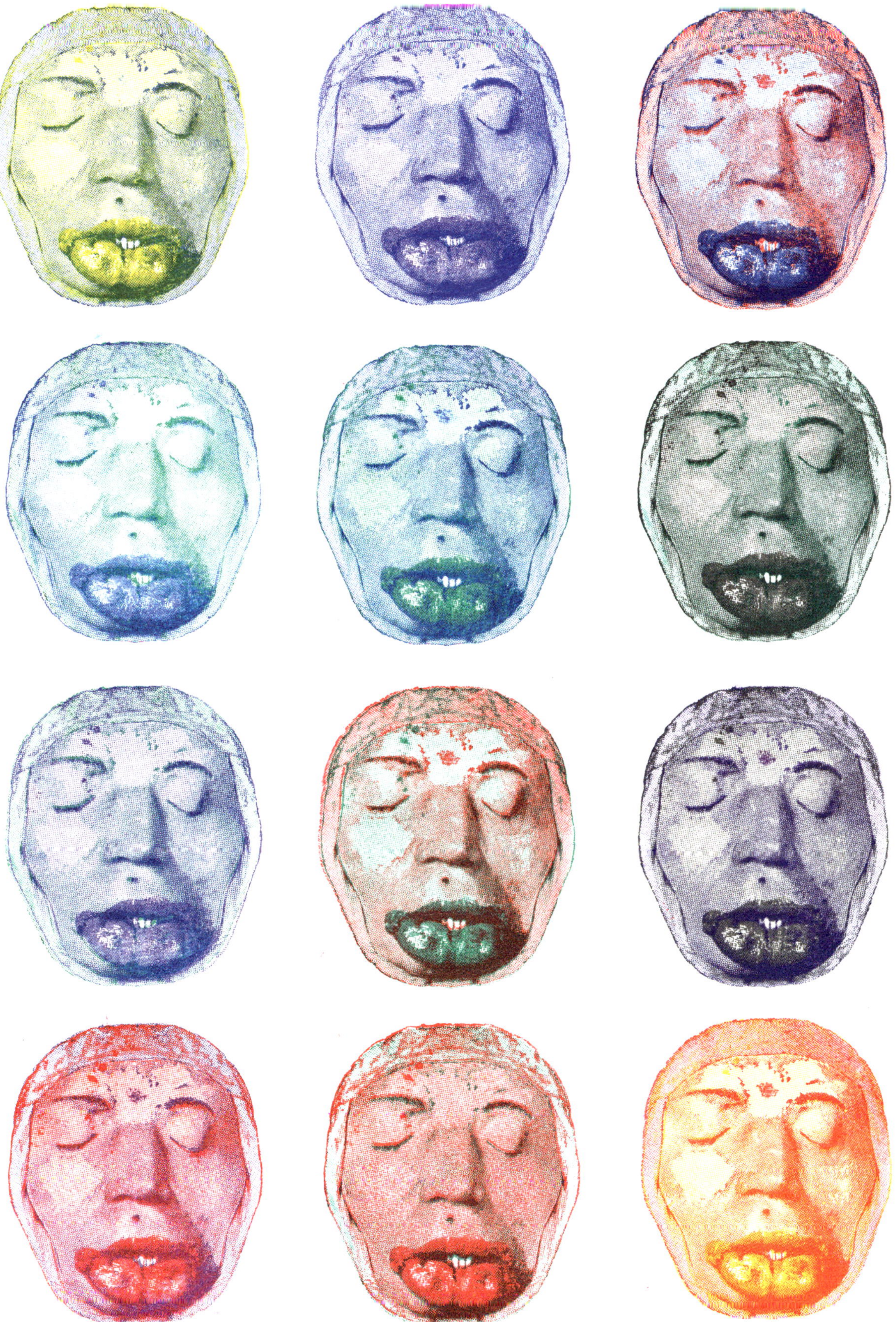

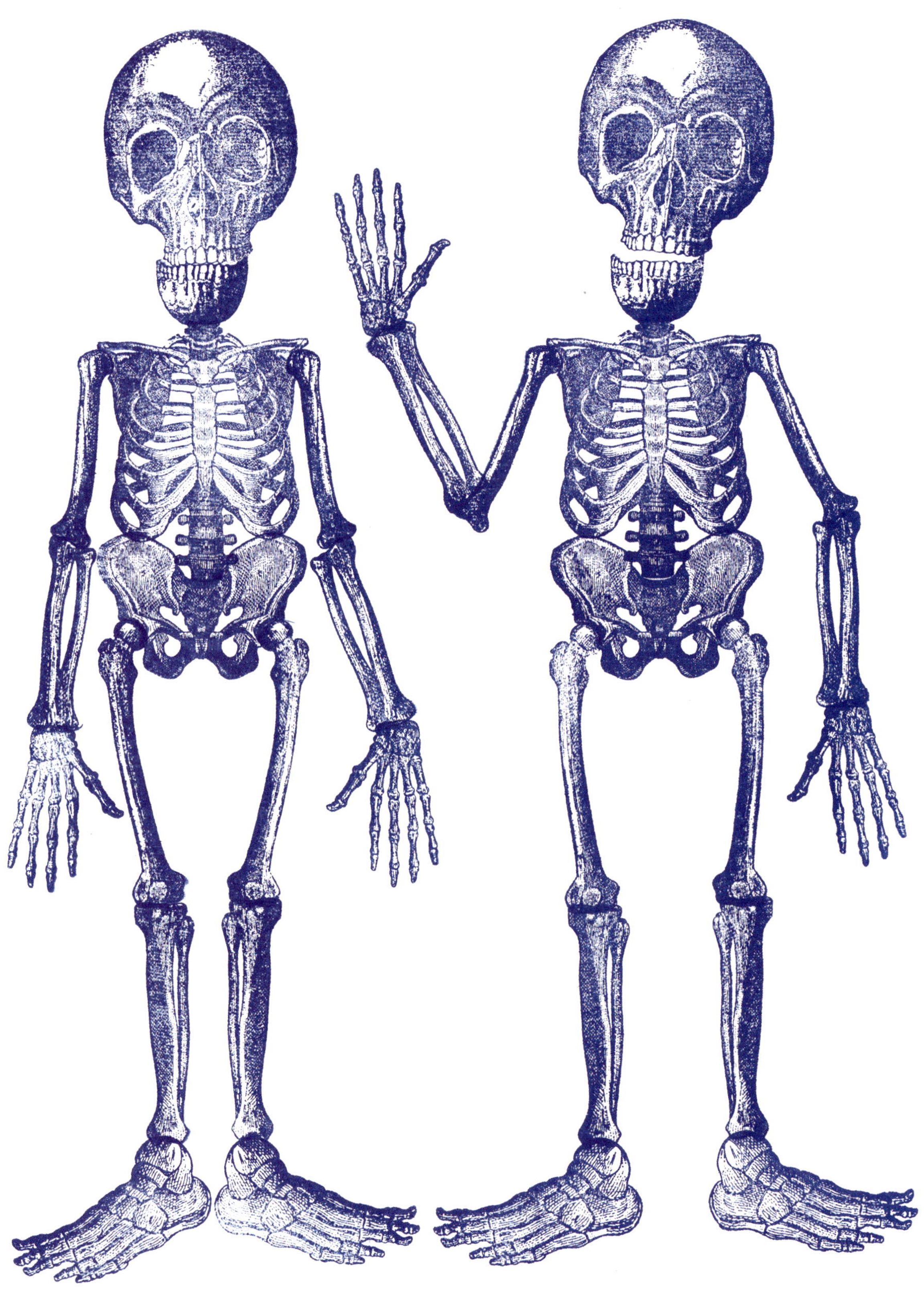

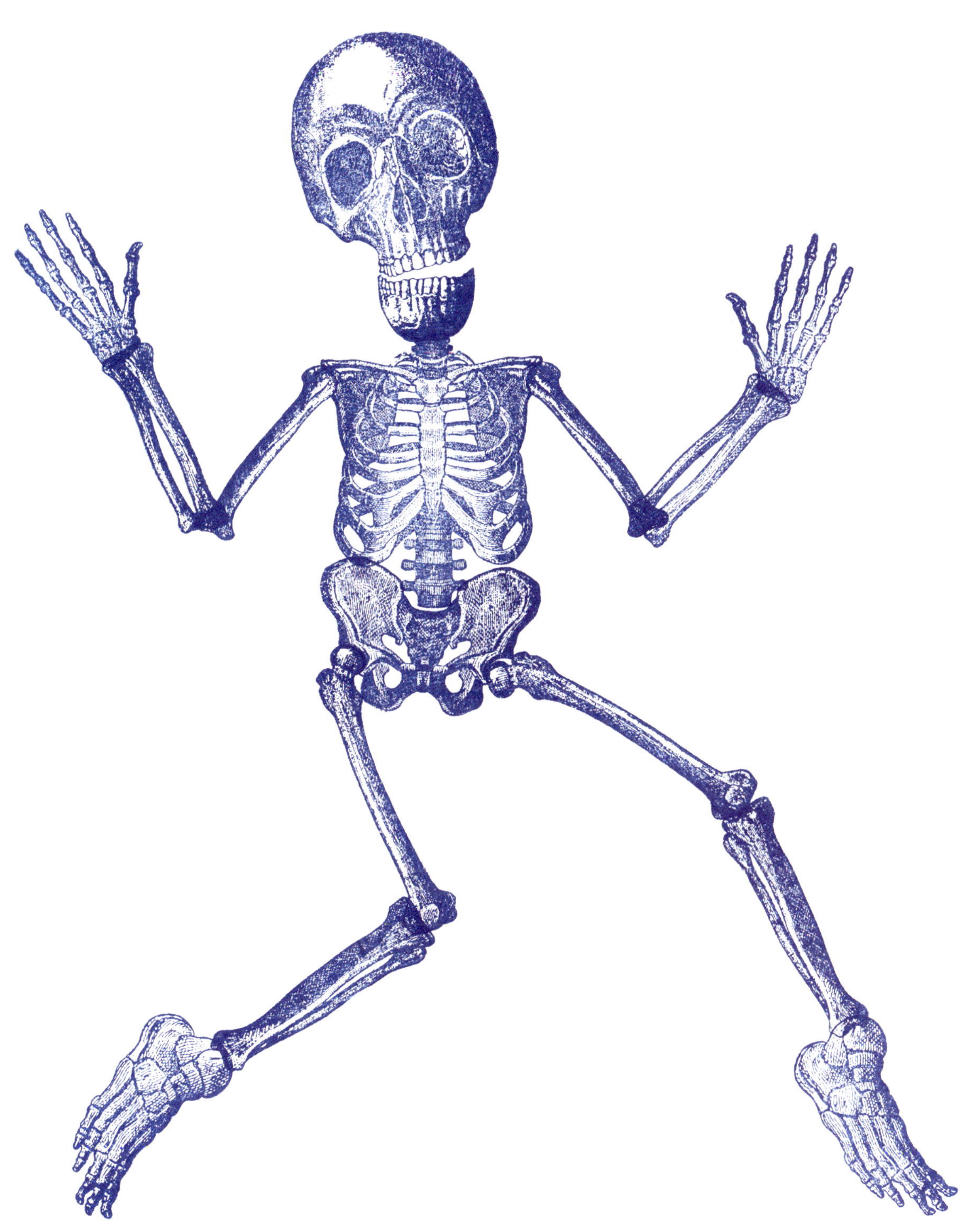

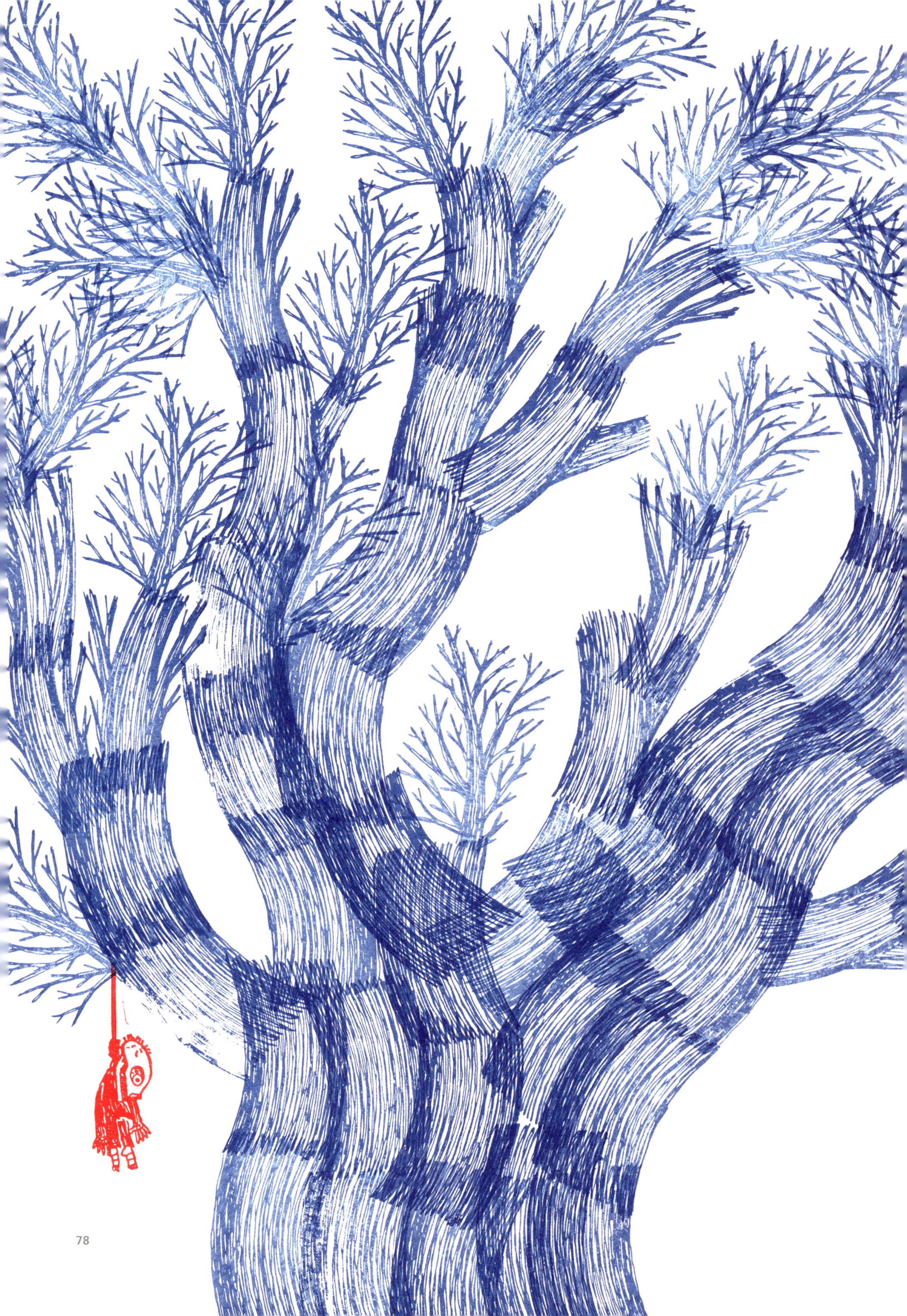

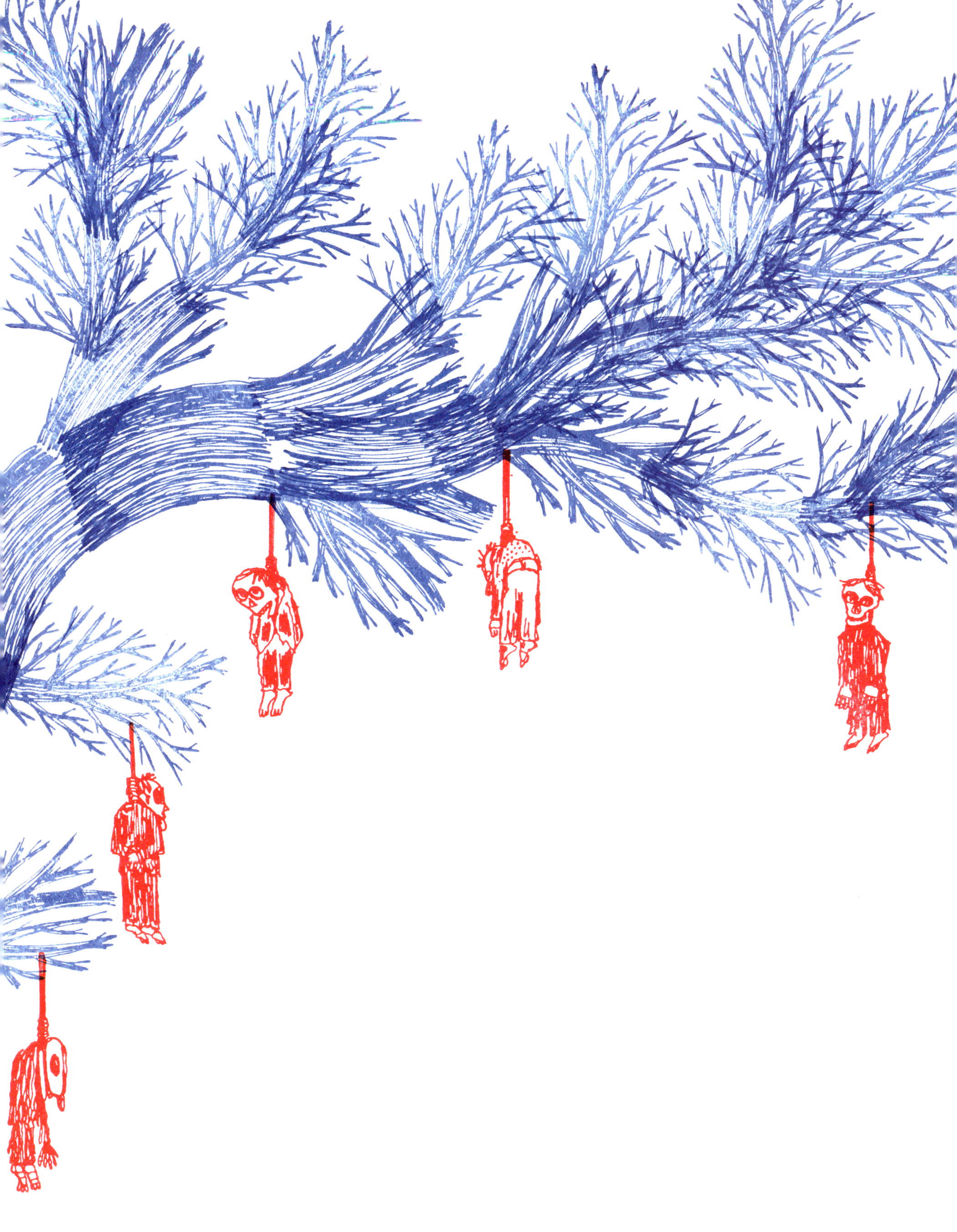

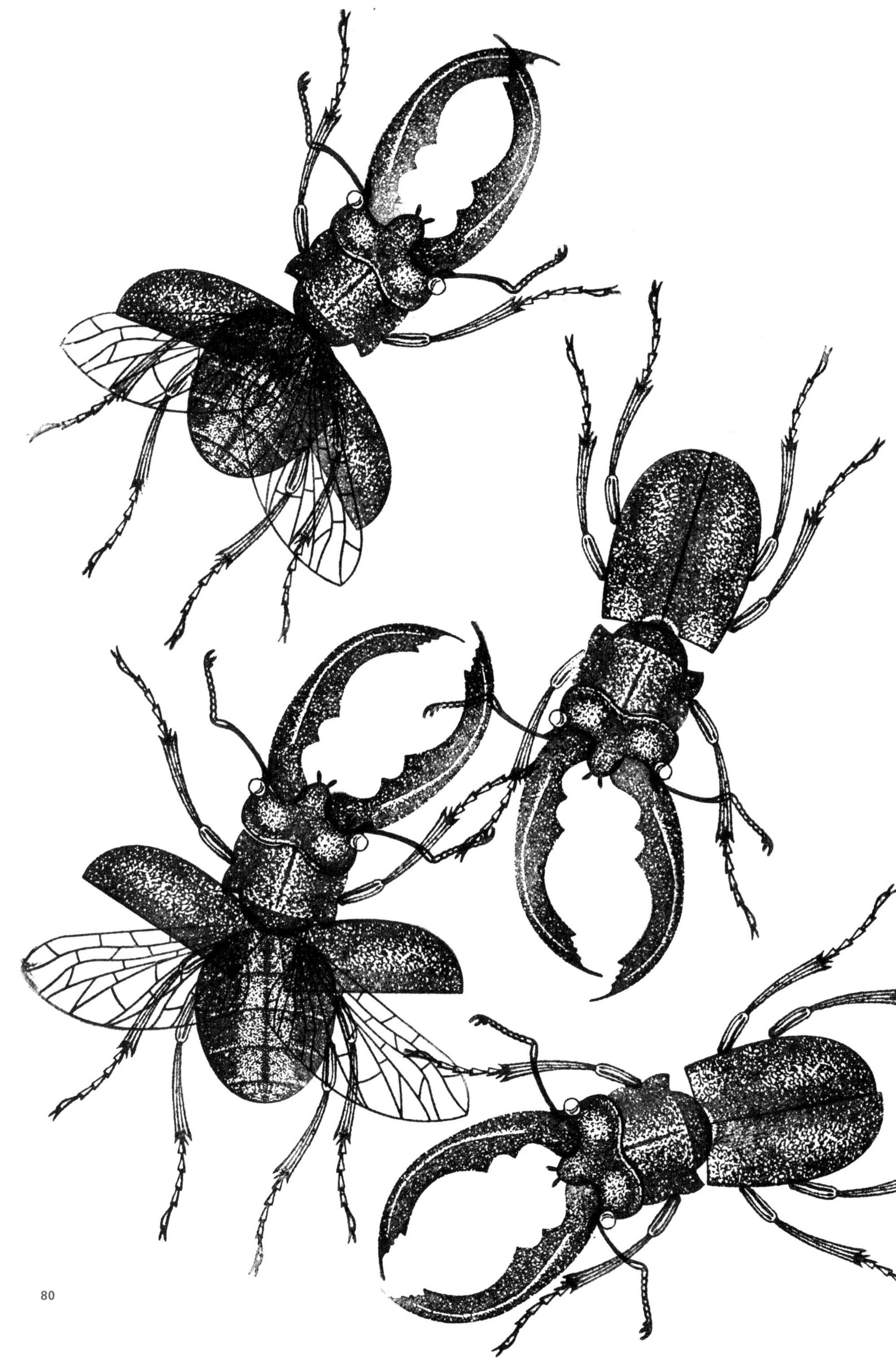

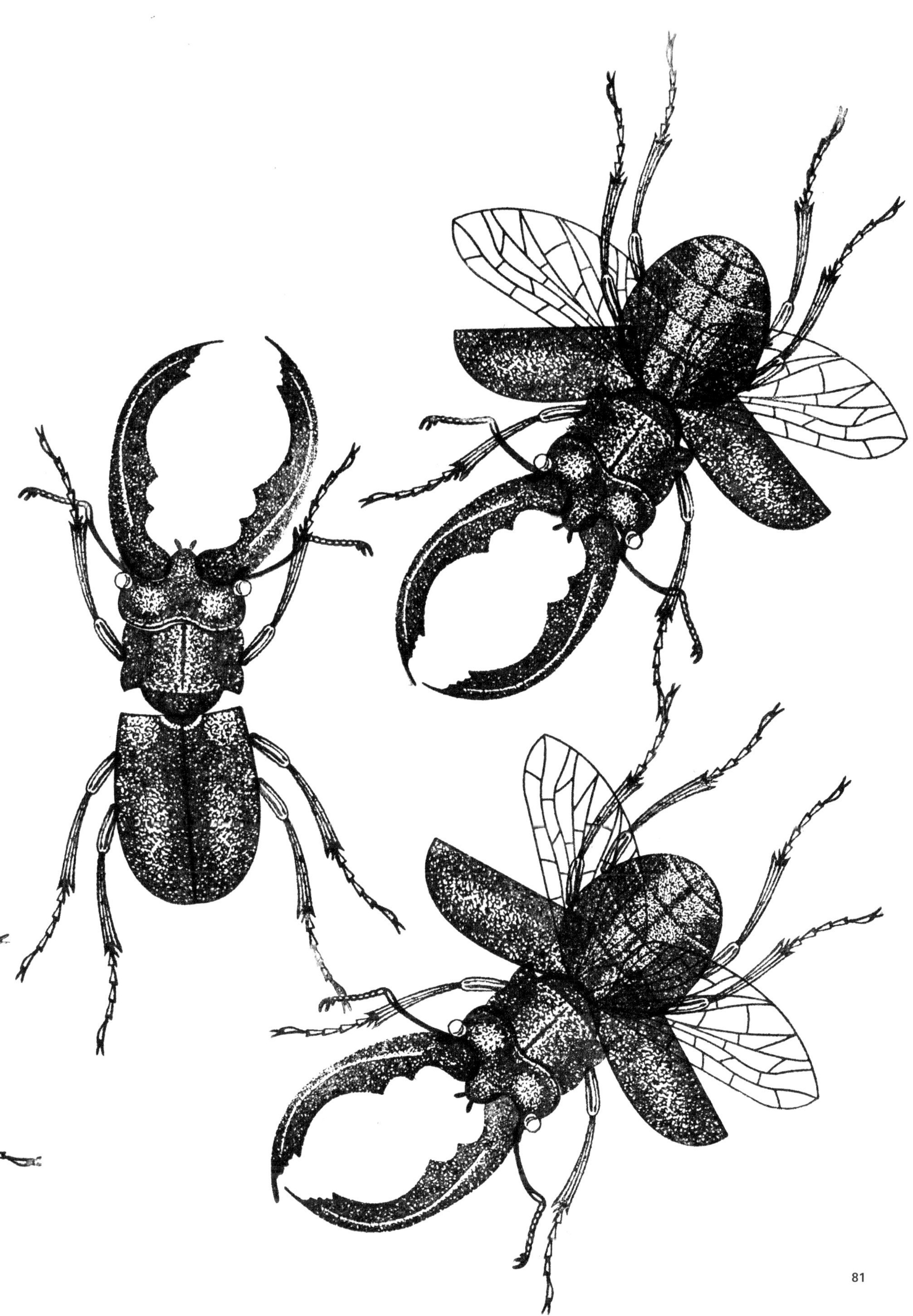

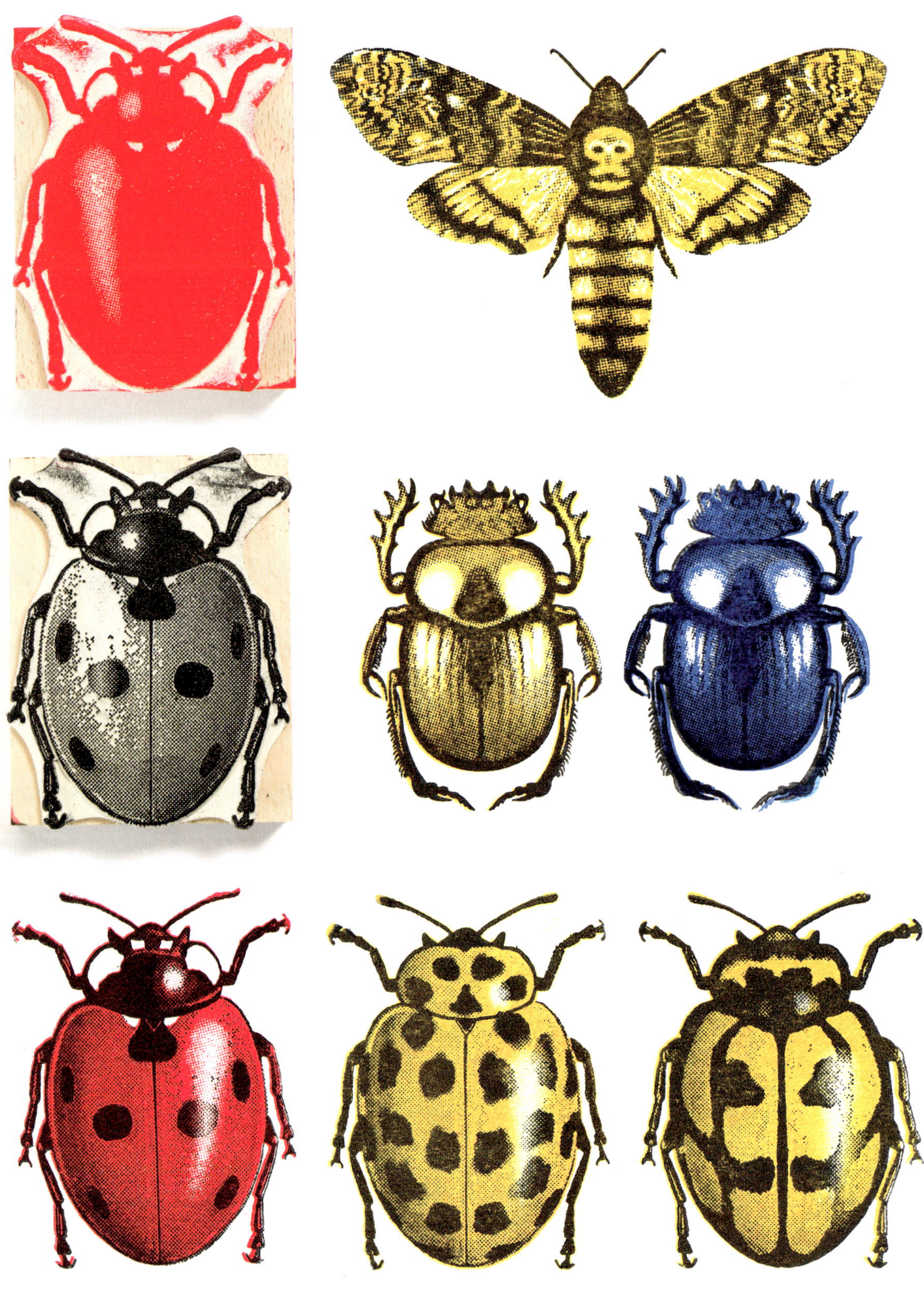

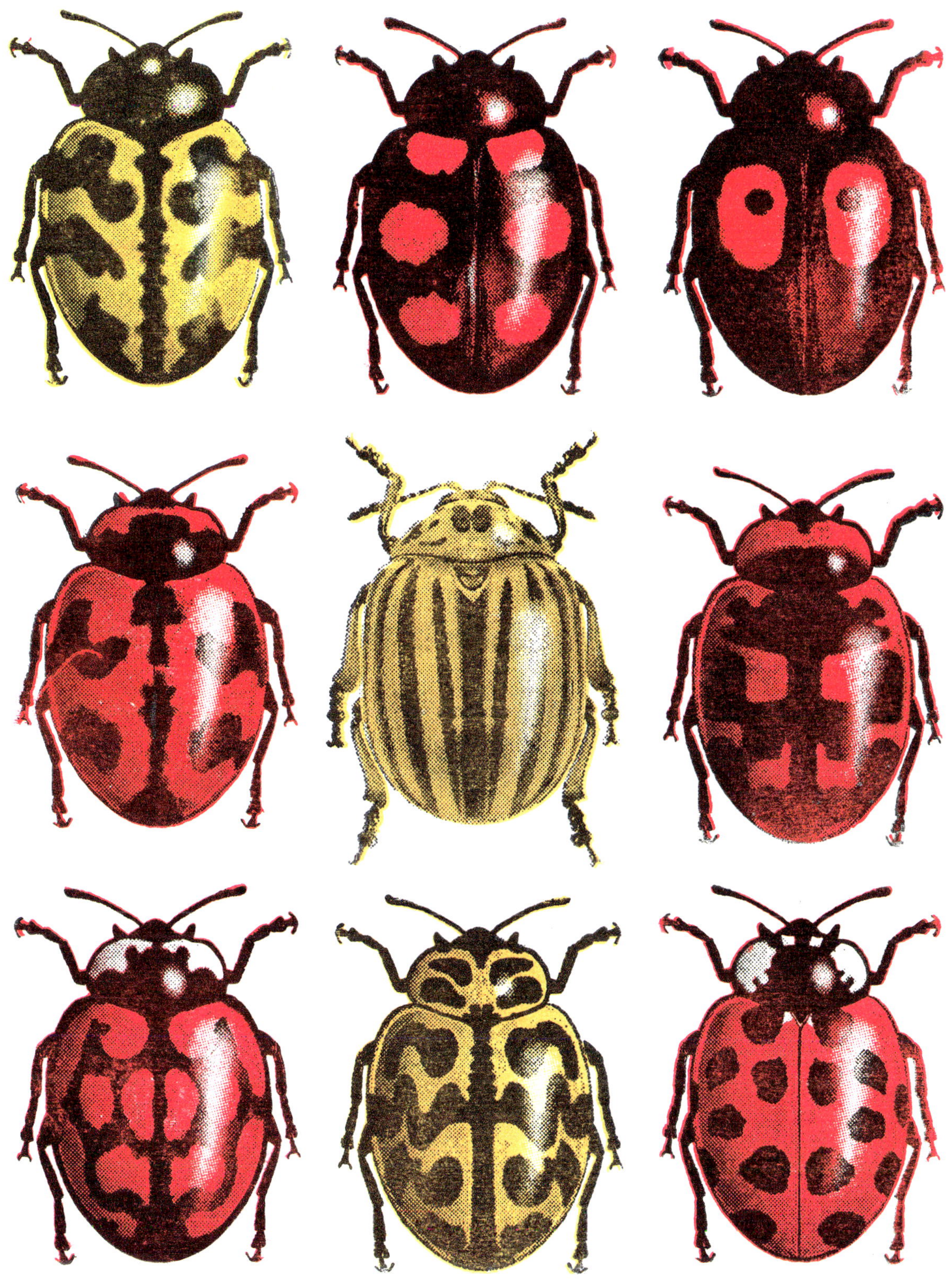

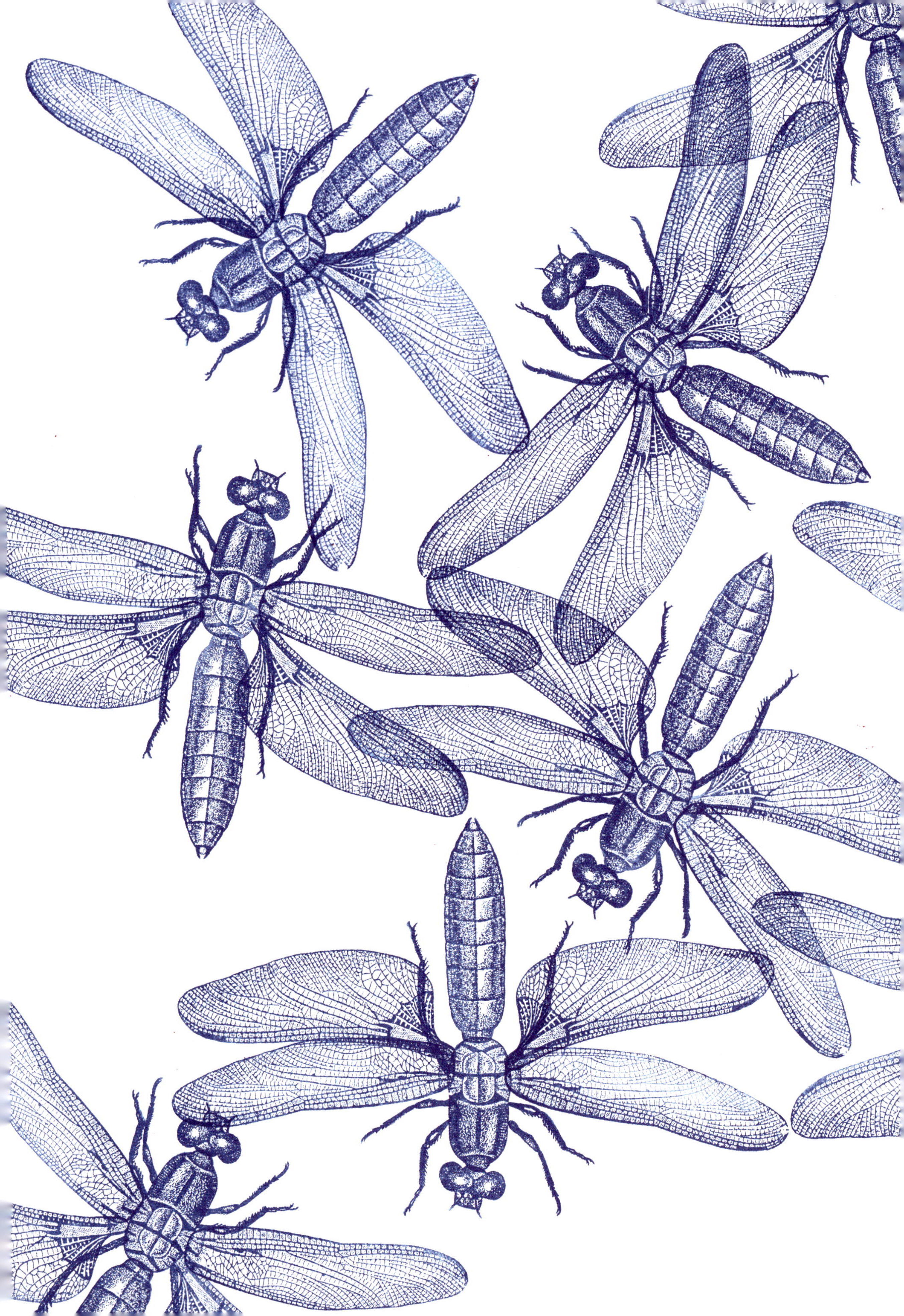

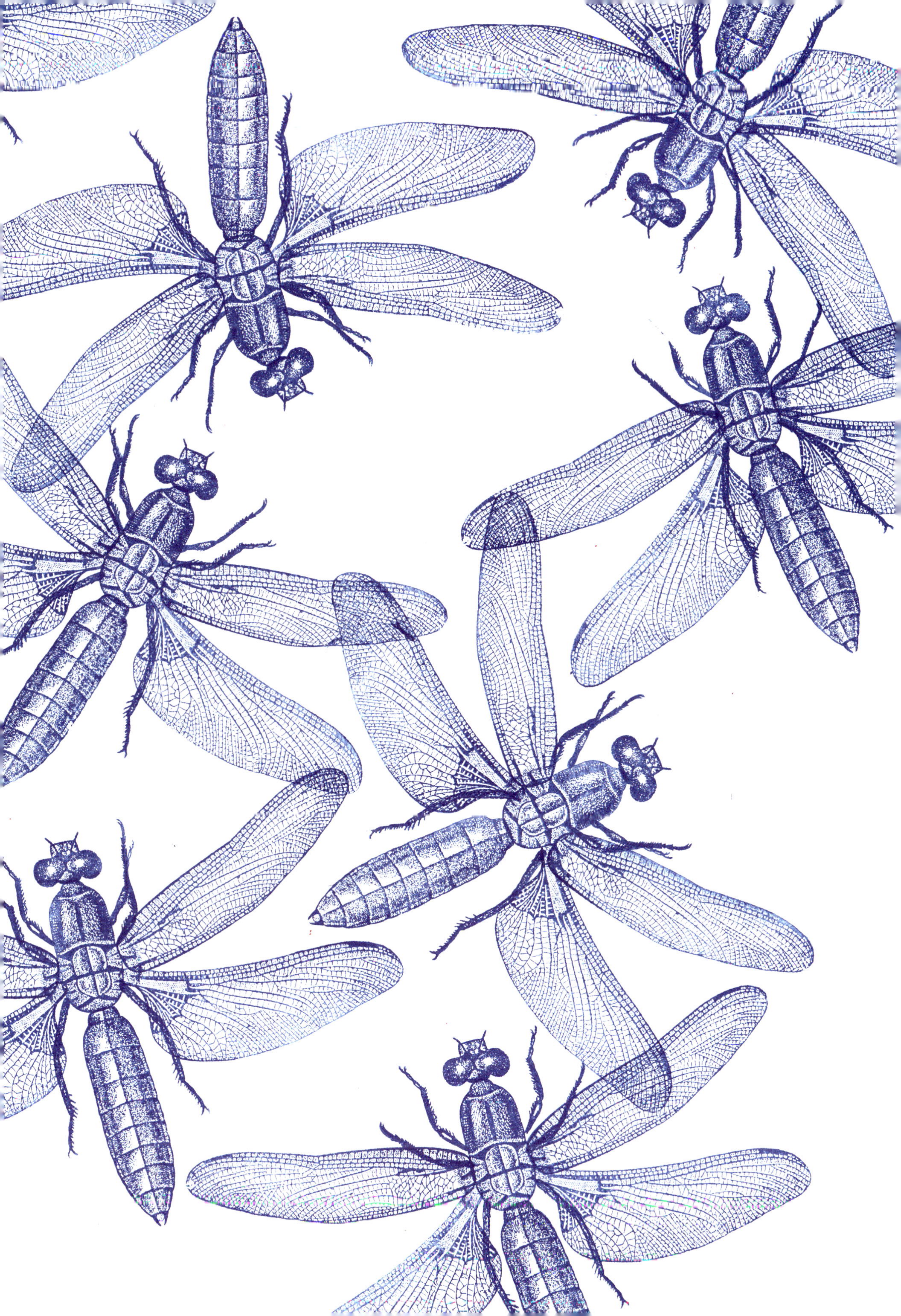

INTERVIEW WITH VINCENT SARDON

by Richard Kraft and Lisa Pearson
Translated by Philippe Aronson

Why rubber stamps?

I'm not very good at answering this kind of question; I have a hard time seeing the primary causes of my work. My work is not the only thing I have a hard time explaining. There is a long list of such things: eccentric Parisian behavior, the books on display in bookshops, the erratic love life of certain friends, jogging, concept stores, religion, seafood sauerkraut, television, colon cancer, rents in the eleventh arrondissement, skorts, and generally almost everything I see when I venture out of my workshop. My work simply reflects the world, which seems to have been created by an absolute moron. To devote one's existence to designing stamps that are also miniature portable artistic machines seems neither more nor less stupid to me than any other human endeavor. So much for primary causes.

When I was a student I had a ton of shitty summer jobs. Once I worked in an insurance company, where I spent my days making stacks of contract cancellation letters from unhappy clients; I would stamp them before putting them on the shelf. I had a big stamp that read TO BE DESTROYED. I stamped each page. Many of the letters were extremely aggressive. Some of them were very well written; others were filled with grammatical mistakes, which somehow made them even more violent. I won't deny that I enjoyed reading them. My interest in stamps and in a certain kind of written violence that stamps convey and amplify might perhaps date from that time.

I was an art student at the University of Bordeaux, in southwest France. Typically, French universities don't get a lot of funding, and in this sense you could say that mine was exceedingly typical. But we had access to the engraving workshop at the school of fine arts. The professors there considered engraving to be a hopelessly outdated sub-genre, somewhere between historical paintings and cloisonné enamel. And the fine arts students wouldn't have been caught dead in this workshop, so we had the place to ourselves. I started by engraving linoleum, copper, zinc, wood: anything I could find there. We used acid, varnish, iron perchloride and all kinds of quirky, somewhat toxic techniques that I liked a lot. It was around this time that I began to engrave stamps with gouge chisels on linoleum or wood. I was broke, so I bought cheap convenience store

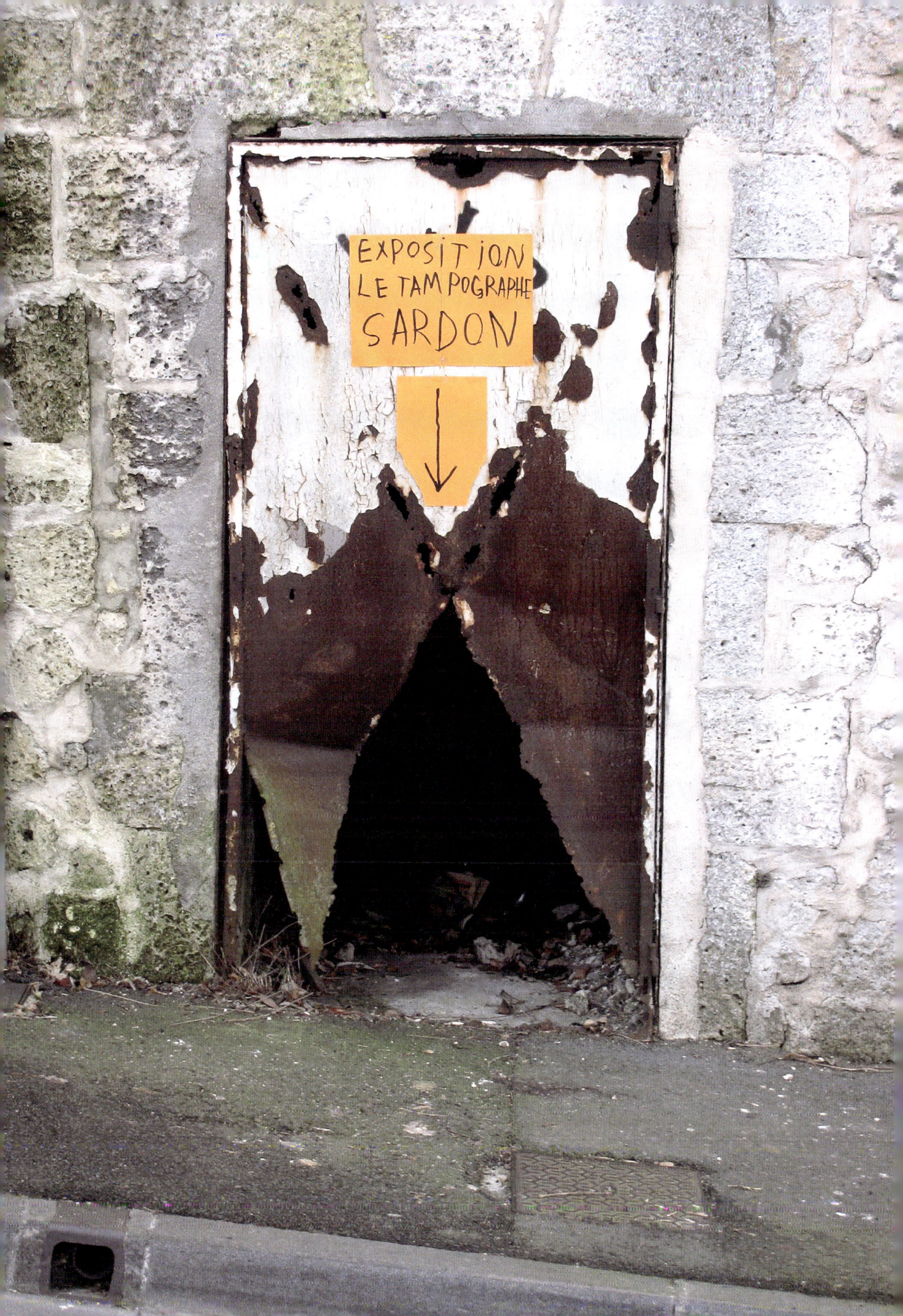
EXPOSITION
LE TAMPOGRAPHE
SARDON

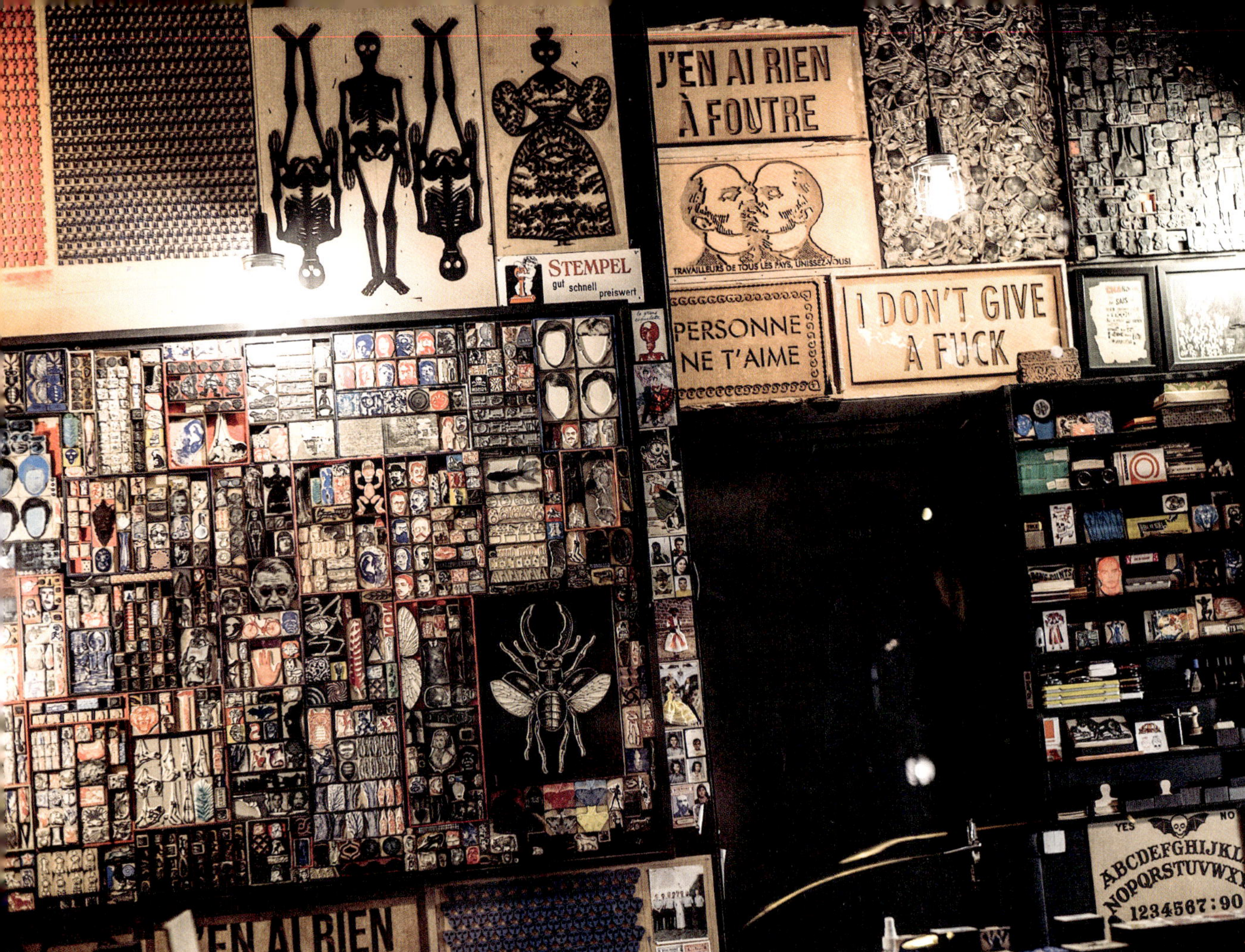

erasers and used them to make stamps, too. With these, I printed fanzines that I would sell for five francs a copy. Once I sold twenty copies, I would call a friend and we would drink the proceeds in a little bar down the road from where I lived.

Once I graduated, I joined the "workforce" (horrible word). My first job was doing illustration. I was obsessed with drawing. I drew all the time. As soon as I had a minute to spare, I'd take my pad out and go at it. I ghost illustrated some stuff for a Gallimard author, a creep with one of those stupid floppy fringe hairstyles who exploited about a dozen kids like me; then I moved to Paris. I was twenty-five years old. I went to show my drawings to newspapers and quickly found work as a political illustrator for *Libération* and *Le Monde*. I was more obsessed than ever with drawing and spent hours honing caricatures of Jacques Chirac, Lionel Jospin, and George W. Bush. I hated every minute of it, but I was in denial. Then, slowly the stamps began to take over. The more I hated working for newspapers, the more this thing was getting bigger. That's how it started.

As an artist you're appropriating and wholly subverting a medium (the rubber stamp) that is often used for petty, arbitrary and often idiotic displays of bureaucratic power.

But when you stamp, it's almost as if you're inverting the action into a refusal (rather than an assertion) of authority. And you do this with a very keen sense of humor, often targeting taboos. In this way, that doesn't seem so different from political cartooning, but clearly the rubber stamps have liberated you, taken you into new territory. What can you do as an artist using rubber stamps, that you couldn't when drawing a political cartoon?

When I was a press cartoonist, I could see the limits to my freedom seated at a comfortable desk in the back of the *Libération* newsroom. These limits had a beard, a nice little gut and glasses, and were known as "publishing director." It was he who decided how long the leash around my neck would be, and in which direction I might be allowed to roam. Whenever I deviated from the plan, he would give my leash a yank.

When Ségolène Royal was running for president, I portrayed her as a granny-type lady with the dimly illuminated eyes of a Charismatic Christian. The following week a journalist cornered me in the paper's open space, pen in hand. She began touching up my drawings, explaining that Ségolène Royal was a beautiful woman: she was trim, with a noble forehead, impeccable hair, elegant shoes and an angelic smile. That was the day I realized that my job was doing PR for the French Socialist Party.

Of course it wasn't all bad: you could portray the party's opponents as hideous beings with double or triple chins, yellow teeth, wicked eyes and hair sprouting from their ears; or a two-and-a-half-foot-tall Sarkozy with gigantic platform shoes and a devilish expression. It leant an air of freedom of press to the whole endeavor, but it was just an air. I stopped working for *Libération* not long after this incident.

So, free of the leash, I rented a little workshop just beneath Place de Clichy and filled it with machines, books, and a bed I had scavenged in the street in the eighth arrondissement, that still smelled of the old lady it had belonged to. There I began making hundreds of stamps, exploring the first thing that popped into my head. I warmly welcomed any bizarre or disgusting ideas. It was all very random: when a mental image took over my mind, I got rid of it by turning it into a stamp. I wasn't attempting to transgress any taboos in particular, but my stamps and writing revealed the grimmer aspects of my life in Paris, the city's violence, the brutality of its politics, the sleazy sexuality on display in the Pigalle neighborhood, the hatred I would sometimes see on people's faces. I began to turn my life into material, and it felt more powerful than any caricature about French fiscal reform ever did.

The stamp is never neutral. It packs a symbolic wallop because of the millions of judges, cops, customs officials — agents of public authority — who use them to validate passports, to turn people away at the border, to pass judgment, to pass laws, to sentence, to record proceedings, to excommunicate — all sorts of evil documents that have the power of putting people in impossible situations. Any absurdity presented in this manner becomes ten times more powerful thanks to the magic wand of graphics. It is this mysterious power that fascinates me and that I continue to explore. Once upon a time newspapers had his kind of sacred power, but no more. Thirty thousand copies of *Libération* in circulation, with a drawing of mine on the cover, and nobody gave a shit. In that sense stamps are vastly superior as a tool.

Independence is clearly paramount to you, and humor is one the critical elements of your work. Now that you've got no editors (and with your own shop, no gallery dealers), how do you locate where you draw the line? What demands to be skewered and what seems possibly too fragile or even too dangerous?

I began to show my work in 2007. You could feel that a shit storm was brewing, but it was still relatively far off. Press cartoonists didn't need police protection to get wasted at the bar down the road. The most dangerous thing you might have to face at the office was a lawsuit, or hate mail — two democratic processes that seem, from today's vantage point, almost friendly compared to what my ex-colleagues at *Charlie Hebdo* went through. These days a simple caricature can lead you straight to the Quai de la Rapée morgue. You can be proud and publicly state that terror will never win — the fact of the matter is that it does affect your work.

After the Paris attacks, social media overflowed with drawings and graphic doodads that were all universally and absolutely shitty. Bloodstained doves of peace, pencils brandished like weapons and other such disgusting symbolist idiocies. I wondered if I should jump into the fray, but nothing came except tears, which are about as editorially unpalatable as you can get. I might come up with an idea in ten years' time.

When an idea is funny, it's usually because it contains a kernel of truth. Truth is brutal and candid, and makes you laugh. If you don't understand what is happening to you — say if some ex-colleagues of yours, journalists all, get riddled with bullets at work by a couple of kids — it's hard to find something relevant to say.

In defense of these young and ambitious jihadists, they are not the only group dead set on making it more difficult for artists to express themselves, and one can only salute the impressive efficiency of social media, thanks to which it has only taken a few years to connect the planet's nuttiest conspiracy theorists, medieval holy men, supremacists, apprentice Nazis, testosterone enthusiasts, pro-lifers, cavemen, left-leaning anti-Semites and right-wing Stalinists — all more or less putrid activists now linked together in amorphous, anonymous pressure groups whose nastiness and efficiency puzzle me to no end. I look upon the years before Facebook as an almost carefree period when it was possible to make a joke without worrying about what a dude on the other side of the planet might think, without fearing buzzkill. None of this changes the nature of my work, but I know that somewhere, just outside my field of vision lurks a mountain of horseshit in the shade of which very little manages to flower.

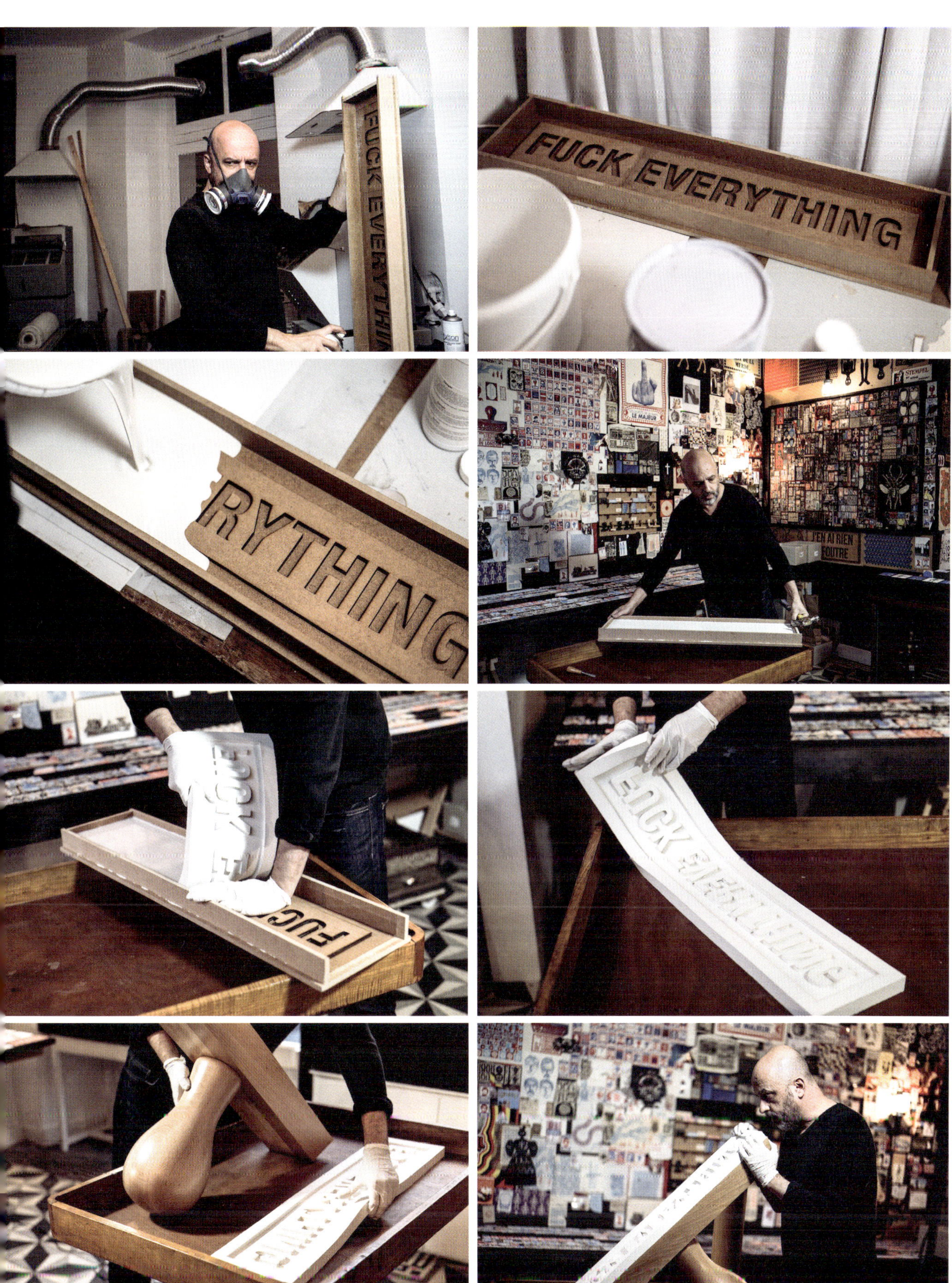
FUCK EVERYTHING
RYTHING
LE MAJEUR
J'EN AI RIEN FOUTRE
STEMPEL

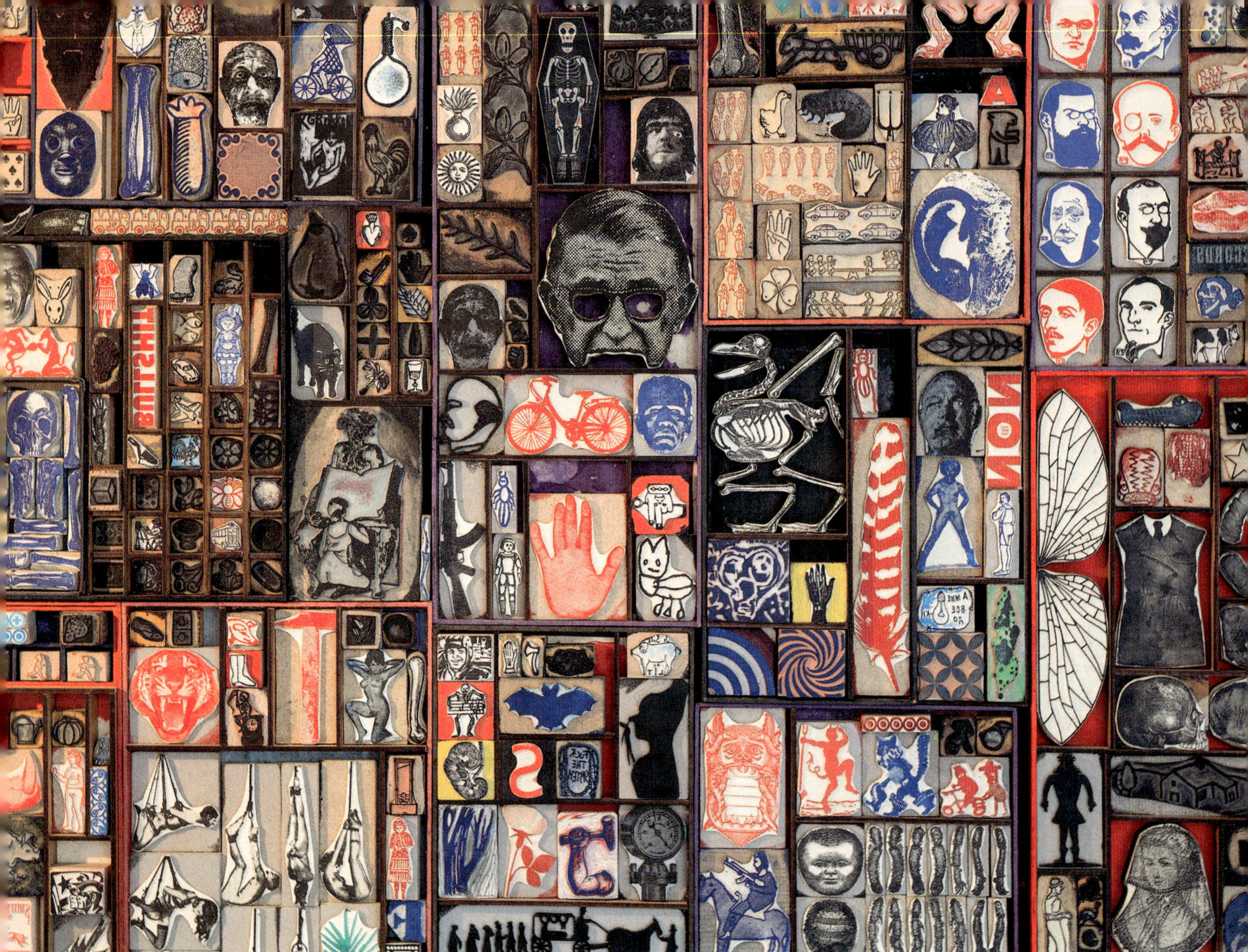

I don't have any targets in particular. I speak from experience. I deal with a few hundred acres of pavement, a small chunk of arrondissement in a city suffering from the same ills as most of Europe's capital cities: gentrification, the closing of minds, bad vibes, the working class exiled to the *banlieues*, the struggle to make rent every month and the alarming proliferation of artists. At times it seems like this city has nothing but artists in it. It's practically impossible to find a guy to fix your toaster-oven, but if you go for a coffee down the street, in less than ten minutes you will have overheard the life stories of three videographers, a children's choreographer, a bald graphic designer and two writers of experimental fiction.

I have noticed for some time now, on the other side of the boulevard, that television production companies are slowly but surely taking over the old, empty rundown cavernous industrial spaces. I see younger and younger people than before, and fresher complexions. I see fewer and fewer old ladies; the neighborhood drunks who would stagger from bench to bench have almost all disappeared, giving way to better-dressed alcoholics. This is the foul air I attempt to report on.

Besides the immediate world around you, your work also seems to be in dialogue with a range of influences. Pére Ubu and Alfred Jarry make appearances as does Dada. There are artists like Warhol, Pollock, Dubuffet, Chaissac and Yves Klein. Could you talk a bit about the artists, writers and other figures that you love and perhaps those that you've wrestled with, and those whose work you feel most connected to?

My tastes owe a lot to happenstance. My artistic education was very unsystematic. I always read what came to hand. My parents' library contained bestsellers of varying degrees of atrociousness. I was powerfully bored in our village and had no interest in playing with my classmates — primates whose behavior was unintelligible to me. So I began to read shitty books such as *Papillon*, *Emmanuelle*, *The Kon-Tiki Expedition*, *Les prodigieuses victoircs de la psychologie moderne* (roughly: *Great Breakthroughs in Modern Psychology*) the *Kama Sutra* that my father had unsuccessfully attempted to hide under the bookcase, books on UFOs, psychic powers, werewolves, vampires, and there was even an instruction manual on how to turn ordinary canine house pets into attack dogs.

One day I came upon a paperback edition of *The Red Grass*, an angst-ridden novel by Boris Vian. It impressed me deeply, though I still don't quite know why. After reading it, I took my savings, hopped on my bike and cycled to the neighboring town to buy more books by this author about whom I knew nothing. I came home with a paperback of *I Spit on Your Graves* — the title of which I was immediately taken by, though my grandmother, seeing me reading the book on the couch in the living room, did not share this enthusiasm.

The first time I saw the names Alfred Jarry and Père Ubu, was in a book of essays by Vian. Reading *Ubu Roi* and to a lesser extent, *Faustroll*, was what led me a few years later to show my work to the Pataphysicians, and to join the Collège. I felt that in them I had found a group of people capable of appreciating the utter uselessness of my work.

As I grow older, I am more and more attracted to autobiographical writing, and less and less interested in fiction. I still enjoy reading books about flying saucers, werewolves and duck breeding — I have a lot of respect for ducks. But autobiography is what I like best. I have read Casanova's memoirs several times over, less for the rather repetitive sex than for his con man savvy and depictions of nobility, artists and the common people. I also love reading Jules Renard's *Journal*, in which he describes late nineteenth-century Paris; the pettiness of the artistic world of the time is very similar to what you find today. I like the books of Sophie Calle, and the letters of Gaston Chaissac, which don't have a lot in common, except the fact of being by artists who combine writing and conceptual art. I love Riad Sattouf's work. I also like Jean Dubuffet's painting and theoretical writings, though his rather rigid moral stance irks me. Which is why I caricatured him in a set of stamps that reproduce some of his more mechanical works. In the same way, it was extremely tempting to design a set of stamps caricaturing the work of Andy Warhol and Roy Lichtenstein. Each artist has his own mannerisms, and stamps are an efficient way of accentuating them. Yves Klein, for example, turned the nude bodies of his models into giant human stamps during the great libidinous happenings that apparently made a deep impression on those who witnessed them. This of course lends itself ideally to a set of depressing, bureaucratic and utterly sexless rubber stamps.

Radical artists are often easy to caricature; the more lyrical ones, Gaston Chaissac comes to mind, usually work within a system that one can easily isolate, exaggerate, and transform into a set of rubber stamps. There is an element of satire in what I do, but oddly enough I am unable to caricature an artist I am indifferent to. The work I attack as it were has to hold an attraction for me.

You grew up in Bayonne very close to Spain which is where your family's from—is that right? You made a Bayonne set of stamps with protesters marching and then the police beating the crap out of them. When you look back on what you witnessed as a child (and particularly as a child of immigrants), how has that affected your sense of identity as a French citizen, and has that infiltrated your work as an artist?

My family comes from northern Spain, and I did indeed grow up in French Basque country. The Pays Basque is a lovely mountainous region situated on the Atlantic coast. The Basques are known far and wide for having exterminated the whales in the Gulf of Gascogne, deforested the Magdalen Islands and Newfoundland, invented the odd-looking beret (that has at various times adorned such disparate heads as those of Che Guevara and Saddam Hussein), and for speaking a language somehow related, according to despairing linguists who have had the misfortune of studying it, to hieroglyphic Egyptian, Paleo-Berber, Hebrew, Sumerian, ancient Peruvian and perhaps, Klingon. The Basque language is proud of possessing words that could harken back to Paleolithic times. Thus the word "axe" in Basque has a common root with "rock." The Basque language also has over fifty different and nuanced verbs to describe being bored shitless in the countryside, and I spent my childhood exploring their every shade and gradation.

Basque Country is unfortunately cut in half by the France-Spain border. This geographic breakdown generated extremely strong nationalist sentiment. At the end of the nineteen fifties in Franco's increasingly doddering dictatorship, nationalistic feeling spawned ETA, a separatist group blending respectable revolutionary aspirations with a pronounced taste for political assassination, car bombs and racketeering. It should also be pointed out that, after overthrowing the Spanish Republic in 1939, Franco led a vicious campaign of violence against all political opponents.

As my family fought against Franco on the side of the anarchists, it became clear by the end of the civil war in 1939 that escape was imperative if they wanted to steer clear

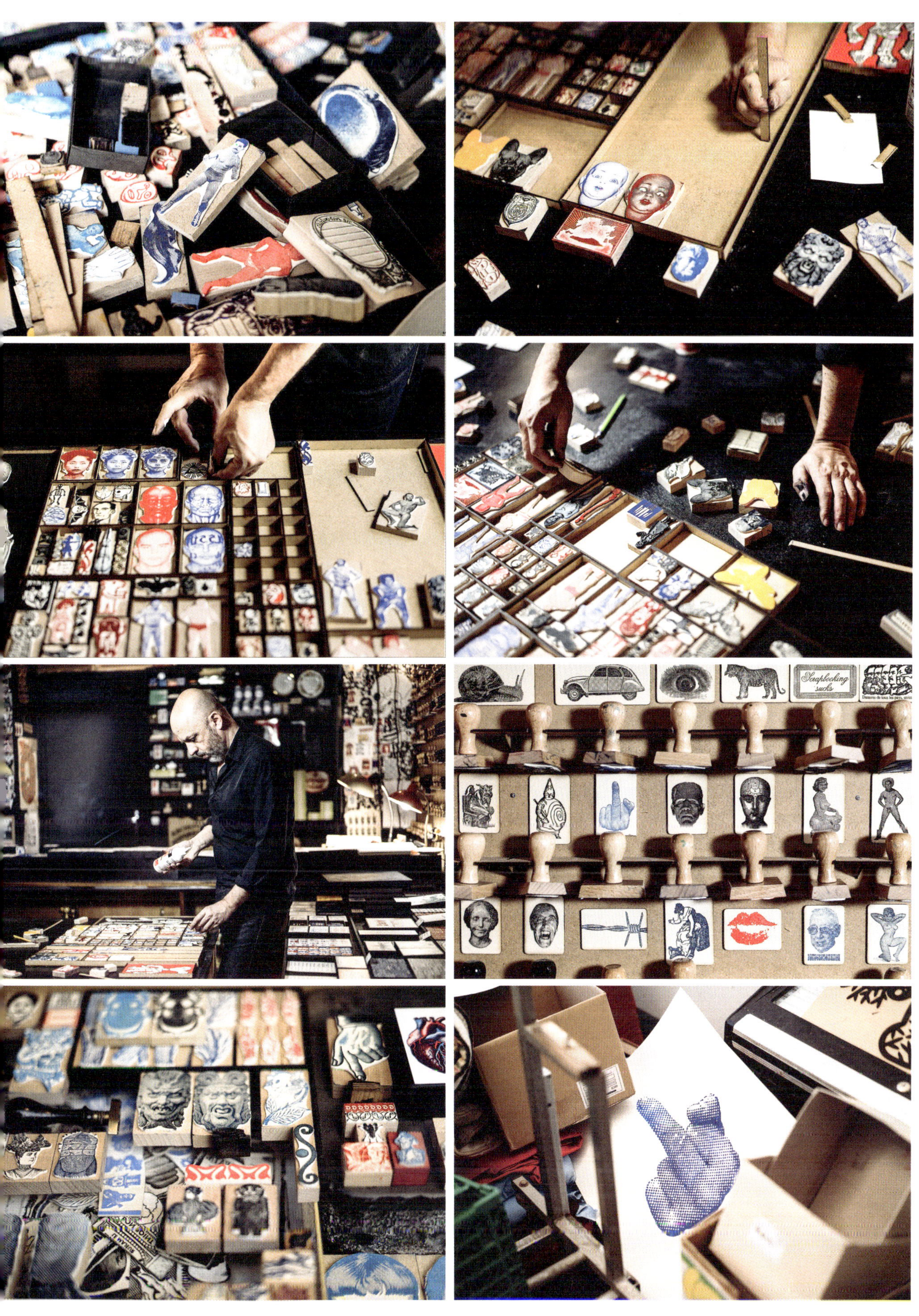
Scrapbooking sucks

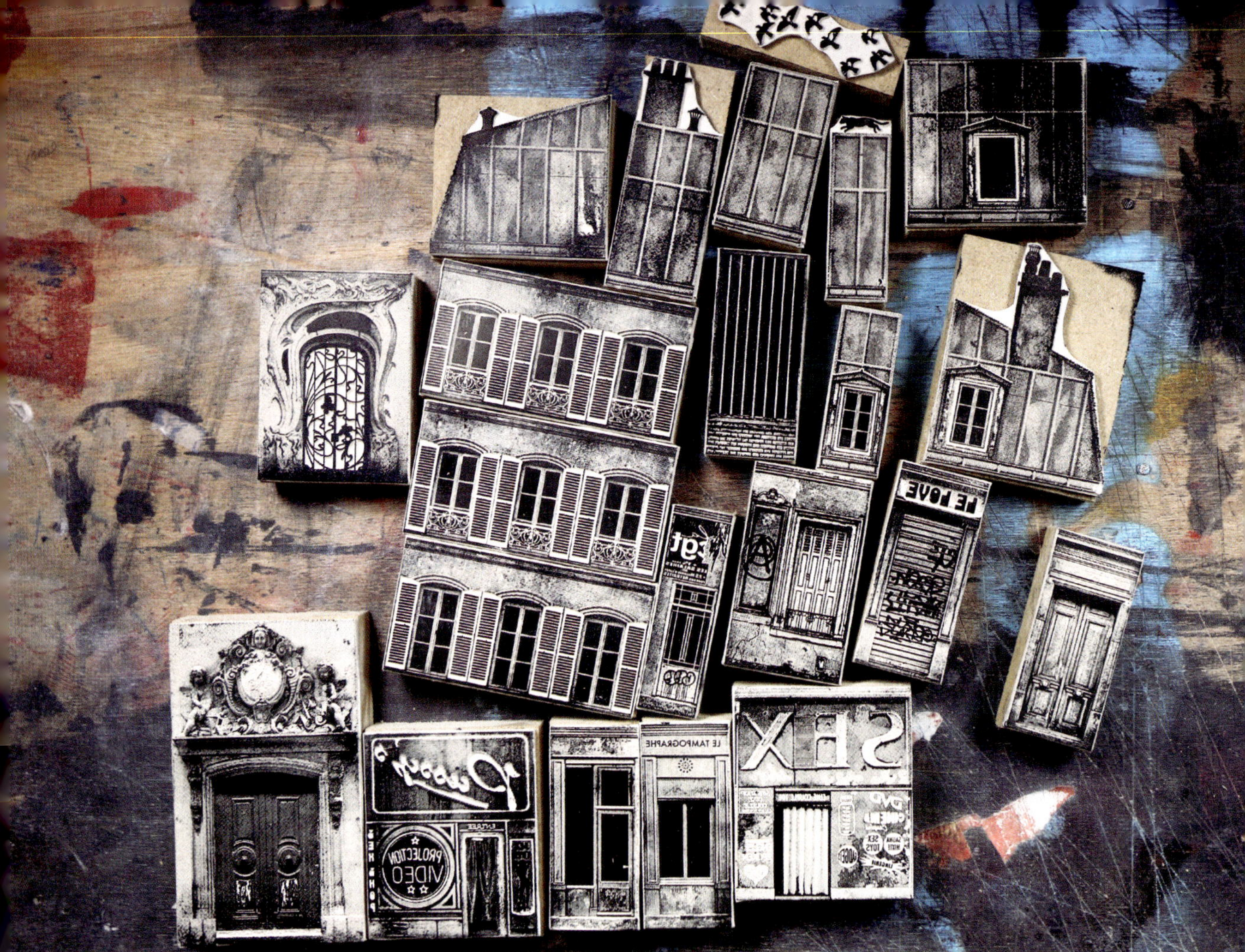

of the summary executions, mass graves and other atrocities that Franco's forces were then committing with ingenuity and pleasure, in a sort of dress rehearsal of what was soon about to engulf Europe. So my grandfather walked across the Pyrenees and was welcomed by French constables who led him to the Gurs internment camp, a muddy quadrangle of wooden cabins rife with dysentery. This might appear to be a rather chilly welcome from a French government that was still an ally of the democratic Spanish Republic. But as Franco was allied with the Nazis who were flexing their muscles in France's direction, they weren't welcoming too warmly these leftist losers. The local press didn't hesitate to designate said refugees as "communist vermin, both arrogant and impossible to assimilate," which is rather interesting in light of current French attitudes toward welcoming refugees from the Middle East.

By the time I was born in the early nineteen seventies, the Gurs internment camp had been closed for some time. Spanish Republicans had morphed into the quiet graybeards one could see reading the Spanish paper on public park benches. By then the ones crossing the border were Basque militants. Franco liked to use a tourniquet to kill them — an ingenious strangling device used to constrict and compress victims' throats, practically decapitating them in the process. So the streets of Bayonne were soon filled with dissidents using the town as a rear base to continue the fight against Madrid. The walls were covered with nationalistic slogans and the stenciled faces of political prisoners on posters or monumental frescoes not unlike the political paintings one could find in Belfast. My taste for effigies and somewhat primitive printing techniques may stem from that.

Demonstrations were common currency, and the town was overflowing with police officers, constables, riot police, soldiers and secret service snitches. Paranoia became a lifestyle. As a child, I remember the smell of tear gas would sometimes waft in through the open windows of my room; Basque militants were known to throw feces on the police. Those were the days.

In the nineteen-eighties, my little town became the scene of executions and machine gun strafing committed by contract killers recruited by Spanish police, who thought they had found an effective solution to the Basque problem with this underground m.o. Mercenaries were hired, machineguns handed out, and bars shot up at random, killing Basques, non-Basques, militants and people who had come to watch the ballgame and have a few drinks — and who all died in the same way, regardless of their views on Spanish federalism and the rights of sovereign peoples.

I came away from all of this with extremely lukewarm feelings for nation states, be they French, Basque or Spanish; as a rule their projects leave me cold. I don't see myself in any of these countries; I am French purely by chance. I feel at home nowhere, and see this as a privilege and a form of freedom. I was deeply relieved when I left my little town at the age of eighteen, and I have never set foot there again. Paris has become my ecosystem, though I have noticed of late and with trepidation that somewhat like the idiots of my childhood, people are again becoming proud of their roots and cultural specificities. And this makes me want to split again.

You've embraced your status as an outsider in myriad ways, not least of which is how you define and sell your art. Besides having your own shop—like an outpost really—that eschews art world commerce, you've turned the ideal of individual, unique authorship inside out. Not only do you sell stamps that make multiple impressions in unforeseen contexts, the person buying the stamp can then do whatever he likes with it, crediting you or not. Where does Sardon begin and end?

I have on occasion attempted to work with gallerists, succumbing — as I thankfully almost never do anymore — to a bout of idiotic optimism, or because poverty had scrambled my brain. I made sure to avoid inviting friends to the openings. I was afraid of seeing condemnation in their eyes. My friends are very strict about morality and dishonest ventures. Moreover, having to listen to this or that gallerist talk for hours about his tax evasion issues and the poltergeist haunting his Swiss chalet, only strengthened my resolve to self-distribute my work.

In Paris several artistic circles coexist while remaining apart. You have the official contemporary art scene, the tacky Saint Germain des Près galleries, the alternative galleries that are quite happy to let their artists starve, the extremely chic Marais galleries, horrible conveyors of figurative painting, and a growing number of concept-stores in which you will find variously discouraging selections of design, art, decoration and Risograph prints. I tend to think I wouldn't fit in at any of those places. Maybe I'm wrong. But I prefer not having to waste energy putting up with other people.

So I rented a space next to my studio. I redid it from floor to ceiling, and turned it into a stampographical gallery open once a week to the public. It is here that I welcome the folks who come to buy my stamps and demonstrate their various uses. Not only do I avoid meddlesome intermediaries, but I also get a pretty clear view of how my work is perceived.

I don't really know what people do with the stamps. It escapes me. Sometimes people send me photos — embarrassing or heartening, depending on whether they were used in a hideous scrapbook or to print my illustrations on anonymous buttocks. Both uses are legitimate as far as I'm concerned. I sell things that are both tools and works of art; the potentialities contained within the tools — that's what interests me. I am less captivated by seeing what people actually do with the stamps. In truth, some things are so ugly I would gladly refrain from taking credit for them.

My work is destined for amateurs, not artists. I am steadfastly opposed to my work being used by professionals. My work is for innocent people. I am not a great fan of artists, and when an artist walks into my gallery, I sniff him or her out immediately. The air becomes rarefied, all color disappears, and I get a strong urge to head outside for a stroll.

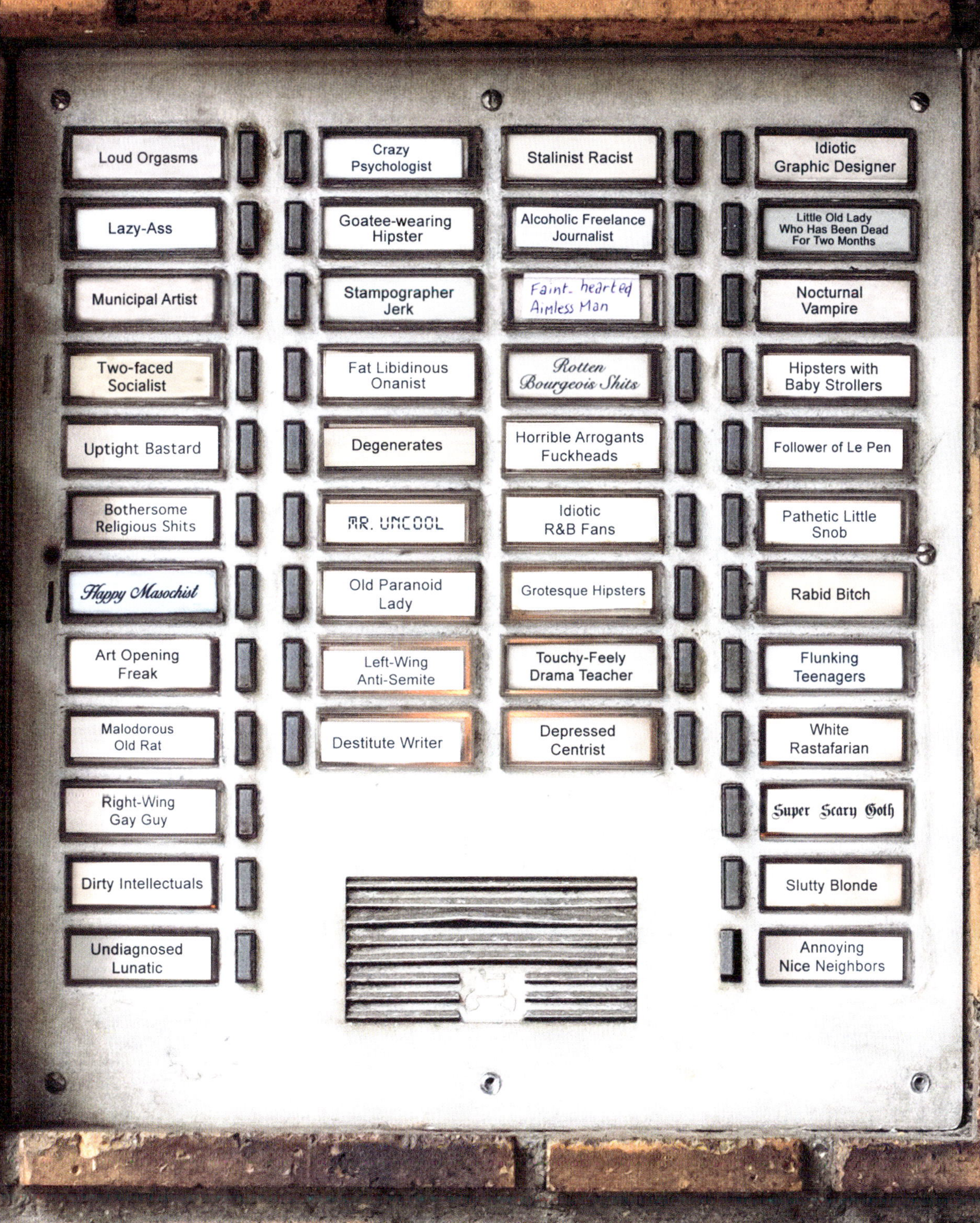
Loud Orgasms
Lazy-Ass
Municipal Artist
Two-faced Socialist
Uptight Bastard
Bothersome Religious Shits
Happy Masochist
Art Opening Freak
Malodorous Old Rat
Right-Wing Gay Guy
Dirty Intellectuals
Undiagnosed Lunatic
Crazy Psychologist
Goatee-wearing Hipster
Stampographer Jerk
Fat Libidinous Onanist
Degenerates
MR. UNCOOL
Old Paranoid Lady
Left-Wing Anti-Semite
Destitute Writer
Stalinist Racist
Alcoholic Freelance Journalist
Faint-hearted Aimless Man
Rotten Bourgeois Shits
Horrible Arrogants Fuckheads
Idiotic R&B Fans
Grotesque Hipsters
Touchy-Feely Drama Teacher
Depressed Centrist
Idiotic Graphic Designer
Little Old Lady Who Has Been Dead For Two Months
Nocturnal Vampire
Hipsters with Baby Strollers
Follower of Le Pen
Pathetic Little Snob
Rabid Bitch
Flunking Teenagers
White Rastafarian
Super Scary Goth
Slutty Blonde
Annoying Nice Neighbors

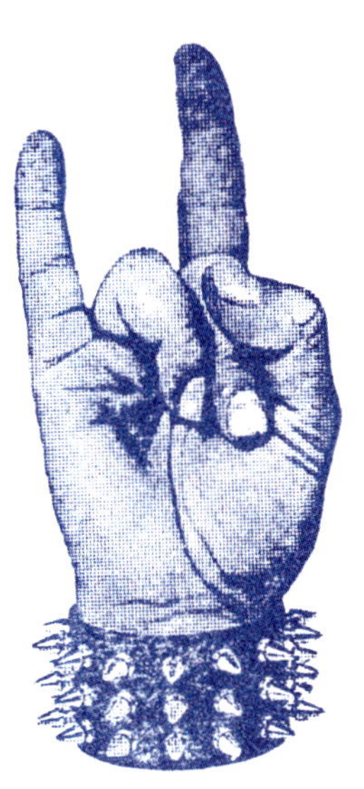

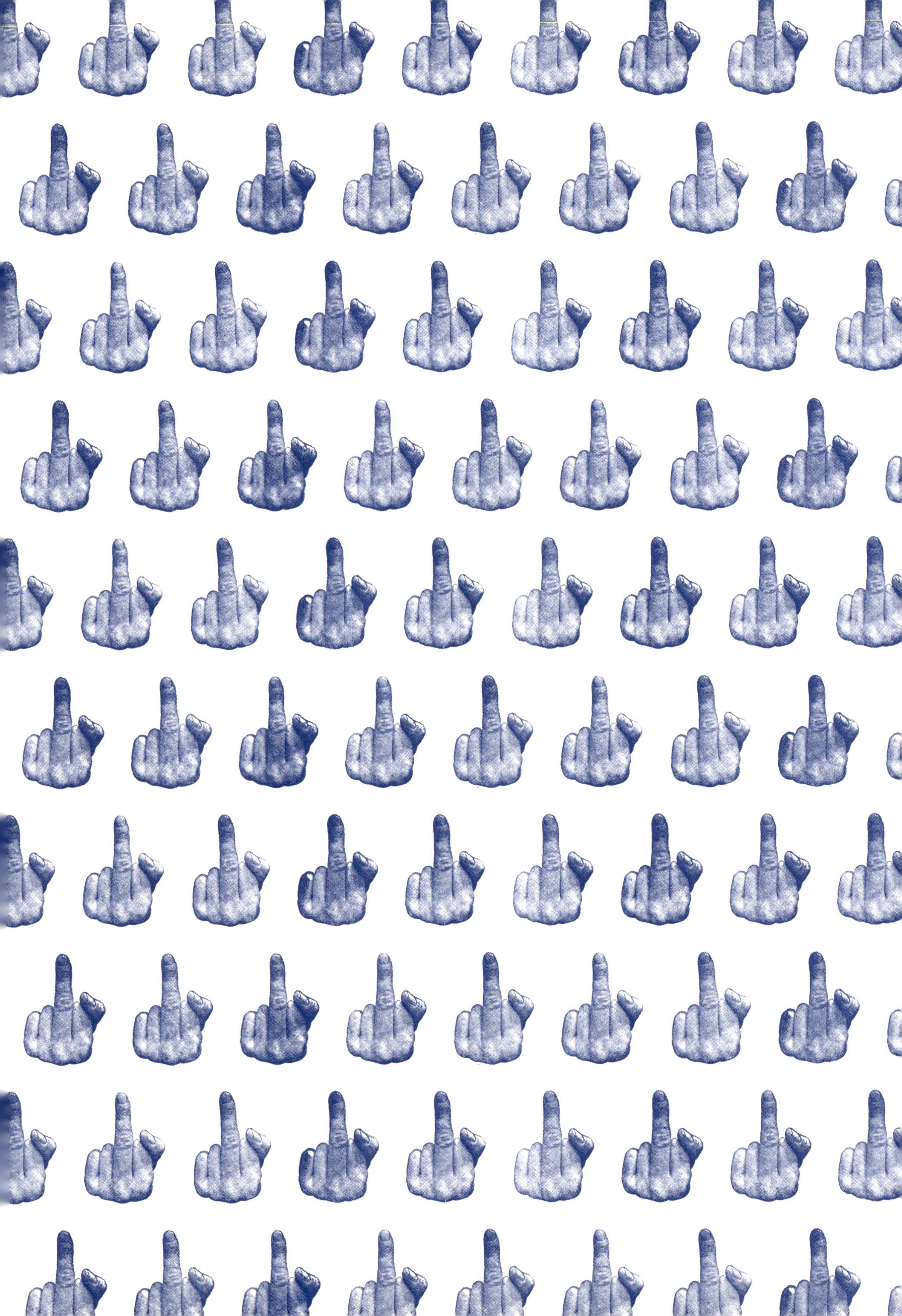